T0269956

COUNTRY NEVER TROD

*William Lewis Manly's 1849 Voyage
down Utah's Green River*

MICHAEL D. KANE

TWODOT®

ESSEX, CONNECTICUT
HELENA, MONTANA

A · TWODOT® · BOOK

An imprint of Globe Pequot, the trade division of
The Rowman & Littlefield Publishing Group, Inc.
4501 Forbes Blvd., Ste. 200
Lanham, MD 20706
www.rowman.com

Distributed by NATIONAL BOOK NETWORK

British Library Cataloguing in Publication Information available

Library of Congress Cataloging-in-Publication Data available

ISBN 978-1-4930-6095-5 (paper)
ISBN 978-1-4930-6096-2 (electronic)

CONTENTS

Manly and McMahon's 1849 expedition (present-day boundaries).

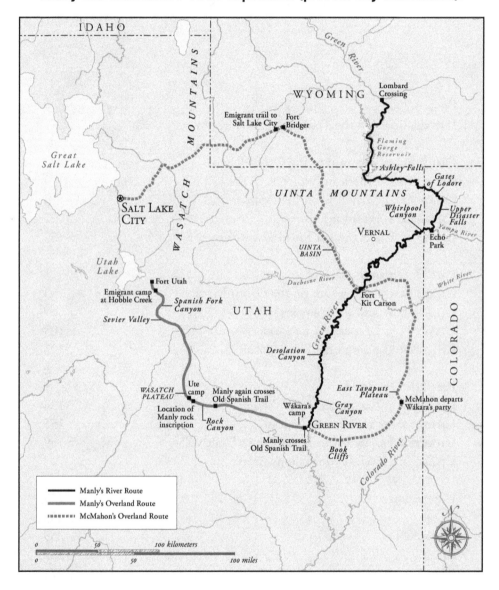

IDAHO

WYOMING

Green River

Lombard Crossing

Emigrant trail to Salt Lake City · Fort Bridger

Flaming Gorge Reservoir

Ashley Falls

Gates of Lodore

Great Salt Lake

UINTA MOUNTAINS

Whirlpool Canyon

Upper Disaster Falls

⊛ SALT LAKE CITY

VERNAL ○

Echo Park

Yampa River

Utah Lake

UINTA BASIN

Duchesne River

White River

Fort Utah

Emigrant camp at Hobble Creek

Spanish Fork Canyon

UTAH

Fort Kit Carson

COLORADO

Sevier Valley

Green River

Desolation Canyon

WASATCH PLATEAU

Ute camp

Manly again crosses Old Spanish Trail

East Tavaputs Plateau

McMahon departs Wákara's party

Location of Manly rock inscription

Rock Canyon

Wákara's camp

Gray Canyon

GREEN RIVER

Manly crosses Old Spanish Trail

Book Cliffs

Colorado River

───── Manly's River Route
───── Manly's Overland Route
▪▪▪▪▪▪ McMahon's Overland Route

0   50   100 kilometers
0   50   100 miles

PREFACE

GROWING UP IN THE OPEN LANDS OF UTAH, WYOMING, AND NEVADA, I constantly found myself drawn to the vast deserts and high, rugged, snow-capped mountains. There, in solace, I'd search for paths less taken. Immersed in a dazzling display of the sun's rays streaking across a new-born day, or a brilliant sunset followed by a star-filled sky, my mind would fill with thoughts of the pioneer, forty-niner, immigrant, or farmer of the 1800s. What was it like for those Americans pushing westward as their country expanded in the 1800s, searching over the horizon for fruitful lands, freedom of choice, and a better life for self and family? Later in life, as I began to explore and research the lives of these men and women, I truly found my passion.

Understanding the lives and dreams of the white settlers of western America requires exploring their writings, comparing and verifying their authenticity. Fortunately, we have a wealth of historical records from the western frontier in the mid-1800s—a time of open plains, mountains, and lakes of a newly discovered America. The first step is to establish facts, but as historian Robert Shafer writes, "What happened is supposedly an easy or elementary question; why it happened is much more difficult and challenging."[1] Beyond bare facts, then, we must compare and contrast their written accounts, place them in context, and ask why these brave men and women made the decisions they did. Such examination may decipher the truths as they experienced them.

As I read countless tales of triumph and tragedy in the American West, I was introduced to a forty-niner, explorer, and humanitarian whose story most people have never heard—and those who know of him cannot fully agree on the details of his story. His name is William Lewis Manly. In August, September, and October 1849, he and his travel companions boldly floated down what to them was the unknown Green River in what is now Wyoming and eastern Utah, traversed wilderness lands of central Utah, and joined one of the first wagon trains to venture south through Utah Territory toward Los Angeles. Writers have spent more time on the later portions of Manly's journey, when the emigrant wagon train found unimaginable hardship in Death Valley.[2] My focus, however, turned to his earlier river running. Historians have debated how many miles Manly and his men traveled down the Green River, as well as what land route they took in their arduous journey across the vast Utah Territory. Many have considered the evidence and concluded that he traveled the Green River only as far as the Uinta Basin, largely following what others had accomplished. But after many months of my own research, I came to believe that he went much farther—all the way to the Old Spanish Trail near what is now the town of Green River, Utah.

Piecing together Manly's story helps write a vital chapter in the annals of American history and reveals a vibrant strand in the rich tapestry of the adventurers who explored the West. Based on my findings, I argue that Manly and his companions were the first known people to venture down and document 415 miles of the Green River—all in an abandoned ferryboat and three wooden dugout canoes. This was a full two decades before John Wesley Powell's historic adventure of 1869. Long before Manly's group reached their goal of navigating all the way to California, however, they met a notorious Ute Indian named Wákara,[3] who advised them to leave the river before it grew even more treacherous. Manly and four of his men then walked 175 miles across unforgiving Utah lands in ten days. With Manly's innate abilities to survive in the wilderness and open lands, he and his men overcame immense challenges and succeeded in the harshest of environments. Despite encountering perilous whitewater rapids on the Green, the isolation of deep canyon recesses, inhospitable deserts, and high mountain passes of the Utah Territory, everyone in the party eventually made it back to the safety of civilization.

A complete understanding of their experience also requires considering the story of the West from a different viewpoint, that of the earlier inhabitants of the lands the Euro-American explorers and settlers claimed for themselves. For Manly and many others, the land was an unexplored and unpeopled wilderness, but of course it had been inhabited by tribes and bands of American Indians for thousands of years. Too often the perspectives and stories of these people are revealed only in the records of the white settlers, but those records allow historians to piece together a picture that brings the natives' experiences from the background to the foreground. I have relied on that scholarship, in addition to Manly's own descriptions, to provide a more complete picture. Though he writes from the racialized viewpoint of his era, he shows an uncommon bond with some of the native inhabitants, and he acknowledges his reliance on their knowledge and aid for his survival during his journey.

In the course of my research, I realized that reading dusty books and poring over old maps would not be enough to establish what really happened to Lewis Manly. I was an outdoor adventurer long before I pursued postgraduate studies, and I have helped guide thousands of people down the wild rivers of the West. So I hollowed out two logs of my own, prepared horses and other supplies, recruited my son and some experienced friends, and retraced each mile of his journey down the river and overland. This book is his story and mine.

The dreams and aspirations of completing this book were dependent upon many who helped me. Barbara, my wife, stood strong and never wavered, supporting me on countless days away from her to research and follow the paths Manly trod. My son, Dallas, not only ran the waters of the Green with me but walked every step of the land expedition and was a shining example of fortitude, constantly showing an undaunted will to succeed. My time spent with him will never be forgotten. My two daughters, Sierra and Morgan, never complained of my absence and made me feel complete with their love and support. My mentor and close friend, Merlin Goode, and his son Clint acted as guides down the Green and must be commended. Both were as a beacon of light and direction through the entire expedition. My debt to them can never be repaid.

I express heartfelt appreciation to the Department of Parks, Recreation, and Tourism at the University of Utah for allowing me the opportunity to learn, apply, and enjoy the fruits of academia, which has given me untold gratification.

Many thank-yous to Dinosaur National Monument and the Bureau of Land Management for assistance in obtaining river permits and advice on running the various sections of the Green River. Also, many state and federal government employees gave valued input and direction as this project unfolded. Thanks to all.

Over the course of getting this book published, I have received candid reviews from a number of anonymous scholars who helped me see where I'd leapt to conclusions and needed to improve the manuscript. Not everyone agrees with the conclusions I come to here, but I have tried my best to answer the critiques I have received. Thanks also to Nathan Waite, who has been a tremendous help in revising the narrative over the past many months. And I am grateful to the staff at Rowman & Littlefield for seeing this project's potential and making my dream of a book about Manly a reality.

Last but certainly not least, I must express gratitude to the many historians and private citizens who reside along the trail that Manly walked. They opened their doors to our expedition team as we passed by and assisted with direction and local historical input. The generosity and spirit of the American people can never be underestimated.

An earlier, condensed version of my research into Manly's travels, coauthored with Nathan Waite, was published as "Avoiding Mormons, Running Rapids, Encountering Western Utes: William Lewis Manly's Voyage Down the Green River and across Utah in 1849," *Utah Historical Quarterly* 89, no. 3 (Summer 2021), 215–230.

I have made every effort to authenticate and verify all researched material presented in this book, and I bear responsibility for any errors, inaccuracies, omissions, or any other inconsistency herein. Any misrepresentation of events, people, places, companies, or organizations is unintentional.

Michael D. Kane
West Jordan, Utah
February 2021

Introduction: On the Trail with Lewis Manly

In 1869, with the financial support of the US government, Major John Wesley Powell led a now-famous river expedition. Starting at Green River, Wyoming Territory, Powell and his men traveled down the Green to its confluence with the Colorado River, then down the Colorado to its confluence with the Virgin River in Nevada. The explorers traveled 385 miles across Utah and Arizona Territories and successfully ran the entire length of the Grand Canyon. With this journey, Powell received considerable notoriety and acclaim for hardships endured and environments assessed.[1]

Twenty years earlier, and far less well-known, a twenty-nine-year-old American forty-niner made history on the Green River, too. En route

William Lewis Manly (1820–1903)

PHOTOGRAPHER UNKNOWN; PUBLISHED IN MANLY, *DEATH VALLEY IN '49*, II

to the goldfields of California, William Lewis Manly and his companions were traveling across the open lands of what would shortly become Utah Territory, and later Wyoming, when they came to the bank of the Green River. At the crossing, it dawned on Manly that he was "sitting on the bank of the river whose waters flowed to the great Pacific,"[2] and he and six other men decided to risk all and venture down the Green in the hope of reaching California by way of the river. Their decision to float a river and traverse lands unknown to them rather than traveling on the established emigrant trail began a grand adventure

I

down the Green and marks a unique chapter of forty-niner history—one filled with tales of bravery, sacrifice, and survival amid impossible odds in some of North America's most unforgiving landscapes.

Previous writers had grappled with the later portions of Manly's journey, carefully tracing his path through Death Valley, and that part of the story was better known.[3] But I gravitated to the early part. Just how far down the Green River did Manly float? It would probably be easier to determine if Manly had stored his papers somewhere else. More than forty years later, in 1894, Manly wrote about what happened to his records of the journey in his book, *Death Valley in '49*:

> I got out my memorandum I had kept through all my journey. As my letter [describing the journey west] was liable to be quite lengthy I bought a quantity of foolscap paper and begun. I took my diary as my guide, and filled out the ideas suggested in it so [my parents] would understand them. [. . .] So I worked away, day after day, for about a month [. . .] I had all the facts recorded which I found noted down in my diary. [. . .] My notes began in March, 1849, in Wisconsin, and ended in February, 1852 [. . .] over three hundred pages of closely written foolscap paper. [. . .] By the aid of my notes I could very easily remember everything that had taken place during my absence, and it was recorded in regular form, with day and date, not an incident of any importance left out, and every word as true as gospel. I had neither exaggerated nor detracted from any event so far as I could recollect. [. . .]
>
> I placed my narrative and some other papers in the chest and gave the key into [Samuel Zollinger's] charge [. . .] I wrote to Mr. Zollinger to send the account I had written to my parents in Michigan [. . .] I afterward learned that in time they received the bundle of paper and read it through and through, and circulated it around the neighborhood till it was badly worn, and laid it away for future perusal when their minds should incline that way. But the farm house soon after took fire and burned, my labor going up in smoke.[4]

Such was the process of recording and losing the account of William Lewis Manly's westward journey in 1849. Manly tells us he was "persuaded so earnestly by many friends to write the account" that he went on to write the story again, which appeared in an article titled "From Vermont to California" and in an expanded form in *Death Valley in '49*.[5] With these written documents, Manly recorded for history one of the most remarkable journeys across the western landscapes of America in the 1800s.

It did not take long after Manly's publication for historians and writers to start weighing in on his Green River adventure. In 1902, Frederick S. Dellenbaugh authored *The Romance of the Colorado River*. Dellenbaugh was seventeen years old when he joined John Wesley Powell's second expedition down the Green River in 1871. Dellenbaugh was not aware of Manly's story when he first published his book, but he learned of it later and included a short description in the third edition of *The Romance of the Colorado River*, published in 1909. In that edition, Dellenbaugh recognizes Manly's accomplishments and is complimentary of his achievements in running the Green in 1849. Without explaining why, since Manly himself does not specify the end point of his river voyage, Dellenbaugh states that Manly disembarked in northeastern Utah, in the Uinta Basin. Dellenbaugh wrote: "Manly's account appears entirely truthful. He tells of canyons, rapids, *etc.*, till near the mouth of Uinta River they met the Ute chief Walker."[6] Dellenbaugh's book is the first published attempt to pinpoint how far Manly floated down the Green. Since that time, many books, articles, and other literary references by historians have followed Dellenbaugh's lead and declared that Manly floated to the Uinta Basin, or the mouth of the Duchesne River, a distance of 290 miles, before leaving the river under Wákara's advice.[7] And certainly there are reasons to conclude he went only as far as the Uinta Basin; as I discuss later, Manly fails to describe important landmarks downstream from there, and the timeline makes more river miles appear less likely.

When I studied the issue, however, I began to wonder about the conventional wisdom. Reading Manly's book and articles closely, I realized he provided details about land formations, human encounters, and landmarks that are *downriver* from Whirlpool Canyon in the Uinta Basin.

Even more revealing, his account of his overland travels makes more sense if he had gotten off the river much farther south. Manly's book, *Death Valley in '49*, also includes an independent account of his fellow voyager Morgan S. McMahon, who separated from Manly when they got off the river, and McMahon's account offers further evidence that the company traveled beyond the Uinta Basin. Comparing the accounts to other historical events, maps, diaries, and interactions with fellow travelers at the time, I became convinced Manly traveled 125 miles farther south on the Green than Dellenbaugh gave him credit for. If I was right, Manly traveled all the way into southeastern Utah, where the Old Spanish Trail crosses the Green River in the San Rafael Desert, floating a total of not 290 miles but 415 miles, in thirty-three days.

I ultimately decided not to rely solely on the historical method, though. As Robert Shafer put it, "History is a science,"[8] and I decided that one of the important tests for determining the accuracy of Manly's expedition would fall to the method of scientific observation. Using empirically verifiable evidence as a barometer, I could gauge Manly's statements or claims as real or unreliable. Manly himself seemed to be challenging me to prove him right or wrong; he wrote, "Those who traveled over the same or similar routes are capable of passing a just opinion of the story."[9] Retracing Manly's steps afforded me the opportunity to objectively test the distances and claims made by Manly and his fellow explorers. I decided that if I were going to do a proper comparison, I would have to duplicate his water and overland travels as closely as possible, utilizing the same forms of travel and going at the same season of the year. In doing so, I hoped to be able to compare notes with Manly, see the same land formations, travel the same historical trails, and undergo similar experiences. In undertaking such an endeavor, the words of another historian, Paul D. Leedy, rang in my ears: "In order to appraise accurately the meaning and relationship of events . . . the historical researcher should always seek to get as close to the *original events* as possible in the hope of thus better reconstructing them."[10]

As I detail in Parts II and III, I organized just such an expedition. My schooling is in Parks, Recreation, and Tourism, and my doctoral dissertation was centered in history, but first and foremost I consider myself an outdoorsman. Like Manly, I have spent much of my life running rivers, including more than a decade outfitting and guiding thousands of people down the Snake River near Jackson Hole, Wyoming. I even had the opportunity to help run US president Bill Clinton down the Snake—twice, in 1995 and 1996. But a historic reenactment of a voyage down the Green River was new to me.

I gathered a crew that included my nineteen-year-old son, Dallas, and we embarked on August 13, 2006. In all, we floated 415 miles on the Green River in wood canoes we built ourselves, similar to the watercraft Manly constructed and described. Then we walked and rode horses 175 miles to Hobble Creek in what is now Utah County, Utah. Along the way I gained invaluable insights into Manly's journey, and I have spent the last decade analyzing in detail all aspects of his 1849 expedition. Even more, though, I had a great adventure in the wild lands of Utah, and I learned a lot about myself, my son, and the men we traveled with.

Retracing Manly's route firsthand created a window of opportunity to look into the past and appreciate his accomplishments, failures, and convictions about a land of free-flowing rivers and open space he so passionately cherished:

> I was always a great admirer of nature, and as I sat there alone I could see miles on miles of mammoth mustard waving in the strong breeze which came down over the San Francisco Bay just visible to the northward, and on the mountain summits to the west could see tall timber reaching up into the deep blue of the sky. It was a real contented comfort to be thus in the midst of luxuriance and beauty, and I enjoyed it, coming as it did at the end of the lone and dreary road I had been traveling for the past twelve months. Up the Platte; across the Rockies; down the Green River cañons in my canoe; across the mountains to Salt Lake; out over the "Rim of the Basin," and across the desert.[11]

So the doors of a newly forming America swing open for him to begin his westward adventure. I was more than happy to follow along.

Part I

From Vermont
to the Green River

CHAPTER ONE

American Explorers of the West

WILLIAM LEWIS MANLY STANDS AMONG AN ELITE GROUP OF AMERICAN explorers. Few people of his time were willing to set out into "the great unknown," as John Wesley Powell put it, and discover what lies beyond the edge of the map. This fraternity of frontiersmen had daring and courage, and their accomplishments are deeply woven into the fabric of early American western history as generations of settlers have followed their determination and the trails they blazed.

Though these explorers were spread out over the nineteenth century, their writings and views are strikingly similar. Meriwether Lewis, William Clark, John Wesley Powell, William H. Ashley, and William Lewis Manly were all explorers of the American West who had a deep sense of adventure and an abiding respect for the untamed lands they trod daily. (Though each took into account the peoples already living on these lands, none would have acknowledged that this made the land any less wild and untamed.) Their words and characteristics further reveal commitment to the path they chose.

Meriwether Lewis, who together with William Clark led a two-year expedition to explore the Louisiana Purchase, wrote:

> We were now about to penetrate a country at least two thousand miles in width, on which the foot of civillized man had never trodden; the good or evil it had in store for us was for experiment yet to determine, and these little vessells contained every article by which we were to expect to subsist or defend ourselves. . . .

I could but esteem this moment of our departure as among the most happy of my life.[1]

Meriwether Lewis was likewise branded by his biographer as "a man of high energy . . . but this was tempered by his great self-discipline. . . . He was born to leadership, and reared for it, studied it in his army career, then exercised it on the expedition. . . . He knew his profession and was proud of it and one of the best at it."[2]

Writing of his experiences exploring the Grand Canyon six decades later, John Wesley Powell displayed the same adventurous spirit, tempered by both anticipation and anxiety:

We are now ready to start on our way down the Great Unknown. . . . We are three quarters of a mile in the depths of the earth. . . . We have an unknown distance yet to run; an unknown river yet to explore. What falls there are, we know not; what rocks beset the channel, we know not; what walls rise over the river, we know not. Ah, well! We may conjecture many things. The men talk as cheerfully as ever; jests are bandied about freely this morning; but to me the cheer is somber and the jests are ghastly.[3]

On another occasion, Powell—whose biographer called him "a man of almost pathological optimism"—wrote:

At one time, I almost conclude to leave the river. But for years I have been contemplating this trip. To leave the exploration unfinished, to say that there is a part of the cañon which I cannot explore, having already almost accomplished it, is more that I am willing to acknowledge, and I determine to go on.[4]

Though William H. Ashley left behind scant records, he was cut from the same cloth as his fellow explorers. This pioneering mountain man who traversed the American West trapping beaver was eulogized by Rev. William G. Eliot in 1838 as "the most efficient leader that he ever knew."[5]

Ashley "demonstrated to himself and his men . . . his own strength, courage, and resourcefulness in the face of physical challenge and danger." Although he was often intense, "he carefully controlled his outward emotions and responses, giving the impression not only of a maturity beyond his years, but a determination, perseverance, steadiness, and restraint, which set him apart from ordinary frontier emigrants."[6]

Looking back on his own adventures, Manly expressed the same willingness to explore lands unknown:

> Reading people of to-day, who know so well the geography of the American continent, may need to stop and think that in 1849 the whole region west of the Missouri River was very little known; the only men venturesome enough to dare to travel over it were hunters and trappers who, by a wild life had been used to all the privations of such a journey, and shrewd as the Indians themselves in the mysterious ways of the trail and the chase.[7]

Manly's character was forged in his explorations when things grew dire. Confronted with the possibility of his own demise in the harsh deserts of southern California's Death Valley, he wrote:

> I tell you, friends, it was a trying moment. It seemed to be weighed down with all the trails [sic] and hardships of many months. It seemed to be the time when helpless women and innocent children hung on the trembling balance between life and death. Our own lives we could save by going back, and sometimes it seemed as if we would perhaps save ourselves the additional sorrow of finding them all dead to do so at once. I was so nearly in despair that I could not help bursting in tears, and I was not ashamed of the weakness.[8]

Besides determination and "frontier grit," this group of early Euro-American explorers also shared an appreciation for the beauty, majesty, and inspiration of the land. Meriwether Lewis wrote:

I had a most pleasing view of the country, perticularly of the wide and fertile vallies formed by the missouri and the yellowstone rivers, which occasionally unmasked by the wood on their borders disclose their meanderings for many miles in their passage through these delightfull tracts of country.[9]

Manly likewise described his feelings about the wilderness he encountered:

And now to see the clear, pure liquid, distilled from the crystal snow, abundant, free, filled with life and health—and write it in words—the song of that joyous brook and set it to the music that it made as it echoed in gentle waves from the rocks and lofty walls, and with the gentle accompaniment of rustling trees—a soft singing hush, telling of rest, and peace, and happiness.[10]

As Powell journeyed down the Green and Colorado Rivers, he was impressed with the simplicity and beauty of the water flow and surrounding areas, writing: "The curves are gentle, and often the river sweeps by an arc of vertical wall, smooth and unbroken, and then by a curve that is variegated by royal arches, mossy alcoves, deep, beautiful glens, and painted grottos."[11]

All five men appreciated the lands they traversed and lived for exploring them. William Manly, though standing in the shadows of the others' accomplishments, displayed similar character traits and wrote of his experiences in similar language. Like the other four explorers, he left his mark on the map of the American West.

CHAPTER TWO

Early Life on the Frontier

WHEN HORACE GREELEY DECLARED, "GO WEST, YOUNG MAN, AND grow up with the country,"[1] thousands of hardy souls took up the challenge, and throughout the nineteenth century, countless stories of adventure from the western frontier wove their way into the fabric of Americana. These pioneers envisioned open lands and boundless opportunities in the uncharted territories of the West as they followed the setting sun toward towering mountains and unknown rivers. One such young man was William Lewis Manly.

Born to Ebenezer and Phoebe Calkins Manly on April 6, 1820, Lewis (as he was known) spent his early life in the small farming community of St. Albans, Vermont, only fifteen miles from the Canadian border. Surrounded by dense forests of pine, hemlock, maple, beech, and birch trees, the farm life created an atmosphere of "New England ideals," hard work, and love of God, family, and country. Later he wrote favorably of what could be accomplished with "Yankee energy."[2] The Manly farm produced crops of flint corn, rye oats, potatoes, and turnips. The livestock consisted of dairy cows, sheep, pigs, oxen, and horses. During the cold winters, the main source of warmth in the home was the enormous fireplace, which consumed logs four feet long. Later in life, Manly remembered the sweet taste of wild strawberries, raspberries, whortle berries, and blackberries in summer, as well as apples from the orchards.[3]

Lewis Manly learned early in his life to depend on himself, helped along by family. In fall 1829, his family decided to start a new life in what was then the western frontier—Wisconsin and Michigan Territories.

Manly's parents and sister were to travel by water, while his aunt and uncle, by the name of Webster, set out ahead overland. Nine-year-old Lewis was allowed to go with the advance party. As he set out on the months-long journey, his parents offered their parting words: "Weigh well every thing you do; shun bad company; be honest and deal fair; be truthful and never fear when you know you are right."[4] Traveling over poorly maintained roads of dirt and mud, the small party made its way south of Cleveland, Ohio, near Lake Erie, where they stayed for the winter months. During this absence from his family, he quickly learned how strong his ties to them were, and how much he loved and respected his mother, father, and sister.

After receiving a letter from Manly's father, directing them to newly acquired property in the Detroit area, the Websters and Lewis left Cleveland in April, as the waters on the lakes and rivers began to thaw. Traveling around the southern tip of Lake Erie, they arrived at the Huron River only to find it impassable. Securing passage on a steamer, they loaded the wagon and their personal belongings and steamed up the lake northward toward Detroit. They carefully unloaded their wagon when they arrived, only to find the roads once again almost impassable.

Traveling slowly in the deeply rutted, muddy roads, Lewis and the Websters eventually arrived at a large house thirty miles west of Detroit. Lewis's family had already arrived, and he was reunited with his father, mother, sister, Polly, and a younger brother, Calvin. "Mother saw me first," Manly recalled, "and ran to the wagon and pulled me off and hugged and kissed me over and over again, while the tears ran down her cheeks."[5] Polly, who was two years older than her brother, patiently waited for her moment with Lewis, and after her mother's affections had been bestowed, she "locked arms with me and took me away with her."[6]

After this display of love and affection by all, Lewis recounted his deep-seated feelings towards his family:

We had never been separated before in all our lives and we had loved each other as good children should, who have been brought up in good and moral principles. We loved each other

14

and our home and respected our good father and mother who made it so happy for us.[7]

This tender moment of love and affection helped form the roots of Lewis's moral character, which he relied on and demonstrates to readers again and again in writing about his later adventures. Throughout Lewis's growing years, his thoughts were often of his family, and particularly his mother, Phoebe, who provided a bond of love, attention, and moral stability.[8]

Manly's strict New England upbringing is evident in his later writings. He was taught that cruel treatment of people or animals was wrong and that to swear was a sin. One day he saw a father curse a small child who fell while learning to walk; the father's insensitivity remained a painful lifelong memory. The first time Manly saw a slave sold at auction he said, "With my New England notions about the sin of slavery it made a very deep impression on me to see a fellow creature, black though he might be, sold at auction as I would sell a steer."[9]

Manly's mother and sister both focused on anchoring his moral and ethical values, while his father, Ebenezer, took time to teach his son the knowledge and skills that would be so vital later to his survival in the untamed lands of the West. At the emotional reuniting of the family in Michigan, Lewis's father gave him a gift that would prove as important as the strong ethical bonds his mother and sister provided. "Lewis," he said, "I have bought you a smooth bore rifle, suitable for ball or shot."[10] Ebenezer understood the necessity for Lewis to be able to stand on his own and rely on his abilities.

With this gift, Lewis quickly became proficient in the outdoor skills of hunting and survival, to the extent that he began to provide food for his family. As he later wrote, he "became quite an expert in the capture of small game for the table with my new gun . . . Father said to me:— '. . . come home nights—but keep on till you kill a deer.' So with his permission I started with my gun on my shoulder, and with feelings of considerable pride . . . and I got so steady that I could hit anything I could get in reach of."[11]

The Manly family began their new life of farming on two hundred homesteaded acres of government land purchased in Jackson County, Michigan. With the Manlys' strong work ethic, they soon harvested the rewards of a thriving farm. There were two houses on the farm, rough oak log homes with stone fireplaces, wood floors, and oak-shake shingles on the roof. The barn was also built of logs and provided a secure and safe place for the oxen, cow, and horse. Pigs, chickens, and sheep were all quickly added to make the farm productive. Essential duties of raising the farm included clearing brush, plowing and planting the grounds (the Manlys had four yoke of oxen and plow), and erecting fencing for protection. Describing the pattern of work, Manly wrote of "father and uncle splitting out the rails, while a younger brother and myself, by each getting hold of an end of one of them managed to lay up a fence four rails high, all we small men could do."[12]

As the farm became plentiful with wheat, corn, and potatoes, Lewis's role grew, and he increasingly found himself in the wilderness lands that surrounded the farm. His family came to depend more and more on his hunting wild game, fishing, and gathering fruits such as wild cranberries and whortleberries as they ripened at different seasons of the year.

From the age of nine to nineteen, Lewis enjoyed the benefits of a close family and spending time in the wilderness. Daily he would learn valuable lessons of survival as well as continuing to develop his moral character. It is within this setting of open lands and farming that Lewis remembered and compared his home in Michigan to the one he left in Vermont as "a real paradise."[13]

As Lewis Manly grew into manhood, more and more people felt the American West calling to them. At the age of nineteen, he stood five feet, nine inches tall and carried a strong desire to become independent and strike out on his own. While employed chopping and splitting rails for the Michigan Central Railroad and making thirteen dollars per month, he experienced a prolonged illness. He recounted, "I suffered a great deal and felt so miserable that I began to think I had rather live on the top of the Rocky Mountains and catch chipmunks for a living than live here and be sick."[14] Seeing that his three younger brothers were themselves turning into men who could manage the two hundred acres of farmland, Manly began to seriously ponder venturing off on his own.

Shortly after Manly turned twenty, he approached his parents about his desire to venture into the western wilderness, and once again they both provided valuable advice and the freedom for him to make his own decision. Manly's mother told him:

> You must be a good boy, honest and law-abiding. Remember our advice, and honor us for we have striven to make you a good and honest man, and you must follow outreaching, and your conscience will be clear. Do nothing to be ashamed of; be industrious, and you have no fear of punishment.[15]

Manly made up his mind; the lands of the West held his future and fortune. Striking up a friendship with a man named Orrin Henry, he found a traveling partner. They both quickly constructed a wood-plank boat and chest, loading it with the necessary provisions of clothing, quilts, and guns, and were soon ready for departure. As the final good-byes were uttered and tears shed, Manly's father once again spoke wisely as to the unknown challenges that awaited him. "You will have to depend upon yourself in all things," he told his son. "You have a wide, wide world to operate in—you will meet all kinds of people and you must not expect to find them all honest or true friends."[16] With that eloquent yet simple adieu, Manly embarked on a lifelong journey into nature and society.

As Manly was continually challenged, moving westward, he understood the opportunity to live in a country abounding in relatively untrammeled wilderness. Still, he would miss his Michigan home. "I was always a great admirer of nature and things which remained as they were created," he wrote, "and to the extent of my observations, I thought this the most beautiful and perfect country I had seen between Vermont and the Mississippi River."[17]

Manly began his first independent wilderness adventure uneventfully, floating down the Grand River in Michigan to the waters of Lake Michigan, where he found passage by schooner and crossed the lake into the Wisconsin Territory. Traveling 130 miles on foot, he noted: "Walking began to get pretty tiresome. Great blisters would come on our feet, and, tender as they were, it was a great relief to take off our boots and go barefoot."[18] Manly finally reached the small community of Mineral Point, in the heart of the Wisconsin wilderness, but after a short stint splitting wood and hunting, he resolved to return to his family in Michigan due to the lack of work. "Prospects were surely very gloomy for me here away out west in Wisconsin Territory," he remarked.[19]

Traveling back east to Milwaukee, he gained passage on a steamboat bound for the north end of Lake Michigan and then south, down Lake Huron to the city of Detroit. Manly then boarded a train on the Michigan Central Railroad, arriving very close to his parents' farm, and walked two and a half miles to a wonderful reunion at his farm home. "I had a right royal welcome," he recalled, "and the questions they asked me about the wild country I had traveled over, how it looked, and how I got along—were numbered by the thousand."[20] As rewarding as it was for Manly to be reunited with his family, it only took a couple of months for him to again feel the desire to seek his destiny in the western lands of America. Recovering from an illness he called "bilious fever" (or Michigan malaria) he contracted there, and saving some money, Manly once again readied himself and embarked westward in the fall of 1840.

Learning from his past struggles from his first exodus westward, Manly traveled eastward to Detroit and took a steamer back around Lake Huron and down Lake Michigan to Chicago. He remembered the city as "a small, cheaply built town, with rough sidewalks and terribly muddy streets, and the people seemed pretty rough."[21] Finding his way northwestward, Manly arrived in Madison, the territorial capital of Wisconsin, then turned westward once again and returned to Mineral Point. There, Manly again found employment in mining and chopping wood, but the following year he used his expertise in trapping and hunting to earn a more stable income.

As the summer season began to unfold, Manly ventured northward in the Wisconsin woods with Asabel Bennett and a Mr. Buck. The deep and trusting friendship with Bennett would remain throughout Manly's life and play a significant role in the years to come. In the remote wilderness of Wisconsin, Manly's outdoor skills and sense of survival began to take shape. In the fall, winter, and spring months, he successfully hunted bear and deer and trapped foxes, minks, and raccoons. In addition to his time spent hunting, Manly built a cabin to live in and a canoe for crossing and floating numerous rivers. He tanned his own hides and sewed his own buckskin clothing as well as making his own tomahawk with a blade two inches wide and three inches long.

On one occasion after Manly had shot an eagle, he saw "an Indian" steadily coming toward him. Not knowing the man's intentions, Manly wrote: "I . . . brought my gun to bear on him. He stopped suddenly and made signs not to shoot, and I let him come up." On another occasion, describing a common day, Manly remembered, "I would kill one [porcupine,] skin it and drag the carcass after me all day as I set traps, cutting off bits for bait, and cooking the rest for ourselves to eat." It was a daily test of survival in a land of challenges, which Manly relished.[22]

Emerging from the dense Wisconsin wilderness in May, with prized animal pelts that were by his own account far better in quality than other trappers had obtained, Manly and his partner, Mr. Buck, met with remarkable success. Their buyer "told us we were the best fur handlers he had seen, and paid us two hundred dollars in American gold for what we had."[23] Others at Mineral Point were simply amazed that both men were still alive. Manly invested his trapping money in government land. "This was the first $100 I ever had," he recalled, "and I felt very proud to be a land owner. I felt more like a man now than I had ever felt before, for the money was hard earned and all mine."[24]

As Manly explored the open lands of the Michigan and Wisconsin wilderness, he fast became familiar with the waterways of both small and large rivers. He found it much more efficient to depend on boats or canoes rather than strike out overland. As noted, Manly's first experience building a boat was in 1840, before he left on his first adventure from his Michigan home, when he and his partner, Orrin Henry, "purchased three nice whitewood boards, eighteen inches wide, from which we make us a boat" to paddle to Lake Michigan.[25] Manly's next experience involving watercraft took place when he returned home to Michigan. Instead of walking or using wagons, he purchased steamer fare and ferried to the top of Lake Michigan and down Lake Huron to Detroit. It was during this voyage, at a stop called Mackinaw, that Manly noticed a well-crafted birch-bark canoe for the first time. This canoe caught his eye for its simplicity and speed in the water. "At the shore line the Indians were loading a large white birch bark canoe," he remembered. "One man took the stern seat to steer, and four or five more had seats along the gunwale. . . . Their crafts danced as lightly on the water as an egg shell."[26]

Returning within the year to the Wisconsin Territory, Manly again utilized his knowledge and skills to construct a canoe for his travels. "There were three pine trees, the only ones to be found in many miles," he wrote. "We made us a canoe of one of them."[27] With that canoe Manly and his partner, Mr. Buck, traveled down an unnamed stream: "We found it rather difficult work, but the stream grew larger and we got along very well."[28] The fact that Manly remembered the brook gradually increasing in size suggests that they traveled a significant distance. After mastering canoe travel, both men built another boat later on as the winter season turned to spring. Manly once again purchased four boards to build a boat and floated down the Black River toward the Mississippi.[29]

Manly found success traveling both up and down the many rivers he encountered for two important reasons. First, he had learned the skill to construct various types of boats from processed lumber, as well as the ability to carve out canoes from standing trees. Both required a specific design to meet the demands of the different rivers he traveled. Second, he had gained valuable experience understanding water currents, back eddies, sandbars, and log jams, and he learned how to safely maneuver through the many challenges that river running brings. Unbeknownst to Manly, these skills, which he honed as he traveled up and down free-flowing rivers throughout the Wisconsin wilderness, would become paramount to his survival on future rivers when he turned westward toward California.

Chapter Three

Westward Ho

As eight years of mining and hunting in the remote regions of Wisconsin played out, Lewis Manly felt drawn to the excitement of growing opportunities farther west. "Thus in 1845 I had a slight touch of the disease [westward fever] on account of the stories they told us about Oregon," he recounted. "I began at once to think about a outfit and a journey and found that it would take me at least two years to get ready."[1]

Manly was only one of thousands who felt the same excitement about the golden lands to the west. In the book *The Age of Gold*, H. W. Brands gives insight into the intense enthusiasm as countless people traveled on the open plains, over mountains, and across seas to the American West:

> They came by the tens and hundreds and thousands, then by the tens of thousands and hundreds of thousands. They came by sailing ship and steamship, by horse and mule and ox and wagon and foot. They came in companies and alone, with money and without, knowing and naïve. They tore themselves from warm hearths and good homes, promising to return; they fled from cold hearts and bad debts, vowing never to return. They were farmers and merchants and sailors and slaves and abolitionists and soldiers of fortune and ladies of the night. They jumped bail to start their journey, and jumped ship at journey's end. They were pillars of their communities, and their communities' dregs.[2]

The North American continent would never see such a frenzied movement of people again. In *Women's Diaries of the Westward Journey*, Lillian Schlissel estimated that between 1841 and 1848, the number of westward migrants increased from 100 to 4,000. As significant as that is, it pales compared to the 1849 figure: 30,000.[3] Major Osborne Cross wrote:

> The banks of the South Platte [in Nebraska] seemed to be lined with large trains, moving on both sides of the river.... They could be seen as far as the eye extended. . . . As the emigrants passed Fort Kearny this spring, the wagons were counted by the guard daily, and on the first of June better than 4,000 had passed, not reckoning those that were on the left bank of the river, which could not be seen from the fort. While on the journey to Oregon, I had a good opportunity of ascertaining the number of persons with each wagon, and it was a small average to estimate four toeach one; which would make, at this time, nearly 20,000 persons ahead of us.... The number of animals in advance of the regiment could not have been less than 50,000.[4]

George A. Smith, a leader of the Mormons recently settled near the Great Salt Lake, recounted that some twelve thousand wagons crossed the Missouri below Kanesville, Iowa. "The world is perfectly crazy after gold," he wrote. "It is estimated that 40,000 men are on their way overland in search of the yellow dirt."[5] When Captain Howard Stansbury of the US Army Corps of Topographical Engineers headed west to explore the Salt Lake Valley in 1849, he commented: "We have been in company with multitudes of emigrants the whole day. The road has been lined to a long extent with their wagons, whose white covers, glittering in the sunlight, resembled, a distance, ships upon the ocean. We passed a company from Boston [the Boston-Newton Company], consisting of seventy persons, one hundred and forty pack and riding mules, a number of riding horses, and a drove of cattle for beef."[6]

Manly's first thoughts of heading to the West Coast occurred in 1845, as rumors of opportunity circulated. "They said it was in a territory of rich soil, with plenty of timber, fish and game," he wrote. "The climate was very mild in winter, as they reported, and I concluded it would suit me exactly."[7] That year only an estimated five thousand people began the exodus west. But that would soon change. As Manly recounted: "In the winter of 1848–49 news began to come that there was gold in California. But not generally believed till it came through a US officer, and then, as the people were used to mines and mining, a regular gold fever spread as if by swift contagion."[8] As the doors of opportunity began to swing wide, exposing the lands westward, Manly found himself with a head start: he was already on the western frontier in the Wisconsin Territory, he was prepared for the challenge ahead, and the wilderness was an environment he relished.

After discussing the challenges and opportunities, Manly and Asabel Bennett agreed that their fortunes were waiting in the goldfields of California. They consented to traveling together, Manly providing his outdoor skills in hunting, herding livestock, driving wagons, and protection while Bennett supplied a wagon, livestock, camping supplies, family, and food. The men arranged to depart Mineral Point, Wisconsin, and head west to the lands of promise in the spring of 1849.

As preparations ended and the trek was to begin, a mistake in communication led to the separation of the two parties. Manly realized that he needed a good, strong horse to successfully make the arduous journey, so he traveled by steamboat to Prairie La Crosse, where he purchased a Winnebago pony for thirty dollars. Though not entirely impressed with his new pony ("I found him to be a poor, lazy little fellow," he complained), Manly nonetheless held out hope that with good care and feed, the horse would improve.

Together, horse and rider crossed the Bad Ax River to meet the Bennetts at the predetermined location in Prairie du Chien, a small city on the east bank of the Mississippi River. When Manly arrived at the designated location, a letter from Asabel Bennett was waiting, explaining that his departure would be delayed for two or three weeks due to poor grass conditions. With this limited information and no firm date given, Manly thought that perhaps the Bennett family had returned to Mineral Point to wait out the several weeks. So he traversed back across the state of Illinois to Mineral Point, only to find the Bennett family had left two weeks prior. Troubled with the confusion, Manly hastily traveled back to Prairie du Chien, crossing the Mississippi River and traversing all of Iowa to the western city of Council Bluffs (an estimated distance of 350 miles) near the banks of the Missouri River.

Along the way, Manly constantly searched for his traveling companions. "I looked first for a letter, but there was none," he remembered. "Then I began to look over the cards in the trading places and saloons, and read the names written on the logs of the houses, and everywhere I thought there might be a trace of the friends I sought. No one had seen or knew them. . . . Pretty blue."[9] What Manly did not know was that the Bennetts had arrived safely in Council Bluffs before him and had crossed the Mississippi at Kanesville, north of the city.

As it turned out, Manly would be reunited with the Bennetts four months later in the Utah Territory. But for now, dejected and discouraged, he faced a dilemma. He had limited money, and all his essential provisions—clothing, outfit, gun, and other survival gear—were in the Bennett wagon. He soon realized that if he was going to continue on to California, he needed a change in plans.

Carefully weighing his options, Manly met and struck a deal with Charles M. Dallas of Linn, Iowa,[10] a merchant headed west with ox teams and goods. They agreed to travel together and exchange services. Manly would be employed as an experienced teamster and outdoorsman, driving one of the ox-driven wagons and cows in exchange for transportation and board. Manly described the train as a "small band of five wagons, ten men, one woman and three children."[11] They moved at a slow pace, leaving St. Joseph, Missouri, late in the spring of 1849, traveling across the open flatlands of the Platte River. Before long, Manly began voicing his concerns about Dallas, who he felt acted dishonestly by stealing a stray horse from a military escort. "I did not like this much, for if we were discovered, we might be roughly handled," he wrote. "My New England ideals of honesty were somewhat shocked."[12]

Manly's writings concerning his trek across Nebraska at times become very vague, lacking in detail as to the many hardships he and other emigrant parties faced. He seldom mentioned extreme weather conditions, Indians, wagon failures, or personal struggles. Such difficulties, along with the loss of oxen and other livestock from dehydration or lack of foliage and the loss of wagons and personal belongings from needing to reduce weight, were common and could be catastrophic. One emigrant wrote of Wyoming: "From Fort Laramie grass began to fail our stock . . . I have counted about one thousand wagons that have been burnt or otherwise disposed of on the road. . . . From Deer creek to the summit, the greatest amount of property has been thrown away . . . iron, trunks, clothing, etc., lying strewed around to the value of fifty thousand dollars in about twenty miles. I have counted about five hundred dead oxen along the road, and only three mules."[13] David Staples, traveling in the Boston-Newton Company in 1849, within miles of Manly, wrote in his diary as he drew close to the Wind River Mountains: "July, 18th . . . We passed 64 dead oxen in the last 3 days, 34 which we passed today. . . . July 19th . . . We passed 25 dead oxen and 1 mule."[14]

In addition to these common but extreme hardships, the most devastating to all travelers was the disease of cholera. Manly himself mentions cholera only once, and in a very unconcerned way: "We occasionally passed by a grave along the road, and often small head board would state that the poor unfortunate had died of cholera."[15] The fear of cholera, one of the most deadly diseases in America through the mid-1800s, was fed by ignorance as well as the lack of treatment. It caused the death of thousands and left dreams shattered along the two-thousand-mile journey. In his journal, Osborne Cross of the Regiment of Mounted Riflemen wrote: "The cholera now began to make its appearance along this route, the number who had died with it was sufficient evidence that the emigrants were suffering greatly from its effects. They were truly to be pitied, as no aid in any way could be afforded them; on the contrary, they were often compelled to travel when it was almost death to them to be moved. . . . Much fear was entertained that the cholera would increase; we certainly had every reason to suppose so, from the many deaths among the emigrants along the road, and their present helpless condition."[16] Sarah Royce, who was only a few days ahead of Manly on the emigrant trail, wrote: "But another enemy, unseen, and without one audible word of demand or threat, was in that very hour advancing upon us, and made our wagon his first point of attack. . . . The Doctor pronounced the disease

Asiatic Cholera . . . and in two or three hours the poor old man expired."[17] Though Manly wrote little of the illness, it would have been impossible for him not to have seen and felt the effect of cholera in his camp or others. Cholera stalked all camps, much like the wolves that uncovered the graves and consumed the bodies of loved ones left behind.

Given the lack of detail and description of Manly's travels on the emigrant trail, there has been some confusion as to how much time it took him to reach Fort Laramie. In order to reconstruct a more accurate timetable, we need to know how fast he was traveling as well as where he was on specific dates. Mel Bashore, trails expert formerly at the LDS Church History Library, estimates that because of the slow pace of the oxen pulling heavy merchant wagons, the train would likely have averaged ten to twelve miles per day. As for specific dates, we can work with two significant events documented in primary sources. First, Manly recorded that as they headed west, they passed the newly constructed Forts Kearney and Laramie.[18] He then gives an estimated date—a rarity in his record—noting that his company was "several miles from Ft. Kearney I think on July 3rd."[19] Examining the other primary source, however, disproves Manly's estimate.

On the evening of Sunday, June 10, and continuing into June 11, a storm of tremendous force confronted the Fayette Rovers, a company on the trail that was driving a large group of cattle westward. At the time, the Rovers were located near the banks of the Platte River by Prairie Creek and Loup River, not far from Fort Kearney. A member of that company, Adonijah S. Welch, recorded the tempest in his journal:

> June 11—Monday.—It is with no little regret that I record in my journal the occurrence of another stampede, much more serious in its results than the one just spoken of. . . . At last we succeeded in turning them up the river, in which direction we followed them until we thought ourselves within six miles of the camp, and regarded the prospect of saving our cattle, fair. But our expectations were destined to disappointment. The dark cloud which had hung silently on the verge of the northern horizon suddenly rose, and soon obscured the whole canopy of heaven.

It was black as an inky midnight. The rain beat down upon us in such torrents that we soon had not a dry thread of clothing. No object could be seen half a yard distant except when the impenetrable darkness was dispelled by a sudden flash of vivid lightning, which clothed the whole plain and river with a glare of unearthly light, rendering every object distinctly visible for miles distant—an instant[—]then left us in darkness as blind as before. [. . .]

A census was taken about ten o'clock, by which it was found that one hundred and twenty-seven out of two hundred and eighty were missing. Parties have been out all day, but only two were brought in. [. . .]

June 12—Tuesday [. . .] We took a course along the summits of the bluffs, which ran parallel with the river, back toward the Loup. [. . .]

Near night we struck the trail of about fifteen cattle, and soon after met two trains, one of which had found a yoke of cattle near Elm Creek, belonging to the "Canton Boys," who drove two wagons belonging to our "ten." [. . .] we rode on until we arrived at Dry Creek where we made our encampment.

We reluctantly abandoned the pursuit and returned to our old camp on Dry Creek, where we slept soundly, and the next morning we started for *home,* at which we arrived on the day after, subsisting on the way on hard bread—all that was left of our stock. We were joyfully welcomed back to the "Rovers," who gave us a rich repast of the meat of a buffalo they had just killed. Our sick men were nearly well.—Seventy oxen had been found during our absence, having been stolen by a company from Tennessee, who had found, and forced them to swim the river. They were recovered by Dibble and three others, who swam the river and drove them back. Baxter is now in search for the rest, and it is confidently believed that they are still in possession of the company ahead.[20]

The relevance of this story to Lewis Manly becomes clear in the company's records dating from several months later. Mindful of their lost cattle, the Rovers kept a vigilant eye on other emigrants' herds, inspecting them as they passed or were passed. They arrived in the Salt Lake Valley in September and then traveled south to the area of Fort Provo and Hobble Creek, where they rested their cattle and waited for cooler weather to continue the soon-to-be-opened trail to California. While waiting, the Rovers spotted some of their missing cattle in the Dallas camp, which had arrived shortly after them. To determine ownership, a trial was held between the Rovers and Dallas. William Lorton, who was also in the Fort Provo area, recorded this event in his personal diary on September 26: "Had a trial . . . between [Charles M.] Dallas & the Rovers. I was called on as witness. The cattle were of those that stampeded on the Platt. The honorable body decided in favor of the Fayette Rovers."[21]

From this trial it can be verified and documented that on June 11, when the Fayette Rovers' cattle were lost on the Platte, the Dallas company (with Lewis Manly) was in close enough proximity to capture the frightened cattle. Knowing that Manly arrived at the Green River on August 19, the timeline based on Welch's date of June 11 makes much more sense than the one based on Manly's date of July 3. If Manly's company was near Prairie Creek on June 11, which they would have had to be to capture the Rovers' cattle, then they would have seventy days to travel the 705 miles to Green River.[22] This averages out to just over ten miles a day, well within the parameters Mel Bashore laid out. If on the other hand they were near Fort Kearney on July 3, they would have had to travel roughly the same distance in just forty-eight days, or nearly fifteen miles a day, without any rest or recovery days.[23]

Moving across the western landscape toward Fort Laramie, Manly came in contact with a religious exodus that rivaled the quest for religious freedom from the European continent in the 1700s. One of the unusual perspectives that Manly recorded in his accounts of 1849 was his understanding and perceptions of the Mormons, or members of the Church of Jesus Christ of Latter-day Saints, including their religious views and mannerisms. Manly often reminded readers that he was raised on "New England ideals" and principles. Though not of the Mormon faith, he found that the Mormons were a constant presence in the western migration, and in discussions with others along the trail, Manly began to formulate his own views of the Mormons and their beliefs.

The first encounter with Mormons Manly recorded was a party traveling from Salt Lake City back to the United States. He wrote: "About this time we met a odd looking train going east, consisting of five or six Mormons from Salt Lake, all mounted on small Spanish mules. They were dressed in buckskin and moccasins, with long spurs jingling at their heels, the rowels fully four inches long, and each one carried a gun, a pistol and a big knife. They were rough looking fellows with long, matted hair, long beards, old slouch hats and a generally back woods get-up air in every way."[24]

In 1849, Manly found himself surrounded by Latter-day Saints coming and going to the Salt Lake Valley on the same trail. In fact, the trail itself was commonly called the Mormon Trail. As historians of the Mormon exodus point out, "It became the preferred route for thousands of forty-niner gold-seekers who traveled the Mormon Trail into Salt Lake."[25] Manly recounted another meeting with a small group of Mormons on the trail, and his preconceptions of them: "I had heard much about the Mormons . . . and some way or other I could not separate the idea of horse thieves from this party, and I am sure I would not like to meet them if I had a desirable mule that they wanted, or any money, or a good looking wife. We talked with them half an hour or so and then moved on."[26]

When Manly and his small group of emigrants reached Fort Laramie, Wyoming Territory, he again met "some Mormons, employed as teamsters, and in other ways, and they told us there were some Missourians on the road who would never live to see California. There had been some contests between the Missourians and the Mormons, and I felt rather glad that none of us hailed from Pike county [Missouri]."[27] In this encounter, Manly began to experience, first-hand, the deep-seated views that accompanied the Mormons west. Driven out of their promised land of Missouri, they carried significant resentment of how they were treated. Manly's feelings toward the Mormons, a people he did not fully understand, would contribute to his later decisions regarding his route to California.

Remarkably, in this time period the Dallas company often found itself accompanied or in the area of two men who kept detailed journals, James Mason Hutchings and Captain Robert M. Morris. Their accounts help authenticate and validate Manly's own record, including his claim he crossed Deer Creek on July 31 (mileage marker 619) and his observation that he crossed the Green River on August 19 (mileage marker 862), meaning that he traveled a distance of 243 miles in nineteen days, or 12.7 miles per day.[28] Considering the important role these journals play in validating Manly's claims, it is necessary to document Hutchings's travels and his association with Captain Morris prior to meeting and traveling with the Dallas party leaving Fort Laramie. These background details help clarify times when Manly was vague in his own account, and they add meaning to events and decisions Manly described while traveling with the Dallas party.

James Mason Hutchings was a twenty-nine-year-old British emigrant who arrived in the United States on board the ship *Gertrude* in June 1848.[29] After temporarily residing in New York City, he quickly found his way south to New Orleans, arriving by August 13. In January of 1849, the news of the goldfields in California convinced Hutchings to take on the challenge of venturing west, and he soon began to prepare himself for the journey. Like Manly, Hutchings crossed the Missouri late, meaning he was "six weeks behind the bulk of migration."[30]

With his late start, Hutchings and others in his party decided to join a large military group, which would provide safety and security. While waiting at Fort Kearney for additional militia members, Major Robert Bannon Reynolds from Knoxville, Tennessee, acting as the quartermaster for the military wagon train, hired Hutchings on June 25 to repair wagons and other wood items. Hutchings was quite proud to work as a carpenter for the US military. He recorded the terms and his reaction in his journal:

> If I would consent to become carpenter of the train, I'd greatly oblige them, should receive wages, and rations, and have all my baggage, tools, etc. carried. I told him I had no objections, and consulted my company, and they agreed. Since we were travelling

with the train we could as well work for it as not. Also my baggage being carried would lighten our own wagon considerably. They readily agreed to cook, tend to camp duties and free me entirely. I told the Major; he went immediately to the Captain [Robert M. Morris], and in ten minutes I was in the service of Uncle Sam—a thing of which I had never dreamed.[31]

The military train Hutchings joined was part of a larger military entourage moving west to solidify the newly claimed western lands and protect the thousands of emigrants traveling on the trails. The military presence was enabled by the 1846 "Act to provide for raising a regiment of Mounted Riflemen and for establishing military stations on the route to Oregon," which provided for ten companies of riflemen. As a result, and to Hutchings's benefit, "a train of about 400 wagons carrying supplies for the military posts at Fort Laramie and Fort Hall were to leave Fort Leavenworth on June 1 [1849]."[32] Specifically, the company Hutchings joined, under the command of Brevet Captain Robert M. Morris, was formed to accompany and protect John J. Wilson, who was newly appointed as a naval agent for California and Indian agent for Salt Lake City.[33]

After Fort Laramie, Hutchings's contingent met and began to travel with the Dallas party. Manly wrote of his military escort: "As we passed Ft. Laramie we fell in company with some U.S. soldiers who were going to Ft. Hall and thence to Oregon. We considered them pretty safe to travel with and kept with them for some time, though their rate of travel was less than ours."[34] Both Hutchings and Manly make a point to mention that the man in charge of the military company, Major Reynolds, was accompanied by an attractive young lady, who had originally been traveling with the captain of another wagon train but soon left him for Reynolds.[35] Manly wrote, "The captain of the company had a very nice looking lady with him, and they carried a fine wall tent which they occupied when they went into camp. . . . Everybody though[t] the Captain was very lucky in having such an accomplished companion, and journey along quietly to the gold fields at government expense."[36] Elsewhere Manly referred to her as "the gay young lady."[37] He also mentioned seeking advice from a surgeon in the military company. This was likely a doctor accompanying the politician John J. Wilson.[38]

Adding to the uniqueness of the military force Manly mixed with was the presence of immigrant mule drivers, a common hire by the Mounted Riflemen.[39] Manly remembered the awkwardness of communication, writing, "The Government party we were with had among them a German mule driver who had a deal of trouble with his team, but who had a very little knowledge of the English language."[40]

As the combined wagon trains—including gold rushers, military personnel, a beautiful woman, some Mormon teamsters, and several foreign mule drivers—moved steadily westward into what would become Wyoming Territory, events recorded by Manly, Hutchings, and Captain Morris provide a tightly consistent timeline.

Shortly after passing Fort Laramie, Manly experienced another tremendous storm, which he vividly remembered in his later book:

> The first night on this road we had the hardest rain I ever experienced. . . . Our camp was on a level piece of ground on the bank of a dry creek, which soon became a very wet creek indeed, for by morning it was one hundred yards wide and absolutely impassible. It went down, however, as quickly as it rose and by ten o'clock it was so low that we easily crossed and went on our way. We crossed one stream where there were great drifts or piles of hail which had been brought down by a heavy storm from higher up the hills.[41]

Though not as detailed, Hutchings likewise recorded on July 24, two days after leaving Fort Laramie, "A violent thunderstorm paid us a visit, and serenaded us long after we had retired for the night."[42] Hutchings followed his observance of the terrific storm by recounting that it was "very cold" in the morning and that the roads remained "heavy (caused by the rain)" two days later. Of the memorable storm, Captain Morris recorded in his journal: "July 25th Having had no good grass for some twenty miles before reaching Fort Laramie and none since, with a poor prospect of finding any better for some time to Come, I determined to remain and recruit my animals for a day or two. Stormed and rained severely at 1AM of this night."[43]

Several days later, Manly and Hutchings arrived in the Black Hills, and again both commented on the same events. At their campsite on July 29 they found an unusual number of scattered elk antlers. "From the large number of elk horns lying about we concluded it to be a favorite 'stamping-ground' of theirs and named it 'Elk Horn Valley,'" noted Hutchings.[44] Manly was also impressed and brought to bear his knowledge of the outdoors, writing, "I found here a good many heads and horns of elk, and I could not decide whether they had been killed in winter during the deep snow, or had starved to death."[45] Since both men had time to inspect and review the elk horns, it is clear there was some time for rest when they camped for the evening. The next day brought another event both found worth recording. Hutchings wrote, "This afternoon in visiting the ground where we first took the animals I discovered a coal-mine. Upon trying it we found it burned well, and is of excellent quality."[46] And Manly: "We came out at the river again at the mouth of Deer Creek, and as there was some pretty good coal there quite easy to get."

The following day, July 31, the wagon train crossed the North Platte River. The river was wide and deep enough to require the use of a series of ferryboats to cross safely. Manly remembered the event briefly, writing: "There was a ferry there to cross the river and go up along north side. Mr. Dallas bought the whole outfit for a small sum and when we were safely over he took with him such ropes as he wanted and tied the boat to the bank."[47] Hutchings is more detailed in his account of this same event, focusing on the related financial transactions: "Mr. Dallas bought the ferry-boat this morning . . . for an inferior horse, the owners having grown tired of staying there any longer. . . . We worked hard all day to get the teams over, were charged two dollars a wagon, so he made fifty-eight dollars out of our train, crossed his own over for nothing, and sold it for one hundred fifty dollars."[48] For his part, Captain Morris recorded on July 31, "Marched 5 Miles from Camp No 46 reached a ferry where I crossed all my teams between 11 AM and dark at $1.00 each 21 in number, Camped on the North side of North fork Platte in a Sand bank, drove the mules two miles up the river bank and herded them."[49]

These accounts firmly establish that Manly crossed the Platte near Deer Creek on July 31, and with that information one can calculate the wagon train's rate of travel for the next few weeks. According to William Clayton's *Emigrants' Guide*, the distance from Deer Creek to the Green River is 242¾ miles. Manly arrived at the Green on August 19, meaning the party traveled 12¾ miles per day.

After the Platte River crossing, the entourage followed the path of the winding Sweetwater River to Independence Rock. This outcropping of granite, standing north of the Sweetwater, became a landmark that many travelers remembered. Hutchings described it as follows: "This rock stands in an isolated position twenty-five rods in length and one hundred twenty feet in height at the highest part. On the top there is a hollow in which there is water standing most of the year. The road is generally below the lower side of the 'Rock' and near the river. The rock had its name from some of the early emigrants or trappers spending the Fourth of July, and every year since emigrants have traveled long into the night, or will delay a day or two, so as to be there to celebrate. The rock, unlike the sandy limestone of the North Plat[t]e, is of granite, so also the other rocks on the Sweetwater River."[50]

The exact date Manly was at Independence Rock is not known, but it can be estimated. Hutchings's party camped at Independence Rock on August 6 and was at Devil's Gate (five and a half miles farther) on August 8.[51] But he was ahead of the Dallas party at this point, since the next day he "took the river road back and met Dallas and Colonel Johnson."[52] On that day, August 9, Captain Morris wrote in his journal, "Left Camp On 53 at 6 A. M. reached 'Independence rock' 2½ miles at 7AM, Just beyond this crossed the river and marched five to six miles over a tolerable road when we passed Devils Gate."[53] Morris was very likely with Colonel Johnson at the time, who was in turn with Dallas. Comparing these two journals, we can conclude that Manly reached Independence Rock between August 6 and August 9.

Whatever the exact date, while Manly was at Independence Rock, he took the opportunity to climb the granite outcropping and look for the initials or name of his business partner, Asabel Bennett. "We passed a lone rock standing in the river bottom on the Sweetwater, which they named Independence Rock," he recalled. "It was covered with the names of thousands of people who had gone by on that road. Some were pretty neatly chiseled in, some very rudely scrawled, and some put on with paint. I spent all the time I could hunting Mr. Bennett's name, but I could not find it anywhere."[54] Carving one's name into Independence Rock was a common activity for travelers on the emigrant trail; Kent Ruth, the author of *Landmarks of the West,* writes, "Thousands of names can still be read on Independence Rock, nor have wind and rain completely obliterated the dim wagon ruts at its base."[55]

Knowing that Manly was at Independence Rock in early August 1849 looking for someone else's carvings, I researched the possibility that Manly placed his own initials on the rock. In chapter 3 of Randy Brown's *Historic Inscriptions on Western Emigrant Trails,* the inscription of "W'M 1849" is recorded at Independence Rock. While a common enough set of initials, there is a chance that Manly rudely scribed these initials while there. With the help of my daughter Morgan, I visited Independence Rock myself. After several hours of searching, we discovered the inscription indicated by Brown. Located next to the W and between the W and the M at the top of the initials is a chiseled mark. That mark could be an abbreviation for the small letter "m" signifying the abbreviated name of William. Scribed just below "W'M 1849" is another inscription, which reads, "June 20 1849 A Montgomery." Because the two sets of carvings are in such close proximity, there is a possibility that they were inscribed at the same time. The inscriptions look very similar and could have been inscribed using the same tool. If this was the case, the W'M inscription would not be Manly's, since he was on Independence Rock between August 6 and August 9. Casting further doubt on the possibility that it is Manly's inscription, as previously discussed, is the fact that Manly was generally known by his middle name, Lewis.[56] Later on his journey, Manly did record his name on a rock while traveling down the Green River. According to his book, "I painted in fair sized letter on the rock, CAPT. W. L. MANLEY, U. S. A."[57] Thus, it is likely that had he inscribed something at Independence Rock, Manly would have included the initial "L."

Leaving Independence Rock, the Dallas party steadily continued westward. "We traveled on up the Sweetwater for some time," Manly recorded, "and at last came to a place where the road left the river, and we had a long, hard hill to pull up. When we reached the top of this we were in the South Pass of the Rocky Mountains, the backbone of the American continent."[58] Manly reached the South Pass on August 14, as confirmed by Hutchings's journal, which records that his group and Dallas's group were there on that date.[59] Captain Morris recorded his awe at seeing the mountains, including the presence of snow at the higher elevations: "The Wind river Mountains present the fines[t] outline of any that I have ever see, being strongly defined and bold and rugged, for the past three days there has been considerable snow upon the more elevated [peaks]. . . . After leaving the 'pass' the Mountains extend to the right and left until lost in the distance."[60] Manly also noted the lateness of the season and the presence of snow on the peaks of the Wind River Mountains: "We were now on the Sweetwater River, and began to see the snow on the Rocky Mountains ahead of us, another reminder that there was a winter coming and only a little more than half our journey was done."[61] This became an ever-growing concern for Manly. "In talking with the men of the U.S. troops in whose company we still were," he wrote, "I gathered much information concerning our road further west. They said we were entirely too late to get through to California."[62] According to Hutchings's biographer, he "left nearly six weeks behind the mainstream of the migration."[63] For his part, Manly commented, "We thought the lateness of the season meant a doubtful place to winter, and we wondered where it possibly might be."[64]

Chapter Four

Decision at the Green River

As his party got closer and closer to Salt Lake City, Manly became more worried about having to spend the winter among the Mormons. His team master, Charles M. Dallas, had instructed the group that everyone would have to winter in Salt Lake City before heading on to California. Manly confessed:

> This was bad news for me, for I had known of the history of them at Nauvoo [Illinois] and in Missouri, and the prospect of being thrown among them with no money to buy bread was a very sorry prospect for me. From all I could learn we could not get a chance to work, even for our board there, and the other drivers shared my fears and disappointment. . . . We began to think that the only way to get along at all in Salt Lake would be to turn Mormons. and none of us had any belief or desire that way and could not make up our minds to stop our journey and lose so much time, and if we were not very favored travelers our lot might be cast among the sinners for all time.[1]

With this mounting fear, Manly began to look at his options to avoid wintering in Utah Territory. His resolve was strengthened when he discussed the Mormons with some of his fellow travelers. The military men told him, "If you go to Salt Lake City, do not let them know you are from Missouri, for I tell you that many of those from that State will never see California. You know they were driven from Missouri, and will get revenge if they can."[2] Manly began to search in earnest to find another way to California, one that would avoid Salt Lake City and the Mormon population altogether.

Manly and others soon entered discussions with Dallas as to the future of the company. Manly recounted: "In this dilemma we called a council, and invited the gentleman [Dallas] in to have an understanding. . . . He flew [grew?] quite angry at us, and talked some and swore a great deal more, and the burden of his speech was:—'This train belongs to me and I propose to do with it just as I have a mind to, and I don't care a d—n what you fellows do or say."[3] Hutchings noted the high tension and verbal ordeal on August 14. According to Hutchings, "Dallas informed us that he had bought out all of his men, that the whole train was his—but they had conspired to take it away from him, and he requested to travel with ours, which our Captain permitted, offering him assistance if it were needed."[4] Five days later, all parties would soon find themselves at a crossroads.

On Sunday, August 19, the company reached the shores of the Green River. Hutchings recorded: "This is a fine large stream about the size of the North Platte and well-timbered with cottonwood, and a pleasant addition to the landscape."[5] Captain Morris noted the event on the same day and explained that the company "occupied an hour in feeling for a ford, found a good one by going, down stream about ¾ a Mile, bearing down stream."[6] Manly's first impressions were of "a nice clear stream, with the water as cold as ice and [I] knew it must come from the melting snow in sight to the north of us. This was a good sized stream."[7] Manly and the Dallas party had been at or close to South Pass on August 14, meaning the company traveled 62.5 miles in five days.[8] At 12.5 miles per day, their pace coincides fairly closely with Mormon historian Mel Bashore's estimate of ten miles per day.

Knowing that Salt Lake City was not too far off on the horizon, only 169 miles away, Manly's fear increased, and he was determined that Salt Lake was not a place he wanted to be. Reviewing options to avoid the Mormon domain, Manly and others from the Dallas party discussed the possibility of floating down the Green River. "We put a great many 'ifs' together," Manly remembered, "and they amounted to about this:—If this stream were large enough: if we had a boat: if we knew the way; if there were no falls or bad places: if we had plenty of provisions: if we were bold enough set out on such a trip, etc.: we might come out at some point or other on the Pacific Ocean."[9] The idea drew closer to becoming a reality when Manly found a boat half submerged in the sand along the west shore. It was "a small ferryboat (7×12) filled up with sand upon a bar, and it did not take very long to dig it out and put it into shape to use." Manly further described the dimensions of his newfound craft: "The boat was about 12 feet long and six or seven feet wide, not a very well proportioned craft, but having the ability to carry a pretty good load."[10]

Several important questions arise from Manly's account of this discovery: When was the boat constructed? What was its intended use? Who dedicated the time to build such a craft? As tens of thousands flowed westward, the Green River became a natural obstacle for those crossing through the open lands of what would become the Wyoming Territory. Simply stated, does the boat found by Manly fit the historical context of August 1849 on the American western frontier?

Researching those who traveled west before August 1849, I found evidence of ferries built by two parties crossing the Green River. During their journey westward in 1847, Brigham Young and his Mormon pioneer company engaged in building two ferryboats for crossing the river. They spent three days felling trees and building rafts, which were used to ferry their wagons.[11] Company member William Clayton's diary recorded important facts about the Mormons' newly constructed boats: they were rafts intended to transport wagons across the Green River; they were constructed on June 30, 1847; and "there [were] two rafts[,] one for each division."[12] With seventy-seven wagons to be ferried, or 154 separate trips across the three-hundred-foot-wide Green River, the decision to construct two ferryboats is understandable.

A second emigrant who noted the use of makeshift ferries at the Green traveled not far ahead of Manly. Lieutenant Osborne Cross of the regiment of Mounted Riflemen reached the bank of the Green River on July 20, 1849, and recorded:

The wagons were ferried across, and after making our encampment, the whole of the animals were taken about six miles back of the hills to graze on a small stream which empties into Green river above us, where the grass was pretty good.

There are two ferries here, which are only temporary. The Mormon ferry is about five miles above where we crossed the river, and at the foot of a range of high clay bluffs, which we passed to reach this ferry.[13]

Cross understood at least one of the ferryboats they found had been built by the Mormons in 1847. The builders of the other two ferryboats used by Cross's party remain unknown.

Manly arrived at the Green only thirty-one days after the Mounted Riflemen, and it is plausible that the boat he found was one that Cross had mentioned. Manly himself understood the possibility that the boat was one Brigham Young had constructed; in once again voicing his concerns about Salt Lake City, he wrote, "We had some fears as to the reception we might receive at the hands of Brigham Young, for, perhaps, we had taken their boat when we started down the river."[14] In any case, without the sand-filled ferryboat found on the shore of the river, Manly's idea to float to the California coast could well have been washed away before it began.

As it was, Manly and his recruits did decide to leave the Dallas party and travel down the Green. Before they departed, though, all the members of the various wagon parties had to set aside differences of opinion and work together to cross the river successfully.

Major Reynolds of the military company faced significant challenges at the crossing. Hutchings recorded that Reynolds "came to the ford and didn't like the looks of it so tried another, and one wagon getting into a deep hole in the stream, turned over. The swift current swept out first this thing, and then that, and at the last out swam a big whiskey keg, half full."[15] Manly similarly recounted the same blunder by Reynolds: "Here the wagon master attempted to cross the stream thinking it was not so very deep, but before the head mules got more than half way through they began to swim, and swinging around in all shapes . . . the load was badly damaged, and being principally provisions, was not the best state of affairs."[16]

Once all parties had successfully crossed the Green, Manly needed to trade for or purchase items for his river journey. He approached Dallas and worked out a compromise to the satisfaction of both. "If I could sell my pony to Mr. Dallas," Manly wrote, "and could buy some bacon and flour of him I would make the trial at any rate. So I broached the matter to him and he seemed quite willing to get rid of us. He gave me $60 for my pony and sold us what provisions we thought we should need, as we had an idea we could reach the coast in four or five weeks."[17] Manly further commented that Dallas gave Manly's crew rope and two axes.[18] Dallas was left with only one driver, "but he took a whip himself, and with the aid of the children and his wife who drove the two-horse wagon, they got along very well."[19]

It was at this point, after crossing the Green River, that Hutchings's company separated from Major Reynolds, who was heading to Fort Hall on the Oregon Trail. Hutchings and Dallas took the Mormon Trail leading to Salt Lake City. The next day, August 21, Hutchings made an observation in regard to Manly's party that at once verifies their journey and comments dramatically on it: "We came again in sight of the Rocky Mountain. Heard from Dallas that ten of his men had made a raft and a boat out of a wagon-bed and had started down Green River. Quimby was Captain of the party!!! How foolish! If they escape the waterfalls they cannot escape the hands of hostile Indians that infest the stream nearly the whole of its course. This is certainly the 'Greenhorn's Cutoff to California.'"[20] Hutchings did get some of the details wrong, however. He wrote that ten men left the Dallas party, while Manly recounts that there were seven: "This party was composed of W. L. Manley, M. S. McMahon, Charles and Joseph Hazelrig, Richard Field, Alfred Walton and John Rogers."[21] Hutchings is also incorrect when he referred to the men using a boat made from the bed of a wagon. Manly provided a very detailed account of the ferryboat but made no mention of a wagon-box boat. Most important, Hutchings misidentified the captain of the river-running party as "Quimby," and referred to him in a familiar way as someone he knew. That Manly was made captain is clear from his own writing: "About the first thing we did was to organize and select a captain, and, very much against my wishes, I was chosen to this important position."[22]

Another contemporaneous account corroborates the journey but likewise misidentifies its leader. In his journal, Hugh Brown Heiskell wrote of camping eighteen miles from Beer Springs (now Soda Springs, Idaho) on August 23, 1849. Heiskell recorded, "Another wagon came up at ten o'clock—that had been delayed—there were two men with it. They say that 3 men who were with them, two Dutchmen & a Yankee from Boston by the name of Quensby took 20 days of provisions & embarked in a skiff that was left by some emigrants at Green river for California."[23] Clearly Heiskell's Quensby and Hutchings's Quimby refer to the same person. It may be that both are a related misidentification of Manly or that there was someone with the name Quimby or Quensby associated with the party whom Manly does not identify. A "Yankee from Boston" is not far from Manly's origins in Vermont, but "two Dutchmen" is more difficult to account for, since none of the seven names given by Manly are of Dutch descent. It is likely that Heiskell and Hutchings simply received or passed on incorrect details.[24] Despite getting the particulars wrong, the contemporaneous accounts by Hutchings and Heiskell authenticate that Manly's company did indeed embark on their journey down the river.

Standing on the banks of the Green River on August 20, Manly knew very little about its origin, treacherous nature, or course to the ocean. Through maps and advice given by the military personnel accompanying him, however, he understood that some obstacles would need to be passed, and he knew the river would eventually empty into the Pacific. "Both the surgeon and the captain said the stream came out on the Pacific Coast and that we had no obstacles except cataracts, which they had heard were pretty bad," he noted.[25] The maps he studied and advice he received detailed a river that was challenging but conquerable. One of Manly's traveling companions, M. S. McMahon, had high expectations of a successful voyage and insisted that based on information he received, there were no "bad places on this river." He further noted, "I believe we can get down easily enough, and get to California some time."[26] Manly and his comrades clearly had a very limited understanding of the Green River, even with the map or maps they consulted.

What maps were available to them? From later remarks by Manly and his traveling companion McMahon, the map or maps must have included the following landmarks: Ham's Fork, a tributary of the Green;[27] Fort Uintah;[28] the Uinta (now Duchesne) River;[29] Browns Hole, a long valley straddling what is now the border between Utah and Colorado;[30] and the Grand River, now called the Colorado.[31] No single map has been found from the period that includes all these landmarks, but John C. Frémont's most famous map, documenting his 1842 exploration of the Rocky Mountains, includes everything but Ham's Fork.[32] A later map of Frémont's, from 1848, includes Ham's Fork, Browns Hole, the Uinta River, and the Grand, but omits Fort Uintah.[33] It is likely, therefore, that Manly's military companions had both maps and that he consulted and either took notes or memorized details before parting ways with them.

Additionally, McMahon had a map of some sort in his possession. Manly recounted, "[McMahon] said he had a map of the country, and it looked just as safe to him to go on down the river."[34] In his own account, as discussed later in this book, McMahon makes clear the importance of "our little map" to the river journey.[35] One possible conclusion is that McMahon was given a map by the military in the wagon train. However, with maps in demand as a valuable aid to safe travel, more likely McMahon made a personal copy of the map from the military escorts.

The Green River's journey south begins on the western slopes of Gannett Peak—a mountain with a 13,804-foot summit in the Wind River Mountains in Wyoming. The river meanders through southwestern Wyoming, crosses into northeastern Utah, takes a brief turn into Colorado, then continues southward in Utah until it joins the Colorado River just south of Moab, in Canyonlands National Park. It traverses rugged mountainous regions through most of its 730-mile course, 291 in what is now Wyoming, 42 in Colorado, and 397 in Utah.[36] The Green drains 45,000 square miles of the Colorado River watershed, finally running to the Sea of Cortez in Mexico.

Originally known as the Spanish River, the waterway was renamed the Green River in 1824 because of the green soapstone along its bank, which colors the water. The Green is one of western America's major drainages. In 1859, only ten years after Manly challenged the waters of the Green, Washington Irving wrote about its origin:

The Green River, or Colorado of the West, set forth on its wandering pilgrimage to the Gulf of California; at first a mere mountain torrent, dashing northward over crag and precipice, in a succession of cascades, and tumbling into the plain, where expanding into an ample river, it circled away to the south, and after alternately shining out and disappearing in the mazes of the vast landscape, was finally lost in a horizon of mountains. The day was calm and cloudless, and the atmosphere so pure that objects were discernible at an astonishing distance. The whole of this immense area was enclosed by an outer range of shadowy peaks, some of them faintly marked on the horizon, which seemed to wall it in from the rest of the earth.[37]

Irving described in his poetic style the meandering journey of the Green out of the Wind Rivers through uncharted whitewater, across the canyon country, and on to the Colorado.

John C. Frémont was one of the first Americans to document and record the flowing waters of the Green River. In his 1844 account, he described the origins and destination of the river, and his detailed account indicates that he understood the key role the Green River plays in the western ecosystem:

Following a hollow of slight and easy descent, in which was very soon formed a little tributary to the Gulf of California . . . we made our usual halt . . . entering . . . the valley of Green River—the great Colorado of the West . . . to avoid the mountains about the western heads of Green River—the *Rio Verde* of the Spaniards.

Frémont goes on to explain the history of the river and its naming:

The refreshing appearance of the broad river, with its timbered shores and green-wooded islands, in contrast to its dry sandy plains, probably obtained for it the name of Green River, which was bestowed on it by the Spaniards, who first came into this country to trade some twenty-five years ago. It was then familiarly known as the Seeds-kedée-agee, or Prairie Hen (*tetrao urophasianus*) River; a name which is received from the Crows, to whom its upper waters belong.[38]

In his final representation of the Green River, Frémont described the river's ultimate destination into the Colorado and indicated where the river drains or empties.

> The descent of each stream is rapid, but that of the Colorado is but little known, and that little derived from vague report. Three hundred miles of its lower part, as it approaches the Gulf of California, is reported to be smooth and tranquil; but its upper part is manifestly broken into many falls and rapids.[39]

From explorers of the 1800s to present-day river enthusiasts, the Green has continually piqued the interest of travelers. One of the more recent and eloquent reviews of the character and importance of the Green River is that of Ann Zwinger, author of *Run, River, Run*. She described the Green's origin, winding path, and confluence with the Colorado:

> Out of the Wind River it meanders south across high hay meadows and sagebrush flats, and then snakes through the dry, alkali-splotched Green River Basin. When it snubs up against the Uinta Mountains at the Utah-Wyoming border, it is deflected to run east along their northern flank through Browns Park, a wintering place for traders and trappers and, later, outlaws, and still today isolated and remote. At the eastern end of Browns Park the river angles south and enters Lodore Canyon, incarcerated within its formidable red rock walls. Out of Lodore, it hooks around Steamboat Rock and charges sharp westward through Whirlpool Canyon, idles through Island Park, and dashes through Split Mountain, cleaving it nearly down the middle. It emerges and slows southward across the Uinta Basin. It begins to pare downward again as it bisects the Tavaputs Plateau, working through the pale sediments of Desolation Canyon and the craggy rock of Gray Canyon, bannered with its last white rapids. It crosses the

arid Gunnison Valley, and then works its tortuous course through Labyrinth and Stillwater Canyons, through red rock and white rock, to its confluence with the Colorado River.[40]

Prior to the construction of Fontenelle Reservoir in 1961 and Flaming Gorge Dam in 1963, the waters of the Green flowed freely from origin to termination, fed by a series of lower canyon tributaries from the Uinta Mountains. As the water flow dramatically increased, the nature of the river changed, and it passed through canyons and rapids named Flaming Gorge, Kingfisher, Horseshoe, Hidden Canyon, and Ashley Falls.

After these challenging waters (no longer visible today because of Flaming Gorge Dam), the Green River enters a quiet park of open grass fields and clear-bottomed tributaries. This quiet, secluded arena of breathtaking beauty was known to early explorers and settlers as Browns Hole.

In 1839, Thomas Jefferson Farnham wrote about his overland observations of the river at Browns Hole and its treacherous descent into the Gates of Lodore, where the temperament and complexity of the river again change dramatically.

[Browns Hole] is situated in or about latitude 42° north; one hundred miles south of Wind River Mountain, on the Sheetskadee (Prairie Cock) River. Its elevation is something more than eight thousand feet above the level of the sea. It appeared to be about six miles in diameter; shut in, in all directions, by dark frowning mountains, rising one thousand five hundred feet above the plain. The Sheetskadee, or Green River, runs through it, sweeping in a beautiful curve from the north-west to the south-west part of it, where it breaks its way through the encircling mountains, between cliffs, one thousand feet in height, broken and hanging as if poised on the air. The area of the plain is thickly set with the rich mountain grasses, and dotted with little copses of cotton wood and willow trees. The soil is alluvial, and capable of producing abundantly all kinds of small grains, vegetables, &c., that are raised in the northern States. Its climate is very remarkable. Although in all the country, within a hundred miles of it, the winter months bring snows, and the severe cold that we should expect in such a latitude, and at such an elevation above the level of the sea, yet in this little nook, the grass grows all the winter; so that, while the storm rages on the mountains in sight, and the drifting snows mingle in the blasts of December, the old hunters here heed it not. Their horses are cropping the green grass on the bank of the Sheetskadee, while they themselves are roasting the fat loins of the mountain sheep, and laughing at the merry tale and song.[41]

From Browns Hole, notes Zwinger, "water picks up speed as it steadily drops in altitude at twenty-two feet per mile." The cliffs begin to rise like sentinels standing guard over the river as it cuts through the soft Browns Park Formation entering Lodore Canyon, "where the river breaches the end of a mountain range."[42]

South of Browns Park, the accounts from Manly's time period drew more on hearsay than first-hand evidence. In his 1844 account, Frémont analyzes in his documentary style both the part of the river he had seen and what he had not: "Lower down," he wrote, "from Browns Hole to the southward, the river runs through lofty chasms, walled in by precipices of *red* rock, . . . according to our subsequent observations, four thousand five hundred feet." Frémont chose not to enter Lodore, and he warned future explorers about the difficulties that would be encountered:

> From many descriptions of trappers, it is probable that in its foaming course among the lofty precipices [the river] presents many scenes of wild grandeur; and though offering many temptations, and often discussed, no trappers have been found bold enough to undertake a voyage which has so certain a prospect of fatal termination.[43]

For sixty miles, the Green River flows through canyons and parks, unpredictable and twisting. Then the Green slows, traversing Echo Park; after that, in Zwinger's words, "the river makes a hairpin turn around the prow of Steamboat Rock before it enters Whirlpool Canyon . . . the antithesis of the sunny, sandy openness of Echo Park, where the water is flat, the rocks golden sandstone."[44]

From Whirlpool Canyon, the water begins to meander at a leisurely pace through Island Park. The valley widens and creates a wide arena of spectacular vistas. After a forty-five-degree course change, Island Park gives way to a geological wonder, and one of the most spectacular canyons along the Green River: Split Mountain. In Zwinger's memorable words:

> From the air one can see how the river hooks into the mountain at one end, runs for some five miles right down the middle, then angles out at the other end, as it entered. . . . Split Mountain is one glorious chute, rapid after rapid. . . . The river drops 140 feet in seven miles.[45]

As the water flows from Split Mountain and spills onto the open plains of the Uinta Basin, the Green River's personality once again changes from a cascade down mountain ravines in deep, sheer gorges to a soft, whispering flow through open lands of sage and sandy beaches. Between these contrasts of rock walls and open plains, near what is now Jensen, Utah, the first recorded crossing of the Green River by European explorers occurred on September 16, 1776, by Fathers Francisco Antanasio Dominguez and Vélez de Escalante.[46] Escalante's journal documents:

> The river enters this meadow between two high cliffs which, after forming a sort of corral, come so close together that one can scarcely see the opening through which the river comes. According to our guide, one cannot cross from one side to the other except by the only ford which there is in this vicinity. This is toward the west of the northern crest and very close to a chain of hills of loose earth, some of them lead colored and others yellow. The ford is stony and in it the water does not reach to the shoulder blades of the horses, whereas in every other place we saw they cannot cross without swimming. We halted on its south bank about a mile from the ford, naming the camp La Vega de Santa Cruz. We observed the latitude by the north star and found ourselves in 41° 19' latitude.[47]

In the openness of the Uinta Basin, the river falls at a calm rate of two feet per mile. For 104 miles, it continues to slowly wind its way south. After its leisurely descent, the Green once again drops into a series of canyons. The first is called Desolation Canyon. In the words of one river guide, "Desolation Canyon slowly deepens until it slices through the forested Tavaputs Plateau near Rock Creek. . . . Riffles and rapids—nearly fifty of them—gradually increase in difficulty downriver."[48]

In Desolation Canyon, the river changes pace as it winds its way southward for fifty-nine miles. The canyon walls are red in color and forested with piñon and juniper trees. Desolation Canyon eventually gives way to Gray Canyon. Gray and Desolation Canyons differ in vegetation, rock formation, and color. The rock walls of Gray Canyon, predictably, are gray, but also brown, yellow, and white, and it contains rapids known as Range Creek, Rabbit Valley, Coal Creek, and Rattlesnake. This stretch of river is twenty-five miles in length. Emerging from Gray Canyon, the Green enters the Gunnison Valley or San Rafael Desert. It is there the Green begins its final descent of 120 miles to the confluence of the Colorado River by quietly winding through Labyrinth and Stillwater Canyons. This stretch of the Green River is the "longest smooth-water piece of the Green, although shallow riffles and small waves show up at certain river levels in the first twenty miles below the town of Green River."[49] The river gently winds southward toward its final destiny: joining with and becoming part of the Colorado River. As Zwinger puts it, "There by Congressional proclamation, having fallen over 9,000 feet in 730 miles, the Green River ends."[50] In total, it is the twenty-second longest river in the United States, and it has captured the imagination of river enthusiasts for centuries.

As Manly stood on the river's edge in 1849, one can imagine what decisions he might have made knowing what Frémont had learned. If he had heard that the path of the river was treacherous and impassable, he would have quite possibly remained on his westward course with the wagon train. Instead, weighing his past experience of building skiffs and navigating river currents, he decided to exchange wagons for water, bullwhips for oars. A new chapter in Manly's life was about to begin.

PART II

DOWN THE RIVER

Chapter Five

Setting Out on the Green River

Author's Note: At the end of William Lewis Manly's narrative in Death Valley in '49, *he addressed his readers directly: "Those who traveled over the same or similar routes are capable of passing a just opinion of the story."[1] With these words, he seems to challenge or invite readers to prove or disprove his story by trying the journey themselves. I took Manly at his word and did in fact retrace his route, floating down the Green in 2006 and then, from 2006 to 2013, researching and following his route across what is now central Utah. What follows is a tale that weaves together Manly's accounts, as published in the newspaper series "From Vermont to California" and the book* Death Valley in '49, *and my own account, taken from my personal journal. I should note that I did not get all the facts right in my journal, such as concluding that Manly spent thirty-nine days on the Green River, when my later research led me to conclude it was thirty-three. At the time I wrote in my journal, moreover, I had not considered all the evidence that did not fit my conclusions. Later research helped add nuance to my understanding. As time went on, aided by historians, librarians, and other experts in many libraries, rare-book shops, and private collections, I began to make more sense of Manly's vagueness in describing his travels down the Green River, and using my own experience, I could authenticate or refute his account, as well as the accounts of others who have written about him.*

In addition to my own journal entries, I have included excerpts from other historical accounts documenting voyages down the Green, which help fill in the picture. In particular, I draw on William Ashley's account of travels in 1825, John Wesley Powell's writings concerning his 1869 expedition, and Frederick

Dellenbaugh's narratives of Powell's second voyage in 1871. These accounts tell a remarkably consistent story about the nature and circumstances of traveling the Green, which often paralleled my own experiences. All speak to the same tenacity and survival skills that Manly exhibited in the canyons, parks, and open valleys on the Green River.

As Manly and his six men, Morgan S. McMahon, Charles and Joseph Hazelrig, Richard Field, Alfred Walton, and John Rogers, sat on the banks of the Green River, their anxieties must have been heightened as they watched Charles Dallas's wagon train and the military men slowly fade away to the west on the dusty trail. The exact date that Manly launched down the Green is not known, but with the men preparing the ferryboat for travel "and then set[ting] to work in earnest to carry out our plans,"[2] the most probable date would be August 20, the day after they parted ways with the company.

Manly led out in making sure all necessary precautions were taken; with his previous river-running experience in Michigan and Wisconsin Territories, the men leaned on his expertise and survival skills, though he recounted modestly that being elected captain was "very much against my wishes."[3] With supplies and firearms secured, the Manly party then began its historic voyage down the Green River. Spirits were high, "and it looked as if we were taking the most sensible way to get to the Pacific, and almost wondered that everybody was so blind as not to see it as we did."[4]

8/19/2006, Saturday, Day 1, River Day 1

Lombard Crossing to Seedskadee National Wildlife Refuge

The day is finally here and my crew and I are ready to start our journey down the Green River. All the planning and preparation of boats is complete; food and other necessary supplies have been assembled. For the past two months, the most difficult task was constructing the log canoes that will carry us down the Green River. By using chain-

---

Site of Lombard Crossing, where Manly embarked down the Green River.

saws, drills, and countless work hours, we took two thirteen-foot logs, eighteen inches in diameter, and hollowed them out in the fashion of canoes, attaching them together, to float in a catamaran style. This manner of boat is similar to what Manly used when he hollowed out pine trees later on in his expedition down the Green. Other inflatable boats of various sizes and shapes were added to our fleet for safety.

In preparing for our launch, I am fortunate to have Clint Goode as our head boatman. As a young man, he grew up on the rivers of the western United States. His father, Merlin Goode—a man whom I learned to love and respect—introduced me to river running more than twenty-five years ago but recently passed away from cancer. He will be missed on this trip, not only for his expertise but also for his deep friendship. The third and final member of our crew is Dallas Kane, my son of nineteen years. His physical strength, at six feet, seven inches, and more than 210 pounds, will be needed constantly. I will enjoy the association of father/son and lean on him during those times of needed strength.

As I sit on the bank of the Green and look out over the horizon, I cannot help but think of Manly and his statement about leaving the wagon train, heading down the Green, and "sitting on the bank of the river whose waters flowed to the great Pacific. Each company wished the other good luck, we took a few long breaths and then set to work in earnest to carry out our plans." I also felt the same uneasiness and excitement as the canoes became ready. Unlike Manly, who had no definite understanding of the river and its course, I know what distances need to be covered. A feeling of respect comes over me in that he courageously took on the Green and was willing to match skill and wits with a river he knew little about.

Ready to cast off, I remember Manly's statements of doing the same: "We untied the ropes, gave the boat a push and commenced to move down the river with ease and comfort." We push our boats off at 12:05 in the afternoon and, like Manly, head down the Green to challenges unknown. The first concern is the ability of the log canoes to float and maneuver in the potential shallow parts of the river. August waters are considerably lower than June and July. Within several hundred yards I knew the boats would do well. They lay half submerged and could be maneuvered in the water with ease. As we head around the first bend, my anticipation of reviewing history is foremost. With all the years of study and research, the re-creation of Manly's expedition now becomes the final piece of the puzzle. I am ready.

It is now the evening of the first day and I am amazed at all I saw. Ducks, geese, deer, antelope, moose, beaver, raccoons, and muskrats all find the shores of the Green River home. In addition to the wildlife, the vegetation along the riverbank was abundant. The river provides the much-needed water for drinking and sustaining life. I can understand in only the first day why it was so easy for Manly to find and shoot game for food. . . . Waterfowl and other animals can be seen at every turn. I would also imagine the wildlife in 1849 was much greater than now because there was no or little human intervention. Words cannot express how beautiful and peaceful it is floating down the upper stretches of the Green.

We traveled eighteen miles today. If we had left in the early morning, our distance would have been similar to Manly's first day: "As near as we could estimate we floated about thirty miles a day." The sandbars were a little tricky, but with our knowledge of rivers and the flow, we maneuvered around them without any problem. As evening began to creep up on us, we found a wonderful campsite, prepared dinner, and were in bed by 9:30.

Shortly after writing of their departure, Manly recounted three events from which we can make conclusions regarding his distance traveled, his ability to navigate the river, and the availability of food. Regarding their location he wrote in *Death Valley in '49*, "At the mouth of Ham's Fork we passed a camp of Indians, but we kept close to the opposite shore to avoid being boarded by them. They beckoned very urgently for us to come ashore, but I acted as if I did not understand them, and gave them the go-by."[5] The distance from Lombard Crossing (where the emigrant trail crosses the Green) to Ham's Fork (now identified as Black's Fork) is about fifty-eight river miles. Manly could not have traveled fifty-eight miles in one day, and fortunately, his written articles "From Vermont to California" provide more specificity. There Manly wrote, "The second day out we organized into a company. . . . The next day [Day 3] we passed a number of Indians, and we were very careful not to keep close to shore, although they tried hard to have us land."[6] Based on this timeline, Manly's party traveled an estimated fifty-eight miles by the third day, a more reasonable rate. At several points in his narrative, Manly referred to his rate of travel, which he estimated at thirty miles a day.[7]

Other contemporary journal accounts help establish the river's current in this period. The previous month, westbound traveler William B. Lorton observed the current of the Green at the emigrant trail crossing as eight miles an hour.[8] Manly himself would have been able to observe passing objects as they floated down the river and thereby estimate his speed of travel. After spending several months on wagons pulled by oxen over the emigrant trail at ten to twelve miles per day, floating down the Green would have given the sense of moving very quickly.

Second, Manly noted the abundant wildlife: "The next day after this I went on shore and sighted a couple of antelope, one of which I shot. . . . We scared up a band of elk in the grass meadow."[9] As Manly and his six companions began their expedition down the Green River, food seemed to be of very little concern. Dallas had sold the river party some bacon and flour, and the crew was mindful of the use of their small supply: "To make our flour go as far as possible we ate very freely of meat, and having excellent appetites it disappeared very fast."[10] On the fourth day Manly shot a pronghorn, which was fortunate because, he said, "good appetites we already had," adding, "This was about the finest Rocky Mountain beef that one could see."[11] Manly had excellent marksmanship, and he shot wild game throughout the trip on the river. One target he remembered specifically was a creature he gave a nickname: "Mr. Elk . . . started off on a high and lofty trot. . . . I put a ball through his head and he fell. He was a monster. Rogers, who was a butcher, said it would weigh five hundred or six hundred pounds." The men busily began to prepare the meat for future meals. "We packed the meat to our canoes," Manly recalled, "and staid up all night cutting the meat in strips and drying it, to reduce bulk and preserve it, and it made the finest kind of food, fit for an epicure."[12]

As days turned into weeks on the river, Manly never made mention of starving or finding himself in dire need of nourishment. The group's creativity for making different dishes seemed unending. On one evening, the men took the mutton from a mountain sheep that had been shot and made "a fine soup which tasted pretty good."[13] Manly's skill with a rifle became paramount to the success of his river expedition and to later travels.

The third event, illuminating Manly's river-running confidence, occurred on one of the first days of travel. While using a setting pole, a long pole used to push the boat forward, Manly wedged it in some rocks. Not knowing whether to hold on to the pole or let go and stay with the boat, he chose to hold fast to the pole, which flung him into the water: "I was the one who was very suddenly yanked from the boat by the spring of the pole, and landed in the middle of the river." Unhurt and with the men cheering him on, he explained, "That was nothing as we were on our way to California by water any way, and such things should be expected."[14]

8/20/2006, Sunday, Day 2, River Day 2

Seedskadee National Wildlife Refuge to Green River, Wyoming

Our camping spot was secluded, with no bugs. The morning sun drenched the sky with an amazing display of colors in brilliant oranges and deep reds. I was in awe. We rose early, and Clint took

---

the tandem wood canoes and started downriver. Dallas and I cleaned up camp and were in our canoes by 8:00. As we prepared to leave, an owl perched in a tree above us and observed our morning ritual. It was so unusual to watch him watch us. Some Indians believed that seeing an owl in daylight was a sign of death. I believed it was a sign of good luck and enjoyed his company.

The continued beauty and wildlife unfolded in front of us as we floated by. Again, all animals mentioned were at the river's edge. It has been a long time since I have been on the river, and the quiet peace is wonderful. Around 2:00 in the afternoon we began to float through Green River, Wyoming. The sudden noise and vehicle traffic from nearby roads seemed out of place. I thought about Manly, his constant quiet ride, and envied him.

When we arrived in the town of Green River, we stopped for lunch at Expedition Island, which was John Wesley Powell's starting point for his river expedition in 1869. Standing on the island, I contemplated his thoughts as he, too, left on a journey down the Green. The town was founded at that time and supported Powell as he prepared to leave. His feelings of venturing "down the Great Unknown" must have been similar to Manly's. Both Manly and Powell shared the same adventurous spirit of exploration and were willing to challenge all that crossed their path. Although their undertakings are much greater than mine due to the time period in which they lived and equipment they used, I feel that same adventurous spirit and want to be equally successful in understanding what Manly encountered, achieved, and misrepresented as he traveled southward on a river that he only knew ran to the Pacific Ocean.

Our second day's journey ended on the southern outskirts of Green River, Wyoming. We estimate that we traveled more than twenty miles. It was a long day. I would imagine that we are very close to or just ahead of the mileage that Manly would have covered in his first two days. With only our second day on the river and covering these miles, I am concerned that Manly's claim of floating close to thirty miles a day is unrealistic. As future days are logged, I should have a better idea of his accuracy.

One cannot accurately compare the Green River of 1849 and 2006 and its cubic feet per second (cfs), or how many cubic feet of water flow past a given point per second, thus measuring the rate of flow. The variables are many. Each year's river flow is subject to precipitation, amounts of winter snows, thawing temperatures, and summer rains. Also, the Green in 1849 did not have any dams or reservoirs to restrict or hinder the river's constant flow. Currently, the flow of the Green River passes through Fontenelle Reservoir, fifty miles upriver from where Manly would have made his first assessment of his river speed. Flaming Gorge Dam is located one hundred miles below Manly's estimate. Though I floated the river at the same time of year, it can only be a subjective assessment as to the speed that Manly was actually moving. At the location of the river where Manly made his river speed estimate, I was floating, on average, three miles per hour or fifteen to twenty miles per day.

8/22/2006, Tuesday, Day 4, River Day 4

Firehole Marina to Buckboard Marina

Another clear morning welcomes us. We got up early and were on the river by 7:30. Hopefully, we will make our estimated campsite before the afternoon winds begin to blow. Around 3:00 p.m. it will be hard to paddle because the winds will blow across Flaming Gorge reservoir. The lack of current makes the gorge more difficult to paddle. Manly comments that in this section they "were floating down the rapid stream."[15] I wish we were experiencing this rapid part of the Green. As the river channel widens, we come around a left-hand corner and see Black's Fork on our right, emptying into the Green. The channel of Black's Fork is wide. The reservoir has filled the channel, so there is not a realistic view of how it looked when Manly floated by. I climbed to the top of the rock overlook, which was at least five hundred feet in height, and was able to see the confluence well. I took a picture of Black's Fork farther upriver where it becomes shallow, which is how it must have looked in 1849. Black's Fork is the second detailed site that Manly remembers on his journey down the Green. . . . Manly referred to this river as Ham's Fork. Ham's Fork conjoins Black's Fork several miles upriver from the Green. Manly, however, was correct in knowing that the Ham's Fork waters did empty into the Green at this point. We are on our fourth day. Manly did not include any time frames or days spent on the river in reaching this confluence of the two rivers. We will be camping at Buckboard Marina tonight. It is about three miles farther on the right-hand or west side of the reservoir. We are presently moving across the gorge at about 2½ miles per hour.

How quickly plans change. About 3:00 in the afternoon, a sudden storm blew across the reservoir. The canoes could not maneuver through the choppy water and were blown to shore. At the time the wind started, I was shuttling the truck and was on an overlook watching the guys through the binoculars. Luckily, they pulled ashore by a dirt road, which I found and drove to them. As they lay exhausted by the canoes, I prepared dinner, which they appreciated and enjoyed. We decided not to venture any farther, instead camping at our present location and starting again in the early morning. Dallas and Clint stayed the night with the canoes while I drove back to Buckboard Marina and waited for them to arrive the next morning.

With this sudden change of weather and concern for the crew's safety, I decided not to cross the reservoir in the canoes but to follow along the west side of the reservoir with the supply truck. I feel bad that I cannot support the men and paddle along with them, but the safety of the expedition requires me to keep a watchful eye from the shore. I am hopeful that when Dallas and Clint get closer to the dam and areas that Manly described I can float again. While writing this section, I am sitting by a memorial to Powell:

RIVER EXPLORATION

Shortly before noon on May 26, 1869, four small boats carrying 10 men, led by Major John Wesley Powell, silently floated past this point. It was the 3rd day of a historic trip which began at the town of Green River. These small boats carried Powell's party 1000 miles down the Green and Colorado Rivers, through Grand Canyon and into history—the first men to successfully run these wild uncharted rivers.

> As I read this inscription, I thought how important history is and what an opportunity to point out that Powell was not the first person to venture down these waters by the marina and that the correct interpretation needs to be understood. I have set up a meeting on Friday with the interpretation ranger for the Flaming Gorge area. She is interested in meeting with me and learning about Manly.

Winding through the Green River Basin, the river passes rolling hills and open lands. It is shortly after the location where Manly saw Indians at Ham's Fork that the gentle terrain quickly gives way to deeper canyons, and steep ridges begin to tower over the Green. Manly and his men were soon introduced to dangerous waters and peril to their personal safety. On about the fifth day, after traveling ninety-seven miles, Manly was asleep on the flat-bottomed boat when the men saw that the river was flowing into an upcoming mountain and became alarmed that it might be funneling into a large hole. "A huge range of mountains seemed to stretch clear across the valley," Manly recalled.[16] "The boys thought the river was coming to a rather sudden end."[17] He went on describe their anxiety at the apparent disappearance of the river:

> For the life of me I could not say they were not right, for there was no way in sight for it to go to. I remembered while looking over a map the military men had I found a place named Brown's Hole,[18] and I told the boys I guessed we were elected to go on foot to California after all, for I did not propose to follow the river down any sort of a hole into any mountain. We were floating directly toward a perpendicular cliff, and I could not see any hole any where, nor any other place where it could go. Just as we were within a stone's throw of the cliff, the river turned sharply to the right and went behind a high point of the mountain that seemed to stand squarely on edge.[19]

Just as the river approaches the broad mountain face, it turns dramatically to the right and cascades along the side of the mountain. This

A sudden bend in the Green River is now covered by Flaming Gorge Reservoir.

feature is located south of river mile 318 and only a short distance from present-day Manila, Utah. It is here that the waters of the present-day Green begin to deepen due to the steep canyon walls and Flaming Gorge Reservoir. Frederick Dellenbaugh, the youngest member of the second Powell expedition in 1871, wrote much the same description of the red rocks and sudden turn of the Green: "Nevertheless we could see high up before us some bright red rocks marking the first canyon of the wonderful series that separates this river from the common world. . . . Then in a moment we dashed to the right into the beautiful canyon, with the cliffs whose summit we had seen, rising about 1300 feet on the right, and a steep slope on the left at the base of which was a small bottom covered with tall cottonwood trees, whose green shone resplendent against the red rocks. . . . The canyon was surprisingly beautiful and romantic."[20]

The anxiety Manly and Dellenbaugh felt at this point in their journeys was not unique; the sudden change of the river path and flow created a jarring experience for many later river runners. As Roy Webb wrote: "While geologists might debate the effects of compressional deformation and stream capture, the effect that this remarkable landscape had on river travelers who viewed these scenes from the river or from overland is beyond dispute. . . . From upriver, it appeared that the river was flowing into a cave in the mountains."[21]

Manly's description of the Green's dramatic right turn is perfectly accurate, as is his account of the next turn of the river. "The river ran in this direction," he wrote, "almost parallel with the front face of the mountain, for a while, and then turned again to the left, almost squarely and was in a terribly deep cañon, with an increasing swiftness to the stream."[22] Though now covered by hundreds of feet of reservoir at this point, the Green's path and flow are consistent with Manly's description.

8/25/06, Friday, Day 7, River Day 7

Lucerne Marina to Dowd Mountain

The day started off with an interview on KSL Radio in Salt Lake City, Utah. They gave me a satellite phone before the trip and asked me to call in weekly on an outdoor adventure show. I enjoy telling people about what we are trying to accomplish. After the radio interview, we were on the river by 8:00 a.m. for a rewarding day, during which we traveled close to thirteen miles. It took us longer than expected to load all our gear. We will be away from the truck, which is being shuttled, for the next thirty miles. As we pulled away from Lucerne Marina, we paddled across the last large open area of the reservoir and toward the deeper canyons. This is our seventh day and with this the first two miles across the open waters were significant in determining where the river, now the reservoir, is to turn. As we continually drew closer to the towering cliffs, the view of where the river channel is became confusing. We had to reference the map several times, for without it, we would not have been able to tell the correct direction and distance of the river turn. As we paddled closer to the rock walls, it was clear to see why Manly had a difficult time reading the direction of the river when he floated because we also could not determine the true direction by sight.

I knew I was looking at the same river-directional question that puzzled him. Immediately before us the river turns to the right, but, as we draw closer, the path ahead still cannot be seen. We are in the last large open area of the gorge and, looking at the sudden rise of mountains, unable to determine the direction of the river through the mountains directly ahead of us. . . . With detailed observations of the rocks and geological formations opening to allow the river channel to continue, the location was unmistakable, accurately matching Manly's description. The river does take a sharp turn to the right behind a large outcropping of rock that stands vertically in the air, distinctly rising to a significant degree, even though I was paddling on water four hundred feet above the riverbed in 1849. While most formations described by Manly are covered by this man-made reservoir, the tops of these magnificent rocks still stand in testament to his accounts. Significantly, when Powell floated the river in 1869, he also noted the distinctness of these particular rock formations, calling them Flaming Gorge, which name was also given to the reservoir constructed in 1962.

As we pass this meaningful point, the mountain peaks soar high with rugged rock summits. Manly was observant of these visible rock walls. With this change from open sage lands to deep, rocky, narrow canyons, Manly took notice and referred to the change of environment: "We were now for some time between two rocky walls between which the river ran very rapidly. . . . The mountains seemed to get higher and higher on both sides as we advanced."

Traveling several hundred feet above where Manly floated, I could imagine how deep the canyons must have seemed, as well as imposing, to these novice river men of 1849. The river also would have intensified as the canyon narrowed. Within these canyons, massive boulders can and do fall into the river, creating large obstacles and rapids to block safe passage. Floating through, I estimate the river would have been close to 150 feet wide at this point. As we began to drift through this section of the gorge, the rock walls on the left and right sides of the river often grew closer to each other. In these locations, large rapids due to rocks lying in the riverbed would have been probable. With the rapids, Manly and his crew began to experience many difficulties.

In constantly assessing Manly's correct location, another environmental milestone played a pivotal role pinpointing his timeline: the emergence of large pine trees. From the beginning of the river expedition until now, pine trees have not been observed. Some cottonwood trees have lined the riverbank but not pine trees, which is important, because Manly was soon in need of the sturdier pine trees. I will discuss them in tomorrow's log when we reach the esti- mated location where Manly depended upon these large-trunked trees for safe passage. With this area rich in historical accounts by Manly, I cannot help wishing I were on the bank of the river some four hundred feet below. To be at the river's true level and not on top of the reservoir would have been more meaningful for my under- standing and interpretation of what Manly experienced. I would like to have observed all his experiences firsthand.

Fast approaching is the general area where Manly inscribed his name on a rock overhanging the river. As it is lost forever to the waters of Flaming Gorge, I will never be able to see the inscription he left—a loss to me and to history. As I look out over the gorge, boaters are traveling up and down the river. To them, the gorge is a recreational opportunity for travel, fishing, and fun. I have to ask the question, was this reservoir necessary? The saving of water, creating electricity, and recreational use all combined, was it worth the price of lost historical heritage and damaged environment that became altered forever?

I can only see the tops of the canyon walls that surround me as they stand in testimony to what Manly gazed upon some 157 years ago, while the base of these walls of stone remains forever buried in black waters of unnecessary intervention.

The men now entered an unknown land with sheer cliff canyon walls of vivid pinks and flaming reds, higher than any the men had ever seen. "And when we got in there," Manly wrote, "we found the walls more than perpendicular, for the river bed was wider than the space between the rocks 3,000 or 4,000 feet above our heads."[23] Though John Wesley Powell gave more modest and accurate estimates of the canyon walls twenty years later, he too was inspired by the scene: "At a distance of from one to twenty miles from this point a brilliant red gorge is seen, the red being surrounded by broad bands of mottled buff and gray at the summit of the cliffs, and curving down to the water's edge on the nearer slope of the mountain. . . . We have named it Flaming Gorge. The cliffs or walls we have found to be twelve hundred feet high."[24]

As Manly found himself sinking deeper below the cliffs at Flaming Gorge, he recounted: "We passed many deep, dark cañons coming into the main stream, and at one place, where the rock hung a little over the river and had a smooth wall, I climbed up above the high-water mark which we could clearly see, and with a mixture of gunpower and grease for paint, and a bit of cloth tied to a stick for a brush, I painted in fair sized letters on the rock, CAPT. W. L. MANLEY, U. S. A."[25] This is the only time in Manly's travels westward to California that he recounted writing his name. Not knowing if he was in the United States, Manly proudly declared to all, with "all the majesty we could under the circumstances," who he was and to what country he belonged. Neither of the Powell expeditions of 1869 or 1871 make mention of seeing his name.

CHAPTER SIX

Into the Canyons

CRUDELY MANEUVERING THEIR FLAT-BOTTOMED FERRYBOAT WITH setting poles and paddles, Manly and his men were able to find their way through the first canyons—later named by Powell as Flaming Gorge and Horseshoe, Kingfisher, and Hidden Canyons—without mishap. As the canyons deepened and the waters grew more turbulent, with massive rocks blocking the path of travel, the voyagers were in what was to them a wholly new environment. "I don't think the sun ever shone down to the bottom of the cañon, for the sides were literally sky-high, for the sky, and a very small portion of that was all we could see," he wrote.[1] They also experienced more treacherous waters "in a terribly deep cañon": "We found trouble in managing the boat, and had to get out and wade and lift it off the rocks from time to time as we worked our way along. We went through this cañon with much difficulty, when we came to where two big rocks had fallen from the mountain which almost filled up the channel. Here we had to unload our boat and shove it as far out in the stream as possible, and hold it with a line, while I went below and brought it to the shore safely."[2] In his later account, *Death Valley in '49*, Manly is even more descriptive about these life-threatening encounters in Red Canyon:

> Just before night we came to a place where some huge rocks as large as cabins had fallen down from the mountain, completely filling up the river bed, and making it completely impassible for our boat. We unloaded it and while the boys held the stern line, I took off my clothes and pushed the boat out into the torrent which

ran around the rocks, letting them pay the line out slowly till it was just right. Then I sang out to—"Let go"—and away it dashed. I grasped the bow line, and at the first chance jumped overboa[r]d and got to shore, when I held the boat and brought it in below the obstructions. There was some deep water below the rocks.[3]

Twenty-four years before Manly's experience in surviving these dangerous sets of rapids in Red Canyon, William Ashley used similar tactics to successfully maneuver his boats to safety. Ashley wrote: "After progressing two miles, the navigation became difficult and dangerous, the river being remarkably crooked with more or less rapids every mile caused by rocks which had fallen from the sides of the mountain, many of which rise above the surface of the water and required our greatest exertions to avoid them. . . . Our boats were consequently rowed to shore, along which we cautiously descended to the place from whence the danger was to be apprehended."[4] Twenty years after Manly, Powell entertained the same strategies: "We started down through what we called Red Cañon, and soon came to the rapids, which were made dangerous by huge rocks lying in the channel. . . . We came to more dangerous rapids and stopped to examine them, and found that we had to let down with lines and were on the wrong side of the river, but must first cross."[5] For his part, Dellenbaugh remembered the roar of the river at this spot, which came "rolling up on the air with a steady, unvarying monotony that had a sinister meaning."[6]

The set of rapids downstream in Red Canyon proved much more difficult, and Manly's men were no match. Rather than running the rapids, they found themselves loading and unloading the boat to push it over and around the rock-strewn river, a challenging and risky activity itself. At these large rapids, Manly noticed an inscription made high above the water mark of the Green: "I saw a smooth place about fifty feet above where the great rocks had broken out, and there, painted in large black letters, were the words, 'Ashley, 1824.'"[7] As previously mentioned, explorer and trapper William Ashley had courageously run this section of the Green on May 3, 1825—not 1824 as Manly remembered. The inscription by Ashley was very memorable to Manly because it was a sure sign of a previous Euro-American explorer.[8] Powell also noted seeing Ashley's inscription when he passed it on June 2, 1869, as did Dellenbaugh: "It was on one of the huge rocks above the river on the left that Ashley wrote his name. This was in black letters, sheltered by a slight projection of the rock which acted as a cornice. Thus, it had remained distinct, except one figure of the date, for forty-six years, having been done in 1825."[9] Powell gave the rapids the name they would be known by ever after: Ashley Falls.

Historian Roy Webb painted a picture of what the cascades would have looked like before the Flaming Gorge Reservoir: "Ashley Falls certainly looked impressive. The towering thousand-foot canyon walls had given way to much lower ones, with rolling hills above. At some point in the past huge boulders had fallen off the walls and choked the channel, forming Ashley Falls. The total drop in the rapid is unrecorded, but from photographs it appears to be about ten vertical feet in a very short distance."[10] Stephen Vandiver Jones, the assistant topographer for Powell's second expedition in 1871, left a descriptive and precise review of the falls:

For half a mile above the fall the river is quiet as if preparing for the leap. At the head it is divided into 2 streams by a rock of 50 or 60 tons weight that has fallen into the stream. The water on the right falls almost vertically about 4 feet, strikes against rocks, and again leaps 4 or 5 feet breaking into foam, throwing the spray to the height of several feet. The stream on the left falls about the same distance but is less broken over both precipices. The river is full of sunken rocks, and nearly precipitous cliffs rise on each side to near 400 feet, composed of Red Sandstone. The roar of the falls can be heard nearly a mile above. The course of the river is nearly east, and the rays of the setting sun formed a beautiful rainbow at the lower end of the rock in the middle of the stream.[11]

General Ashley detailed his encounter with his namesake with these words: "It proved to be a perpendicular fall of ten or twelve feet produced by large fragments of rocks which had fallen from the [mountain] and settled in the river extending entirely across its channel and forming an impregnable barrier to the passage of loaded watercraft."[12] Dellenbaugh provided his own detailed analysis: "In the centre of the river protruded an immense rock, twenty-five feet square, and the river rushed by on each side making a sudden descent of about eight feet. It would have been nothing to run had it been free from rocks; but it was in reality the rocks which formed it. They had fallen from the left-hand wall within some comparatively recent time and acted as a dam. Many more were piled up against the left-hand cliff. The river, averaging about two hundred and fifty feet wide, had been narrowed by about one-third and a rapid had then been changed into a fall."[13]

Dellenbaugh also noted, "The only white men on record to reach this place except the Major's other party, was General Ashley."[14] At the time Dellenbaugh was floating the Green and writing his journals in 1871, he was not aware of Manly, who published *Death Valley in '49* in 1894. However, by the time Dellenbaugh published *The Romance of the Colorado River*, in 1902, he had become familiar with Manly's book and gave a brief historical sketch of Manly.[15]

With much the same fortitude and desire to succeed as Ashley and Powell, Manly and his men camped above Ashley Falls, catching trout and resting for the challenging day to come. The constant roar of the massive rapid that lay downriver must have been a concern for everyone throughout the night.[16] When morning finally came for Manly, he knew that he needed to scout and plan for the rapids to be successfully run: "I went down the river to explore and found a place where another big rock was in the river and the full force of the stream came against it forming an eddy next to the shore. This I knew would be a hard place to get by."[17] In his book, Manly noted, "We found that another big rock blocked the channel 300 yards below, and the water rushed around it with a terrible swirl."[18] Despite extensive river-running experience, Manly had never encountered such a large and dangerous rapid as what lay before him.

When Powell later encountered this point in the river, he decided to portage: "We unloaded the boats; then fastening a long line to the bow and another to the stern of one we moored it close to the edge of the falls. The stern line was taken below the falls and made fast, the bow line was taken by five or six men and the boat let down as long as they could hold it; then, letting go, the boat ran over and was caught by the lower rope."[19] William Ashley's plan had been similar: "We were therefore obliged to unload our boats of their cargoes and pass them empty over the falls by means of long cords which we had provided for such purposes."[20]

After he scouted what lay ahead, Manly's first plan was to have all the crew cross the river with the boat and avoid the massive, barn-sized rock. "So we unloaded the boat again," he wrote, "and made the attempt to get around it as we did the other rocks. We tried to get across the river but failed." The specific reason for the failure is not given, but understanding the extreme whitewater, it would have been very hard to maneuver and control a flat-bottomed ferryboat not made for such conditions, using poles and makeshift paddles. Manly's alternate plan was to unload the ferryboat and try to maneuver it carefully around the imposing rocks much like Ashley and Powell accomplished. Six men held poles to maneuver the boat, while one man "was to ease the boat down with the rope as far as he could."[21]

At Ashley Falls Manly and his crew watched as their ferryboat was destroyed against the rocks. RECORDS OF THE U.S. GEOLOGICAL SURVEY, NATIONAL ARCHIVES; PHOTOGRAPH BY E. O. BEAMAN, 1871

Then disaster struck. "As the boat came," Manly wrote, "we all put our poles against it and as we stopped it, the current being very strong, the boat instantly filled with water and came bottom against the rock and up edgeways."[22] Desperately, the men tried to maneuver the boat around the rock and avoid the dangers, but all was lost. In *Death Valley in '49*, Manly recounted: "The current was so strong that when the boat struck the rock we could not stop it, and the gunwale next to us rose, and the other went down, so that in a second the boat stood edgewise in the water and the bottom tight against the big rock, and the strong current pinned it there so tight that we could no more move it than we could move the rock itself."[23]

In comparing Manly's portaging plan with Ashley's and Powell's attempts to guide their empty boats past or over Ashley Falls, several important factors led to the success of Ashley and Powell and failure of Manly. First, Ashley and Powell both used long lines to maneuver their crafts. This was critical, as the length of the multiple cords would determine how much they could control the boat's direction. Manly, on the other hand, had only one rope, and it was limited in length.[24] It would have been impossible for one man with one short rope to guide a seven-by-twelve-foot ferryboat, in a rapid that dropped ten to twelve feet in such a short distance. Second, Manly and his men stood on the large boulder in Ashley Falls and tried to push away their on-rushing flatboat with poles. As the vessel struck the large rock in Ashley Falls, the water pushing the boat from upstream turned the boat sideways and pushed either the starboard (right) or port (left) side of the boat up against the rock, causing the boat to climb or rise above the turbulent water. The enormous force from the motion of water was unrelenting, pushing the opposite side of the boat down under the water, pinning it against the solid rock. Standing on the shore, an observer would have seen one side of the boat out of the water, pinned on the rock, while the opposite side would be submerged and firmly embedded against the rock. Rescuing the craft was impossible; its destruction was imminent.

With Manly's plans dashed against the massive rock in Ashley Falls, and the crew standing with poles in hand, watching their boat as it was literally ripped apart, one can only imagine their shock and discouragement. "Some of the boys asked, 'What do we do now?'" Manly recalled.[25] A meeting was held to discuss their options of survival: "This seemed a very sudden ending to our voyage and there were some very rapid thoughts as to whether we would be safer among the Mormons than out in this wild country, afoot and alone. Our boat was surely lost beyond hope, and something must be done."[26] It was here that Manly showed his leadership and survival skills. The options he gave his men were practical and simple: change course, leave the river, and start walking; or build canoes and continue down the river.

As the men discussed their choices, they would have weighed the risks of survival in an unknown region against wintering with the Mormons. Continuing down the Green in wooden canoes became the option of choice. The hand of Mother Nature played a significant role in supporting Manly's decision to venture farther down the Green in canoes. Trees of significant diameter and height are found growing along the riverbanks in this area. What Manly described as "white pine" were actually ponderosa pines. Dellenbaugh confirmed that during his own journey with Powell, "there was much vegetation, pine, spruce, willow-leaved cottonwood, aspens, alder, etc." on the shores,[27] so there was no shortage of material for the canoes in Manly's day.

Manly would have shared with the men his prior knowledge of building canoes and his experiences on the waters in the northern states and territories. They set immediately to work, dividing into shifts and working night and day with the two axes Dallas had given them on their departure from the wagons. Manly gave no timeline for how long it took to complete the two canoes, each of which he said measured "fifteen feet long and two feet wide," but chopping down two trees two feet in diameter and then hollowing them out to the length of approximately fifteen feet would have been an immense and time-consuming task.[28] When finished, the newly constructed canoes were lashed together for stability and safety, a procedure Manly would have understood from his days transporting trapping gear and pelts. At some point, Manly and his crew also fashioned paddles to maneuver the canoes.[29]

Once again ready for the challenges of the water, the party cast off on the river. Changing the canoes to a catamaran-like craft allowed water to pass between the attached logs, stabilizing each and preventing them from overturning in the rapids. Manly understood river running, the currents, flows, and eddies that constantly presented challenges, and connecting the boats was a good move. Had the canoes been launched without being secured together, they would have been less dependable and would have rolled over or flipped more easily in rapids. However, once again on the river, Manly and the men quickly realized the load of men and supplies was too great for the two combined canoes to support. Safety and stability were compromised, so Manly again directed the men to stop. They cut down another ponderosa pine tree and constructed a much larger canoe designated for carrying gear. Manly wrote, "This canoe we made twenty-five or thirty feet long . . . and into it loaded the most valuable things, such as provisions, ammunition and cooking utensils."[30] This time Manly tells us how long it took to construct a boat: a day and a night.[31]

Because the new canoe carried the gear necessary for their survival, the men decided that Manly should paddle and control it. He noted, "I was the only really expert canoe navigator."[32] The crew's trust in and dedication to Manly allowed all to continue with the hope that they would reach California safely. He had seen them through the disaster of losing their flatboat, and he was confident in his abilities and knowledge of the wilderness. As a young man, he had been admonished by his father, Ebenezer, "You will have to depend upon yourself in all things."[33] He was finding this to be true on the Green River, as he ensured his own safety and that of his men.

8/26/2006, Saturday, Day 8, River Day 8

Dowd Mountain to Flaming Gorge Dam

With such historical artifacts underwater, as I float over them, I only wish I could see exactly where the events took place. I feel cheated as the waters of progress hide the locations of events and confrontations between man and nature. Aside from the rock walls, the only things that remain true to Manly's story, untouched and in full view to surviving this dangerous stretch of river, are the tall-growing pine trees that are, in fact, more than thirty feet high. . . . I am gratified as we paddle through the final waters of Flaming Gorge to see firsthand the trees described by Manly growing continuously up the ridge to the crest of the mountains high above the water's level. . . . The ponderosa pines grow straight with large trunks, some well over two feet in diameter. This tree would have been perfect for making canoes. Hooray for their beauty, hooray for their ability to rise above the waters of the gorge!

With the newly made canoes hewn from ponderosa pines, the pace quickened; Manly recounted that the crew now "went flying down stream."[34] As the men ventured out on the waters, a plan was devised to help direct them and ensure their safety. Manly took the lead, positioned in the rear of the large canoe with Morgan McMahon seated in the front.[35] In recounting the difficult times on the river, McMahon wrote Manly, "We drilled holes through the sides of the 'Pilot'—you, I have no doubt remember which that was, yours and mine, in which we took so many fearful risks, and 'No. 2.'"[36] This remark—the fact that the men named the boats "Pilot" and "No. 2"—helps bring into focus the important relationship and vital link between the men and canoes they built.

Now that the men were in separate boats, communication became a new challenge. Manly devised a plan to warn the other men in the smaller canoes if a dangerous rapid or river condition was to suddenly appear: "[If] I raised my right and motioned back, they were to know that danger was ahead, and they were to go to shore and land their canoes so as to avoid accident."[37] This plan was similar to Major John Wesley Powell's own plan as he floated the same river in 1869: "Then with a flag I signal the boats to advance, and guide them by signals around dangerous rocks."[38]

8/29/2006, Tuesday, Day 11, River Day 9

Flaming Gorge Dam to Little Hole

Morning came early in anticipation of being back on the river. Coming across Flaming Gorge was an ordeal. I missed the river and its soothing waters. The reservoir seemed to take away the river's voice, where all we encountered was flat water for ninety-one miles. Directly in front of us stands the Flaming Gorge Dam, imposing and looking out of place in such a beautiful canyon. As I compare the dam and its man-made strength with that of Mother Nature, my smile is almost a smirk. The interpretative sign close to the boat ramp below the dam explains that the dam stands 455 feet or 140 meters above the river's edge. When I was floating along on the reservoir, everything I viewed was close to 455 feet above what Manly experienced. I wish someone had taken me down that section of river before the dam was constructed. What Manly saw those few desperate days in which he fought for his life and the lives of the crew who followed him can never be recaptured. Now that the reservoir is behind me, I am eager with anticipation. Arriving at the bank below the dam, the river once again sings to us as we greet it and load our boats.

By noon we are ready to go. People are all around, mostly fishing. I see more people now than I did the whole week on the reservoir. An osprey flies overhead with its catch of the day firmly in its talons. The clear water reflects the sunlight as the environment comes alive, showing all nature has to offer. As we paddle down the river, the towering ponderosa pines greet me and welcome my company. It feels good to be on the river again. As I float along, I have my keyboard on my lap and am able to write. The fish below the boat are numerous. Silently floating downstream, I watched the Green unfold with life and energy. I am at peace. The reservoir was dark and unnaturally still. Here, all is alive. In ten minutes of floating, I must have seen more than one hundred fish. Clint tells me that in one river mile there are more than 22,000 fish. As my boat drifts quietly along, a family of river otters boldly frolic in the deep green waters. Floating a river while using a keyboard to record my thoughts is a unique experience for me—marvelous!

Manly must have been relieved as he entered these waters; the calm, constant current allowed them to move at a quicker but safe pace. Clint and Dallas are fishing, and I hope we have some trout to fry tonight. We will be floating through these calm and soothing waters for up to four days. It could never get any better than this. Clint is on the log canoes. They are floating well. The two logs are called "Pilot" and "No. 2." Those are the names Manly gave his two wood logs, and I named our logs the same. Pilot is larger and floats higher in the water; No. 2 sits lower in the water but is doing fine. They are not as large in diameter as Manly's logs because we needed them to be lighter weight so we could carry them, but they seem to be doing fine. Tomorrow we run our first strong rapid. That rapid will give us an indication of how well they will do in larger rapids farther downriver.

This is our ninth day on the river. With all the trials and tribulations Manly encountered, thus slowing him down, and our ability to move faster, yet having to canoe across the reservoir, Manly's time schedule would probably now fall behind our own on this ninth river day. The two main factors influencing time spent on the river are the slow waters of Flaming Gorge for us and Manly's taking additional time to construct his canoes, which we prepared before embarking.

We are now entering Little Hole on our ninth river day, whereas I surmise Manly would have been in Little Hole on the 12th, 13th, or 14th day. These are only estimates, but it is important to continually review and consider his schedule as we move down the river.

Emerging out of Red Canyon with his newly constructed wood canoes and into what is now called Little Hole, Manly described what he saw: "This rapid rate soon brought us out of the high mountains and into a narrow valley when the stream became more moderate in its speed and we floated along easily enough." The river coming out of Red Canyon and into Little Hole does calm but continues to flow in a walled and narrow canyon. To this point, there are three main discrepancies in Manly's journal: (a) It seems improbable that Manly could float thirty miles in one day, (b) the incorrect reference of Black's Fork, and (c) his estimated time schedule.

All other observations fit in order chronologically as we have floated along. I am pleasantly surprised that the estimated days on the river by Manly and our team, without Flaming Gorge and building the canoes, are similar. I think we move faster due to river knowledge and modern equipment; however, I believe Manly logged longer river hours per day. To see what Manly and his men accomplished so far on their voyage has surprised me. Their will to survive and dedication to one another are impressive. They needed to stay together as a team for success. This they did!

The evening is here and the boys are content with dinner and sitting around the campfire. Today was a magical day for me. To be back on the river after the reservoir felt more natural. Everything came alive. To float and see things Manly saw and experienced made me feel complete. Toward the end of the day we rounded a bend where an unusual ponderosa pine tree was growing. I recognized it from a picture Powell's photographer had taken in 1871's second expedition. I stopped and took a picture of it. This trip has been in review of Manly, but identifying locations and events Powell encountered is equally gratifying from a historical perspective.

Floating through Red Canyon in their newly made canoes, Manly found the river once again in a calmer state, with only moderate rapids; then, "starting on again, the river lost more and more of its rapidity as it came out into a still wider valley, and became quite sluggish."[39] Author Ann Zwinger also detailed this stretch of Red Creek Canyon and the silty waters that flow through it, calling it "the first red rock canyon on the Green River." She continued: "The walls are a soft rose red in the morning light, eight hundred feet high, rising back to two thousand on the mountainside to the south."[40] In a letter to a newspaper, O. G. Howland, crew member of the 1869 Powell expedition, referenced this section of Red Canyon and the silty red river conditions at the same location, calling it "Red Creek."[41] Manly incorrectly referenced passing a stream in the canyon on the west, "thick with mud." Red Creek actually enters on the east side of the Green, at the start of Red Creek Rapid.[42]

8/30/2006, Wednesday, Day 12, River Day 10

Little Hole to Browns Park

It is an overcast morning, but no rain. The river sang to me all night as we are camped by a small riffle of water. Fish are jumping by my boat as I write and watch the sun emerge between two cedar-covered mountains. The boys are asleep and warned me not to wake them up for they needed extra sleep. Our camp is next to a large ponderosa pine the size and shape Manly would have used. I cannot even imagine how hard that would have been to cut and shape a 30-foot canoe out of it by hand; I'd had the modern conveniences of chainsaw and drills.

As I am sitting here, an osprey gracefully drops into the Green and catches its breakfast. Today, we will continually float into open waters. We are fast approaching Browns Park, thirty-five miles long and ending at the Gates of Lodore. We have allowed three days to float through this beautiful area. We could have run this section faster, but the day set for our launching in Lodore is September 2. There is no hurry.

Floating down and nearly out of Red Canyon, I see a cave three-fourths up the cliffs on the left side of the river. Dallas and Clint agree to hike up and see what is inside. We all hope for more Indian artifacts. It takes about thirty minutes to climb—nothing but rock inside, but the view of the valley and flowing Green are spectacular. Up this high we can see why the Green was given its name: clear water, reflecting the moss and green rocks that lie in the riverbed.

Climbing down, I slipped and fell into a large bed of cactus. I had cactus spines all over me. After a good laugh, Dallas and I picked most of them out. He got the ones on my backside while I worked on the ones in the front. I can tell I am not as nimble as I once was. I am so glad that I am healthy and able to accomplish this trip.

After several miles, we approach Red Creek Rapid and stop to scout it. It is not much of a rapid but has historical significance to Manly. While there, I notice on the map a stream coming in from the east called Red Creek. Clint explained to me that when it rains, it flows thick with red mud. Referencing Manly's writings, he remembered a swollen stream, coming in from the west. . . . No streams in this section of the river flow from the west side, which Manly could have referred to that fit his description. With that and the uniqueness of Red Creek flowing from recent rains, this creek is the one he must have seen. With the Green constantly winding, twisting, and turning as it finds its way through these many canyons, it is difficult to see the sun and determine directions and is, therefore, understandable that Manly misread the confluence of Red Creek flowing from the east and not the west. This confluence of the Green and Red Creek is the fourth noticeable mistake Manly made in his observations while floating down the river.

After this observation with the crew, we successfully navigate Red Creek Rapid and begin to leave Red Canyon. Emerging out of Red Canyon, the landscape is opening up just as Manly pointed out. We have floated twenty miles from the Flaming Gorge Dam and have arrived at Browns Park. In the map Manly reviewed, this area was known as Browns Hole. When Manly reached this area, he recounted, "It took us 2 or 3 days to pass this beautiful valley."

The beautiful valley Manly refers to here was Browns Hole, the name he mistakenly used in remembering his map when he thought the river was dropping out of sight just before the Flaming Gorge cliffs and Horseshoe Canyon. Browns Park widens, with the meandering Green flowing through it. In the early maps of the 1800s, this area was called Browns Hole, but when Powell floated through in 1869, he renamed the area Browns Park because of its beauty. . . . This beautiful open valley has large areas to farm and irrigate.

While floating in this valley, Manly remembered picking red berries that were close to the river's edge. . . . As I entered the first turn of Browns Park, I saw a large bush growing by the river covered with red berries. After noticing this bush, we saw many more appear as we continued to float through the park. A short distance after entering Browns Park, we arrived at Jarvie Ranch, a historic ranch house. While there, I asked one of the rangers what the red berries were growing along the riverbank. He identified them as chokecherries, which make excellent jam.[43]

Stopping at the ranch was an unexpected pleasure for all of us. The Bureau of Land Management interpretive rangers welcomed us and enjoyed learning about Manly. Likewise, we enjoyed learning about the early outlaw history in Browns Park. In the late 1800s and early 1900s, this area became a hotbed of outlaws on the run. Butch Cassidy and the Sundance Kid were just two of the well-known rustlers who hid in this protected valley. The Bureau of Land Management has restored the Jarvie Ranch located along the bank of the Green. The rangers claimed this area stays warmer in the winter than other surrounding lands—an advantage to outlaws who stole horses and cattle. When they brought the livestock in, they did not need to supply feed and could rely on local, natural grasses. In those winter months, the temperatures were warm enough to allow ample feed to be found. We will be camping below Jarvie Ranch tonight and will spend some time tomorrow walking throughout the valley reviewing as well as enjoying this picturesque valley.

We traveled twelve miles today and, since leaving the dam two days ago, have covered twenty-five miles. Manly would have moved much faster in this stretch. We are traveling more slowly because we cannot enter Lodore Canyon below Browns Park until September 2 due to our permit authorizing us to float through Dinosaur National Monument. Today is the 31st of August, so we will have today and tomorrow to float twenty miles—ample time to cover the distance. I would think Manly enjoyed floating through this area, as we have. These open, calm waters must have been a welcome relief from the turbulent waters of Red Canyon thirty to fifty miles upriver.

As we get ready to leave Jarvie Ranch and float to our evening camp spot, the Bureau of Land Management interpretative rangers continue to offer assistance. They have given us ice to pack in our food coolers and provided electricity to charge my laptop computer. We gave them a commemorative handkerchief of our expedition. It is rewarding to associate with the different government agencies along the way that share the same excitement as we do about western American history of the 1800s. All is well, and our time on the river today has been wonderful. I will close for now.

Powell described Browns Park as "a valley, bounded on either side by a mountain range, really an expansion of the canyon. The river, through the park, is 35½ miles long and passes through two short canyons on its way, where spurs from the mountains on the south are thrust across its course."[44]

Before Powell changed the name, Browns Hole was reportedly named for a trapper named Baptiste Browne who worked at one time for the Hudson Bay Company. Ann Zwinger called the area "a layered landscape: steep dark red slopes, heavily evergreened, form a high near-even horizon, nested with the pale, rolling and notched hillsides and mesas of the Browns Park Formation."[45] Here Manly and his companions discovered a new food source: "We picked red berries that grew on bushes that overhung the water. They were sour and might have been high cranberries."[46] These berries are known as squawbush berries. The plant itself gives off a bitter smell, earning it its other name, skunkbush.[47]

Powell noted the presence of native inhabitants in this area: "Here the walls are comparatively low, but vertical, and vast multitudes of swallows have built their adobe houses on their sides. The waters are deep and quiet; but the swallows are swift and noisy enough, sweeping about in their curved paths through the air and chattering from the rocks, the young birds stretching their little heads on naked necks through the doorways of their mud nests and clamoring for food. They are a lively people. So we called this Swallow Cañon."[48] Though Manly does not reference this canyon, he would have enjoyed floating through such a peaceful sanctuary of seclusion, given that in his own words, he "was always a great admirer of Nature and things which remained as they were created."[49]

8/31/2006, Thursday, Day 13, River Day 11

Browns Park to Swinging Bridge

After another radio interview, we began a day where the water has been calm. We pushed through some little rapids but nothing to worry about. After lunch, we entered a beautiful gorge called

Swallow Canyon. Powell named this canyon because of the large, purple-stoned canyon walls that rise vertically on each side of the river where numerous swallows make their homes out of the mud they carry in their beaks from the riverbank, which reminds me of government housing projects. With the crew a mile or so behind me, I am in this canyon all by myself and the silence is wonderful. I have a downstream breeze gently pushing me deeper and deeper into a wonderland of natural beauty.

Manly would have enjoyed this stretch because of his desire to see the beauty of nature. They would be moving fast in their canoes and, with the towering walls protecting them from the sun, they might have hoped the remainder of the river was just like this. Little did they know that two days later they would be in Lodore Canyon, fighting for their lives.

Swallow Canyon's walls rise at least one thousand feet, with hawks soaring high overhead on the soft, warm breezes. If I ever imagined the most peaceful place on earth, I have just found it. In reflecting what Manly and his crew felt daily, their emotions must have been constantly changing. In this location, they were probably glad of the decision to take the river route. Later, as their lives hung in the balance, Manly's will to survive and leadership skills played a role with the men and their dependence upon him.

Today, in Swallow Canyon, I am experiencing one of the most peaceful moments of my life. I am a lucky man to live in a time when I can enjoy such tranquility. If my mentor and Clint's father, Merlin, were ever with me, it would be right now on these calm waters. Not a sound is heard, as the wind races itself down the canyon walls.

Floating peacefully through this deep canyon, I feel as though it is alive, silently watching me pass through. In this magnificent canyon, floating alone is the solace that I have been searching for since the day I left on our expedition. I must never forget this moment: the strength of the canyon walls with the Green gracefully passing through, untouched with conflict or strife. Our floating ended around 6:00 in the evening. We camped at Swinging Bridge. The campsite is not very good, but we will have to make do. All goes well and the skies are clear. Tomorrow is our last day of calm water. We will be at the Gates of Lodore tomorrow night.

The two-thousand-foot Gates of Lodore.

Manly recounted, "We ran the length of this valley in three or four days and then began to come into the cañons again which grew deeper and deeper and the river rougher till at last the mountains on either side seemed sky high, and nothing but bare rocks."[50] Early Browns Hole settler Sam Bassett described the next feature of the river, the Gates of Lodore, as a "great stone mouth drinking a river."[51] Ann Zwinger vividly portrayed this canyon, which Manly was fast approaching: "Each canyon of the Green has its own distinctive presence but none is as dramatic as Lodore. The cliffs rise two thousand feet, immediate, all the more striking because of the pale landscape from which they spring, almost without transition. The Gates of Lodore hinge inward, cruelly joined, hard rock, ominous."[52]

Thoughts of tragedies recently experienced in Red Canyon must have now given Manly and his crew feelings of foreboding. Later, Powell memorably wrote of his own anxiety at this spot: "The river fills the channel from wall to wall. The cañon opened like a beautiful portal to a region of glory. Now, as I write, the sun is going down and the shadows are setting in the cañon. The vermilion gleams and rosy hues, the green and gray tints are changing to somber brown above, and black shadows below. Now 'tis a black portal to a region of gloom. . . . On the 8th [June] our boats entered the Cañon of Lodore—a name suggested by one of the men [Andy Hall], and it has been adopted. We soon came to rapids, over which the boats had to be taken with lines."[53] Ashley also expressed a tremendous foreboding entering the Gates of Lodore as rapids began to appear. He wrote, "I was forcibly struck with the gloom which spread over the countenances of my men; they seemed to anticipate (and not far distant, too) a dreadful termination of our voyage, and I must confess that I partook in some degree of what I supposed to be their feelings, for things around us had truly an awful appearance."[54] Dellenbaugh concentrated more on the grandeur of the Green entering Lodore Canyon: "The mountains rose abruptly just beyond our camp, and the river cleaved the solid mass at one stroke, forming the extraordinary and magnificent portal we named the 'Gate of Lodore,' one of the most striking entrances of a river into mountains to be found in all the world. . . . The cliffs, red and majestic, rose at one bound to a height of about 2000 feet on each side, the most abrupt and magnificent gateway to a canyon imaginable."[55]

9/1/2006, Friday, Day 14, River Day 12

Swinging Bridge to Gates of Lodore

We awoke today to cloudless skies and no wind. It should be an easy float to the Gates of Lodore. I estimate Manly would have passed here around his thirteenth to fifteenth day. Our schedules as far as time spent on the river have matched fairly closely. The unknown for me is determining how long it took to build the canoes. For the last three days, we have only floated twelve miles per day.

Manly probably made excellent time through these calm waters and would have logged at least twenty miles each day. In retrospect, they did not have much to do other than float. I would think they started fairly early and would end towards evening or dark. They did spend time preparing the game Manly shot, but otherwise their days were primarily spent on the river. This section today continues to be peaceful and calm.

Late afternoon and I can see the canyon of Lodore in the distance. The river has been enjoyable all day. Within the last mile, there have been numerous dead cottonwood trees rising out of the silent waters. Their white trunks, pale from the scorching sun, depict a deathly look as they ominously protrude out of the calm water. They stand like headstones in a graveyard, quietly marking the past life of the trees captured by the river's current years ago. To me, these dead trees stand as a warning for what is to come tomorrow. Manly wrote that it took them two or three days to float through Browns Park. . . . We took extra time to prepare and completed the 44-mile float in four days.

Today, I drifted by a rock wall that had distinct high-water marks on the purple rock. I measured from the current water level to the high-water mark. It was just less than six feet. As I float, I constantly ponder what the water level might have been for Manly. Even though we are in the same month of August that Manly floated, the dams of Fontenelle and Flaming Gorge distort current levels and do not give a true indication of what the water level might have been. I think we are close to what Manly experienced because of the similar number of days we both have spent on the river, but this is only a guess, for I have no scientific way to accurately measure true water levels in 1849.

I am now coming around the last turn towards the Gates of Lodore. Manly and his men would already have realized their journey just became more difficult. As they entered the canyon, with a depth and narrowness similar to the canyons where Flaming Gorge Reservoir now stands, they had to know they would be approaching an area of rapids and danger. The towering mountains on each side of the river look ripped apart for the Green to angrily flow through. I have been down this section before, and I am feeling the intimidation of what lies ahead. The canyon of Lodore and our wood canoes will meet head-on tomorrow.

When we arrive at our campsite tonight, we will be joined by other professional guides to help us through. I am glad that Clint is with us. He has logged more than seventy-five trips through the canyon. During the five-day canyon run, we will be pulling over at various rapids, which Manly described, so as to verify or question his written descriptions. I wonder whether the wood canoes will hold up and continue floating through Lodore. Tomorrow we will begin to see. I do not think it will be easy; it certainly was not for Manly. All is well, and we will be ready.

As Manly entered the Canyon of Lodore, massive boulders blocking the main current became commonplace, as did portaging. "After the first day of this," he wrote, "the river was so full of big boulders, that the only way we could get along was to unload and take our canoes over, and then load up again, only to travel a little way, and repeat the operation."[56] Lucky to not have experienced any mishaps in the upper waters of Lodore, Manly slowly proceeded downriver with the utmost caution and skill, knowing that at a moment's notice all could be lost. The going was slow and frustrating: "Sometimes we could ride a little ways, and then would come the rough-and-tumble with the rocks again."[57] After floating a distance of six and a half miles from the Gates of Lodore, Manly encountered and successfully portaged around two larger rapids, later named by Powell as Upper Disaster and Lower Disaster Falls. Manly recounted the constant hardships the men endured as they passed these falls and deepened their journey in Lodore. "We found generally more boulders than water," he wrote, "and the down grade of the river bed was heavy."

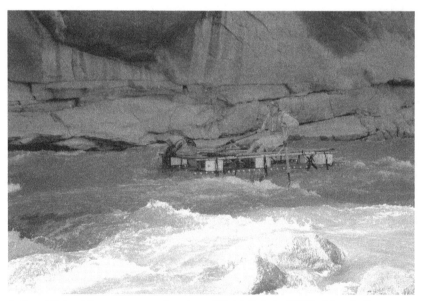

Author Michael Kane maneuvering down Triplet Falls in 2006, riding in the wooden canoes he built to follow Lewis Manly's path down the Green River.

89

Some days we did not go more than four or five miles, and that was serious work, loading and unloading our canoes, and packing them over the boulders, with only small streams of water curling around between them. We went barefoot most of the time, for we were more than half of the time in the water which roared and dashed so loud that we could hardly heard [*sic*] each other speak. We kept getting more and more venturesome and skillful, and managed to run some very dangerous rapids in safety."[58]

General Ashley recorded the identical process of surviving Upper and Lower Disaster Falls by unloading their boats and carrying their gear to safer waters: "A mile lower down, the channel became so obstructed by the intervention of large rocks over and between which the water dashed with such violence as to render our passage in safety impracticable. The cargoes of our boats were therefore a second time taken out and carried about two hundred yards, to which place, after much labor, our boats were descended by means of cords."[59] Powell's men recounted the back-breaking labor of portaging, with one crew member memorably recording, "Have been working like galley-slaves all day."[60] Dellenbaugh described the process in most detail:

We were up very early in the morning, and began to carry the cargoes by a trail we made over and around the huge boulders to a place below the bad water of the first fall. The temperature was in the 90s and it was hot work climbing with a fifty-pound sack on one's back, but at last after many trips back and forth every article was below. Then the empty boats were taken one at a time. And by pulling, lifting, and sliding on skids of driftwood, and by floating wherever practicable in the quieter edges of the water, we got them successfully past the first fall. Here the loads were replaced, and with our good long and strong lines an inch thick, the boats were sent down several hundred yards in the rather level water . . . intervening between the foot of the upper fall and the head of the lower, to the beginning of the second descent.[61]

Though Manly survived this stretch of Lodore with life, canoes, and equipment intact, Powell was not as fortunate; he lost one of his boats, the *No Name*, in Upper Disaster Falls. He wrote of the 1869 expedition:

> I heard a shout, and looking around, saw one of the boats coming over the falls. Captain Howland, of the *No Name*, had not seen the signal in time, and the swift current had carried him to the brink. . . . The first fall was not great, only two or three feet, and we had often run such, but below it continued to tumble down twenty or thirty feet more, in a channel filled with dangerous rocks and that broke the waves into whirlpools and beat them into foam. I turned just to see the boat strike a rock and throw the men and the cargo out. Still they clung to her sides and clambered in again and saved part of the oars, but she was full of water, and they could not manage her. Still down the river they went, two or three hundred yards to another rocky rapid just as bad, and the boat struck again amidships, and was dashed to pieces.[62]

As Manly and his men carefully portaged Upper and Lower Disaster Falls, Manly made a startling discovery: a "deserted camp, a skiff and some heavy cooking utensils." They also found a note of some kind affixed to an alder tree informing passersby that the writers "had found the river route impracticable, and being satisfied that the river was so full of rocks and boulders that it could not be safely navigated, they had abandoned the undertaking and were about to start overland to make their way to Salt Lake." Manly stated that he wrote the names given on the notice in his diary, but since it was burned up, he could no longer remember them.[63] Though the identity of the earlier river runners is a mystery, Manly's account provides details that show it was not Ashley. First, it could not have been posted for a significant period of time without being destroyed by the elements. Also, the party claimed to be heading toward Salt Lake, so it must have been after 1847, when the Mormons founded the city. Finally, the note said the earlier crew had brought heavy

Today, old abandoned campsites are not an uncommon sight on the Green River. In 2006, author Michael D. Kane explored one such site near Lodore Canyon.

equipment with them, which would not have been used if they had been walking or on foot, as Ashley had been before embarking down the river.

Powell, in his initial run down the Green in 1869, noted this same deserted camp, still intact, including "the lid of a bake oven, an old tin plate and other things, showing that someone else had been wrecked there and camped in the cañon after the disaster." He alluded to Ashley's "attempt to run the cañon, some years ago," and assumed it to be evidence of that run.[64]

For his part, Dellenbaugh believed that Ashley did not even enter Lodore Canyon. "In the canyon of Lodore, at the foot of Disaster Falls, we found some wreckage in the sand," Dellenbaugh wrote of the 1871 expedition in 1902, "a bake-oven, tin plates, knives, etc., which Powell first saw in 1869, but these could not have belonged to Ashley's party, for plainly Ashley did not enter Lodore at all. It was evidently from some later expedition which probably started from Brown's Park, in the days of Fort Davy Crockett."[65] By the time he wrote his book, Dellenbaugh had read *Death Valley in '49*, and he mentioned Manly's report of finding the abandoned camp, concluding, "Apparently the cooking utensils, etc., were the same we saw twenty-two years later at that place and thought were wreckage."[66]

After describing more details of the camp, Dellenbaugh went on to refute Powell's theory that it had belonged to Ashley, since Ashley had passed through before the Latter-day Saints established Salt Lake City. Then he pleaded, "Should any reader have knowledge of the men who were wrecked in Lodore between the time of Ashley and Powell, the author would be glad to hear of it."[67]

Taking Dellenbaugh's invitation, I researched who the earlier river runners who left their gear at Disaster Falls might have been, and I uncovered a possibility. One clue was that Powell and Dellenbaugh observed the lid of a bake oven (commonly known as a Dutch oven, made of cast iron). Such ovens were a common item for the emigrants traveling west by wagon. The presence of this and other heavy equipment suggests that those early unknown river runners had not intended to run the Green but were traveling overland and, like Manly, changed plans to float the Green, doing so with the equipment that was in their possession. In reading various diaries and journals of other emigrants bound for the West Coast in 1849, I came across a journal entry by William Lorton, who wrote that on July 28, 1849, just a month before Manly was to come to the Green, "some California emigrants made boats of their wagon boxes and set sail down Green River." This group of river travelers would have been close enough in time to Manly that a note that was posted on an alder tree could have remained intact, and they would have had heavy equipment, including a cast-iron Dutch oven, in their wagons as they traveled westward.

9/2/2006, Saturday, Day 15, River Day 13

Gates of Lodore to Pot Creek

The morning sun rises and bathes the Gates of Lodore with sunlight. The warm, pink colors fall on the deep maroon canyon walls. The crew from Dinosaur River Expeditions arrived late last night to travel with us. I am impressed with their work in getting everything ready. Their support will be essential as we run the rapids with the log canoes. The first noticeable landmark is the looming rock walls as we get ready to enter. . . .

As we prepare to descend into Lodore, we will verify the presence of boulders and rapids in the river. During this day of river running, we will encounter Disaster Falls, the first of the three most dangerous rapids in Lodore Canyon where Powell lost his boat, the *No-Name*, on his 1869 expedition. We will stop there and view the rapid. When Manly floated this section, he wrote about finding a deserted camp where the river was "more than usually obstructed."[68] Disaster Falls is the location that matches his description. I will write more tonight about the experience. Running Disaster Falls will be the first true test of the logs. I am confident as to their success. With Manly running in August, as we are, and recollecting all the boulders in the river, which we see, my spirits are renewed that we are running close to the same water levels as did Manly.

The boats are packed and we are ready to go. As I enter Lodore, the canyon walls tower thousands of feet above me. Their deep red color is magnificent against the blue sky and the green vegetation along the riverbank. Nevertheless, the intimidation offered by these canyon walls and looming rapids are palpable to me, as they probably were to Manly.

~~~

We have just run Disaster Falls. Large rocks lie in the middle of the rapid. One by one, we took turns running the rapid while others stood on the bank with safety lines in case of an accident. As Clint ran the log canoes through, the constant echoing sounds of timber striking the large rocks made me worry that they would hit with such impact the logs would shatter. An hour and a half later, we had all made it through successfully, including the logs, which were still intact. I am glad that rapid is completed. I do not want to run it again. The red canyon walls are magnificent. I think back to Flaming Gorge and what was covered up. I am so glad these waters run free. Our heritage, history, and overall grand scale of America remain intact as do these walls. The water continually drops as we sink deeper and deeper into Lodore. Surprisingly, Manly never wrote about the grandeur of what he encountered.

The evening skies are colored pink as the sun sets over the canyon walls. We are now in camp and safe. Disaster Falls was strong and exciting, just as I had expected hours before. The log boat with Clint at the helm ran smoothly. Others in our crew ran the rapids with inflatable kayaks. The lighter craft give a tremendous feel for the water and rapids. The multitude of large rocks at Upper Disaster Falls were even more than I remembered. Manly had similar recollections when he encountered Upper and Lower Disaster Falls. . . .

Thus, Manly verified that he was in Lodore Canyon and found the rapids frequent and large. To avoid losing possessions and men, Manly had the canoes emptied and supplies carried around the rapids. Carrying the boats or lining them along the riverbank became a much safer way of moving downriver. Manly provides a rare mention of a timeline in Lodore Canyon when he described Disaster Falls: "After the *first* day of this the river became so full of boulders . . ." This places Manly toward the top section of Lodore Canyon, within a day's journey of Upper and Lower Disaster Falls. These rapids are just seven miles downriver from the Gates of Lodore.

Aside from the dangers Manly confronts at Disaster Falls, these rapids hold another significant historical importance noted by Manly. He found remnants of someone before him who tried to run the river. . . .

Historically, this rapid has been targeted as ending the whitewater experience and final river miles traveled by William Ashley's exploring party in 1824. He and an expedition of men were searching for waters that held the prized beaver, which were in demand for clothing purposes in America as well as in Europe. If this find by Manly was, in fact, the exiting point for William Ashley, Manly and his party then become the first American explorers to document and float through all of Lodore Canyon and into the southern reaches of the Green.

As Manly successfully passed through Disaster Falls, he accounts for still more rocks found in the river. Floating today, I experienced the same awareness of large boulders throughout the canyon waters and a noticeable drop of elevation evident as the water fell to lower levels and the canyon wound its way southward. Within the days in Lodore, Manly wrote that their ability to cover long distances of river miles became less: "Some days we did not go more than four or five miles, and that was serious work, loading and unloading our canoes, and packing them over the boulders, with only small streams of water curling around between them." With the rapids becoming stronger and bigger, the noise also intensified. . . .

Cautiously moving along the shoreline when needed, Manly and his men remained safe and continued to successfully challenge the Green. Within these first several days in Lodore, Manly's crew must have worked extremely hard together to survive. Trying to run the river individually would have spelled disaster for each. I estimate that Manly took three or four days to pass through the difficult rapids found in Lodore Canyon.

Manly did not have the safety of experienced guides. I am fortunate to have the well-trained professional guides from Dinosaur River Expeditions to assist us. Today, we ran nine miles of constant whitewater. I felt good accomplishing so much as well as understanding and relating to what Manly and his men experienced. Times like today give me a more accurate perspective on Manly and his challenges. We have camped in a designated campground called Kolb Campground. All helped with dinner and cleanup. The skies are darkening, and we will be in bed by 9:00 tonight.

Surviving the beginning rapids of Lodore Canyon, including Upper and Lower Disaster Falls, Manly continued to move into the deepening canyon with unknown rapids looming. He did not detail the next few miles of dangerous rapids, but O. G. Howland, one of Powell's men in 1869, did. "On the twelfth we made a portage of 150 yards," Howland noted, "loaded up and ran down into smooth water just above heavy rapids and camped. From the scene of the wreck [Lower Disaster Falls] to this point we have worked our way down over bad rapids and falls about four and a half miles."[69]

Manly picked up the story four and a half miles below Disaster Falls. He wrote, "One afternoon we came to a sudden turn in the river, more than a right angle, and, just below, a fall of two feet or more. This I ran in safety, as did the rest who followed and we cheered at our pluck and skill. Just after this the river swung back the other way at a right angle or more, and I quickly saw there was danger below."[70] This rapid is now called Triplet Falls, where the river does in fact make a dramatic right-hand turn, a full ninety degrees. Then, as it fast approaches the towering cliffs of Lodore, it turns back ninety degrees to its left. Manly's description is unmistakable. He and his men ran these rapids successfully. Once again, the name of the rapids came from Powell, who portaged the obstacles: "Here we have three falls in close succession. At the first the water is compressed into a very narrow channel against the right-hand cliff, and falls 15 feet in 10 yards. At the second we have a broad sheet of water tumbling down 20 feet over a group of rocks that thrust their dark heads through the foam. The third is a broken fall, or short, abrupt rapid, where the water makes a descent of more than 20 feet among huge, fallen fragments of the cliff. We name the group Triplet Falls. We make a portage around the first; past the second and the third we let down with lines."[71]

9/3/06, Sunday, Day 16, River Day 14

Kolb Campground to Triplet Campground

Sunday morning and I am up early. All are sleeping in because we do not have far to travel today. We will be going only about 4½ miles. I like that because Manly had days that he was only able to travel short distances: "Some days we did not go more than four or five miles." Today, we will approach the second of the three most dangerous rapids.

   This upcoming rapid is called Triplet Falls. Twenty years ago I ran Lodore and crashed at Triplet. I remember flipping over and wondering if I was going to drown. It was a frightening experience. Since that day, I have never been back in Lodore. My anxieties are high in confronting my old nemesis head on. Clint and I have discussed the rapid and have decided that I will run the log canoes through. I am ready and anxious to see Triplet Falls but know Manly had much the same experience.

"This I ran in safety. . . . Just after this [Triplet] the river swung back the other way at a right angle or more and I quickly saw there was danger below and signaled them to go on shore at once, and lead the canoes over the dangerous rapids. . . .

"They did not obey my signals but thought to run the rapid the same as I did. The channel here was straight for 200 yards without a boulder in it, but the stream was so swift that it caused great, rolling waves in the center, of a kind I have never seen anywhere else."

Manly continued the physical descriptions after running Triplet: "One of the canoes came down into the eddy below, where it lodged close to the shore. . . . The eddy which enabled us to save the first canoe . . . was caused by a great boulder as large as a house which had fallen from above and partly blocked the stream. . . . If the canoe had gone on 20 yards farther with him before we caught it, he would have gone into another long rapid and been drowned."

With these details of Triplet, surrounding geological features, and the upcoming rapid called Hells Half Mile, Triplet and Hells Half Mile can be properly distinguished from each other and placed in correct order of the rapids in Lodore.

When our party gets to Triplet, I will video and take pictures of the river as well as surrounding geological formations. Today is a key day in identifying the descriptions about which Manly wrote. Manly described this stretch of river specifically, so I will be able to objectively observe and form opinions.

Aside from Triplet Falls and the anticipated reunion, last night I reviewed Powell's journey in the book *In the Footsteps of Powell*. Here, the author retraces Powell's voyage of 1871 through pictures Powell's photographer took at various points of interest along their journey. Camping by one of those photographic points, I was able to compare the picture in the book with what I was viewing. In doing so, I was able to locate the exact spot where the Powell photograph was taken. The same large rock completely detailed has remained steadfast for more than 130 years. I felt I went back in time and touched history. The feeling was indescribable. I have always enjoyed that aspect of river running. Floating down a river allows a person to enter into the past. Seeing as well as experiencing what those early explorers did more than 150 years ago is gratifying. With those thoughts expressed, it is time to break down camp and move on. I am ready for the day and what the river will bring.

———

It is now late afternoon, and I am sitting on a rock overlooking Triplet Falls. The large rocks are thirty yards away from me, splitting the river current in half. The identifying landmarks, as I observe them at Triplet, are in order as they were remembered by Manly.

The river at Triplet makes a right-angle turn and then dramatically turns and makes another right-angle turn to the left. It is clear to see. The uniqueness of these two sharp turns in one rapid confirms Manly's unmistakable description of where he was while maneuvering through this particular rapid. After the rapid of right-angle turns, the river drops into a two-hundred-yard straight rapid, which does not happen immediately below Triplet as Manly remembers. Approximately one-half mile downriver from Triplet, the Green forms another rapid called Hells Half Mile rapid. Manly does not separate the two rapids but combines them into one experience. The intensity of these rapids and the fact that one of Manly's men almost dies in this stretch make his combining the two rapids into one large rapid understandable.

As the afternoon sun continually drops over the rim of Lodore we have finished scouting Triplet and looking at all the descriptions made by Manly. The crew is standing by the shoreline at Triplet with safety lines, and I will now run the series of right angles. I am nervous but ready.

———

I have just completed running Triplet Falls in the log canoes, and it was spectacular. . . . After guiding the log canoes through the narrow channel, I pulled over and secured the logs to the shoreline. Hiking back up around the rapid, I rejoined the rest of our crew at our evening campsite. All others will run Triplet as well as Hells Half Mile tomorrow. With Triplet Falls behind me now, I am looking forward to observing Hells Half Mile and the geological formations surrounding this rapid. In this whitewater section, Manly would only have been able to travel a short distance. I would estimate he took two days to run these sets of rapids. The rocks in the river, as he explained, would have required him to constantly line the rapids. My feeling is one of relief for successfully running Triplet and anxiety for the upcoming rapid of Hells Half Mile tomorrow. Another day is logged.

Lucky to survive the dangerous rapids of Triplet Falls, Manly and his men had no time to celebrate or regroup, as Hells Half Mile loomed directly below. As he had with Triplet, Manly vividly remembered the unique characteristics of Hells Half and the challenges that he encountered. "I quickly saw there was danger below and signaled them [the five other men in two canoes] to go on shore at once, and lead the canoes over the dangerous rapids," he wrote. "The channel here was straight for 200 yards, without a boulder in it, but the stream was so swift that it caused great, rolling waves in the center, of a kind I have never seen anywhere else."[72] The description perfectly matches Hells Half Mile. In naming this long series of rapids, John Wesley Powell remarked: "On examination, we find that there is an abrupt plunge of a few feet and then the river tumbles for half a mile with a descent of a hundred feet, in a channel beset with great numbers of huge boulders. This stretch of the river is named Hell's Half-Mile. The remaining portion of the day is occupied in making a trail among the rocks at the foot of the rapid."

Major Powell continued with the account of the next day, June 16, 1869:

Our first work this morning is to carry our cargoes to the foot of the falls. We then commence letting down the boats. We take two of them down in safety, but not without great difficulty; for, where such a vast body of water, rolling down an inclined plane, is broken into eddies and cross-currents by rocks projecting from the cliffs and piles of boulders in the channel, it requires excessive labor and much care to prevent the boats from being dashed against the rocks or breaking away. Sometimes we are compelled to hold the boat against a rock above a chute until a second line, attached to the stem, is carried to some point below, and when all is ready the first line is detached and the boat given to the current, when she shoots down and the men below swing her into some eddy.[73]

Dellenbaugh vividly recalled encountering this section in 1871: "The entire river for more than half a mile was one sheet of white foam. There was not a quiet spot in the whole distance, and the water plunged and pounded in its fierce descent and sent up a deafening roar. The only way one could be heard was to yell with full lung power."[74]

Manly made it through Hells Half Mile, but it was so dangerous he paddled his lead canoe to shore and then tried to signal the men to pull over so they could portage. He failed: "I ran my own canoe near shore and got by the rapid safely, waiting for the others to come also. They did not obey my signals but thought to run the rapid the same as I did. . . . The boys were not skillful enough to navigate this stream, and the suction drew them to the center where the great waves rolled them over and over, bottom side up and every way."[75] Manly's account in *From Vermont to California* is equally descriptive and desperate. "I motioned to the boys to go on ashore but they had run the upper one [Triplet Falls] so successfully that they came on when they saw I did not land. The water close to shore was smooth, but very swift, and by keeping as close to the bank as I could and not touch bottom, I could keep out of the big curling waves, where no canoe could ever live. I ran on to the eddy and stopped, and when I looked back, they were just coming into the suction of the swiftly running current."[76]

Manly could then do nothing but watch helplessly as the following events unfolded:

Alfred Walton in the other canoe could not swim, but held onto the gunwale with a death grip, and it went on down through the rapids. Sometimes we could see the man and sometimes not, and he and the canoe took turns disappearing. Walton had very black hair, and as he clung fast to his canoe his black head looked like a crow on the end of a log. McMahon and I threw everything out of the big canoe and pushed out after him. I told Mc. to kneel down so I could see over him to keep the craft off the rocks, and by changing his paddle from side to side as ordered, he enabled me to make quick moves and avoid being dashed to pieces. We fairly flew, the boys said, but I stood up in the stern and kept it clear of danger till we ran into a clear piece of river and overtook Walton clinging to the overturned boat; McMahon seized the boat and I paddled all to shore, but Walton was nearly dead and could hardly keep his grasp on the canoe.[77]

Manly was very fortunate not to have lost a man, and he gave credit to a large boulder in the river at the end of Hells Half Mile, which created a large back eddy that allowed Walton's canoe to slow and gave Manly and McMahon time to rescue him.

At this point of turmoil and discouragement, Manly once again showed his ability to lead and direct the party. The men are dejected and extremely discouraged; "their clothes were all gone. All they had on were shirt and pants, and consequently felt pretty blue." But Manly got them moving: "Boys, right your canoe, and get the water out of her, and let's go and see how Walton is."[78]

9/4/2006, Monday, Day 17, River Day 15

Triplet Falls to Jones Hole

Last night, listening to the constant roar of Triplet Falls was spectacular. Today, the challenges that await are to complete the rafting of Triplet by my crew and then float a short distance dropping into Hells Half Mile Rapid.

Like Triplet, Hells Half Mile is distinctive and identifiable. Its long corridor of continuous whitewater is unmistakable. . . . On the

---

completion of running Hells Half Mile, I want to pull over and see if there is a large boulder and back eddy that fit Manly's description. In doing so, I will be able to verify or dispute Manly's claim concerning this large rock and its position in the river. In addition, Manly also remembers the walls of the canyon at this location being terraced and impossible to climb out. Those also will be photographed and reviewed. It is time to run Hells Half Mile, a thunderous section of whitewater and sky.

—◦—

It is now about noon, and we have stopped for lunch after successfully finishing our run of Triplet Falls and completing all of Hells Half Mile Rapid, the two separated by half a mile. As we blasted through Triplet, we had to stay to the left side of the river channel. With all crew safe and floating out of Triplet, we soon entered Hells Half Mile Rapid. The rocks in the river are numerous and extremely large. It was intimidating approaching them as they lay waiting for us to make a wrong move. Clint was concerned with the amount of rocks in Hells Half Mile, but he guided the log canoes through successfully. I could readily see that inexperienced men in a canoe, as Manly's men were, increased the odds of crashing or overturning, which, in fact, happened to Alfred Walton, as he almost drowned. . . . The rolling waves which run straight for two hundred yards, as Manly explained, are visible and exciting to run. At the end of the rapid, we pulled over to see if there was a large boulder and if it matched the account and location Manly remembers. To my excitement, there on the right side of the river below Hells Half Mile Rapid was a rock that fit his description. Sheltered directly behind this large boulder is a vast back eddy that Manly could have used to save Walton's life. In observing this rock and having successfully run both Triplet and Hells Half Mile, my conclusion is that Manly was identifying this particular large boulder and back eddy at the end of Hells Half Mile Rapid.

My review of Manly's account of this section of river indicates that he described both Triplet and Hells Half Mile correctly, although he inaccurately combines both of them into one. The turns and lengths of these two rapids match perfectly with what Manly remembered. In addition, they are listed in the correct chronological order of entering and floating through Lodore Canyon.

The remaining two obstacles of river and land formations directly below Hells Half Mile are also consistent with Manly's detail. The impassable canyons that tower above the Green, as well as the next rapid that concerns Manly, are in full view and easily identifiable: "[Walton] would have gone into another long rapid and been drowned. . . . I could not get high enough to see in any direction. The mountain was all bare rocks in terraces, but it was impossible to climb from one to the other." Viewing both rapid and rock, Manly would have to have decided whether he should remain on the river or try to climb to safety. Today, the impossibility of climbing out of the area is evident even from the river.

After all men were safely accounted for, Manly decided to climb out of Lodore Canyon, to see how much farther the treacherous rapids continued: "While we were waiting I took my gun and tried to get up the mountain high enough to see how much longer this horrible canyon would last, but I found the way so steep that I could not get high enough to look over in any direction."[79] With the unknown ahead, and having just experienced their most traumatic day on the river, the men were "in low spirits" and "in silence" as they pushed off the next day. To their relief, the rapids quickly became less challenging, and soon they began to exit the Canyon of Lodore. They had traveled over twenty miles through the canyon and dropped hundreds of feet.[80] Summarizing his own ordeals in Lodore, Powell wrote, "This has been a chapter of disasters and toils, notwithstanding which the Canyon of Lodore was not devoid of scenic interest, even beyond the power of pen to tell. The roar of its waters was heard unceasingly from the hour we entered it until we landed here. No quiet in all that time. But its walls and cliffs, its peaks and crags, its amphitheaters and alcoves, tell a story of beauty and grandeur that I hear yet—and shall hear."[81]

CHAPTER SEVEN

Deeper and Deeper

LEAVING THE CONFINES OF THE CANYON OF LODORE, WITH SMOOTHER water ahead, Manly and his men soon drew their attention to the change in canyon topography and the need for food supplies. "Toward night we were floating along in a piece of slack water, the river below made a short turn around a high and rocky point almost perpendicular from the water," he noted.[1] Manly once again described a landmark very accurately: the Green here silently curls around a magnificent seven-hundred-foot precipice of sandstone, the high rocky point that would be named Echo Rock by Powell and later called Steamboat Rock. The open area is still known as Echo Park.[2] Powell described the rock outcropping as "about seven hundred feet high and a mile long," which the river runs to one side of, then turns and runs along the other side.[3] Dellenbaugh recorded the reason for the area's name: "The little opening between canyons we named Echo Park, first because after the close quarters of Lodore it seemed very park-like, and second because from the smooth bare cliff directly opposite our landing a distinct echo of ten words was returned to the speaker. I had never before, and have never since, heard so clear and perfect an echo with so many words repeated."[4] Ashley also recorded entering Echo Park and viewing the Yampa River, which he named Mary's River.[5]

Manly's attention soon centered on three Rocky Mountain bighorn sheep standing on the ledge about fifty feet above the river as they floated by. "Motioning to the boys, I ran on shore and, with my gun in hand, crept down toward them. . . . I got in as good a range as possible and fired at one of them which staggered around and fell down to the

Steamboat Rock on the Green River was described by Manly as "a high and rocky point almost perpendicular from the water."

bottom of the cliff. I loaded and took the next largest one which came down the same way. The third one tried to escape by going down the bend and then creeping up a crevice, but it could not get away and turned back, cautiously, which gave me time to load again and put a ball through it." With hope of appetites being fed and survival seeming more promising, the men's spirits began to soar: "McMahon was so elated at my success that he said; 'Manly, if I could shoot as you do I would never want any better business.' And the other fellows said they guessed we were having better luck with one gun than with six, so we had a merry time after all."[6]

Twenty years later, Powell also noticed bighorn sheep in this same area. He wrote of his encounter with the camouflaged creatures: "During the afternoon Bradley and I climb some cliffs to the north. Mountain sheep are seen above us, and they stand out on the rocks and eye us intently, not seeming to move. Their color is much like that of the gray sandstone beneath them, and, immovable as they are, they appear like carved forms."[7]

9/4/06, Monday, Day 17, River Day 15, continued

Triplet Falls to Jones Hole

As we prepare to complete our last leg of today's long and exciting journey, I am looking for three final geological descriptions left by Manly. After the encounter with Triplet and Hells Half Mile, Manly remembered floating around a high rocky point where the rock was perpendicular to the water. . . . This description exactly fits a rock formation called Steamboat Rock. This rock is impressive, with the Green flowing around it. I vividly remember it from twenty years ago when I camped in its shadow. Adjacent to Steamboat Rock, Manly describes a terrace or ledge that has bighorn sheep grazing upon it.[8] . . . We are about six miles from Steamboat. It should not take us long to reach and verify or question Manly's next descriptions.

—~—

The evening is upon us, and we have just pulled into camp. Today was the hardest day physically on the river yet the most rewarding. I will start where I left off, anticipating Steamboat Rock. Several miles downriver from Hells Half Mile, the river turned to the left and placed Steamboat Rock in view; I recognized it instantly. Massive, vertically rising like a giant out of the water, Steamboat Rock leaves one contemplating the magnificence of Mother Nature. We stopped at the bow of the rock where the Green crosses in front of it and stood silently, pondering the wonder of Echo Park. Photographing and videoing this huge rise of rock was one of the highlights of the expedition. There we were, once again, in the correct chronological order. Steamboat Rock rises more than one thousand feet in the air with the Green quietly circling around its bow. . . .

After observing Steamboat Rock, I turned to look across the river at the terrace Manly described sloping towards the river. It was spectacular finding the river, Steamboat Rock, and the terrace all in place as Manly remembered. As if that were not enough, on top of the terrace were several Rocky Mountain sheep in the late afternoon sun, grazing upon the wild grasses. In Manly's accounts, after discovering the sheep, he was able to shoot three and provide food

Shortly after Steamboat Rock, Manly described a rock terrace with bighorn sheep on it. When he passed the same location in 2006, Michael D. Kane saw not only the same ledge but bighorn sheep grazing nearby.

for the next several days. With fresh meat, the men's spirits must have been revived. . . .

Following the path of the Green, we left Steamboat Rock and Echo Park behind, winding our way into Whirlpool Canyon. The canyon walls of red sandstone and white limestone gave way to the dark black volcanic rock. As we entered in the twilight hours, there was a sense of eeriness and foreboding. The narrow winding canyon was silent. Within the first few miles, we pulled over to observe a ladder left on a high ridge above the river. The men using the ladder in the 1950s were test-drilling holes in the rocks for a proposed dam site. As I touched the ladder, I began to think of what might have been: a dam destroying an environmental wonderland and depleting our heritage, denying generations the opportunities to see all that is offered. I thank David Brower, Aldo Leopold, Robert Marshall, and others who successfully petitioned the US government to stop this construction to preserve this national treasure [Dinosaur National Monument]. . . .

As I stood on that shelf overlooking the river, I thought of Manly: "I was always a great admirer of Nature and things which remained as they were created." As one of the first documented persons run-

ning the waters of the Green, his historical claims could never have
been verified with construction of such a dam.

The compromise between nature and development must be
carefully weighed and measured to avoid the destruction of nature's
magnificence. Traversing the corridors of the Green River, I understood the importance of my role: the Green River drainage and its
historical significance must be protected to benefit all.

After Echo Park, Whirlpool Canyon fast approached. Ann Zwinger
writes: "Whirlpool Canyon is the antithesis of the sunny, sandy openness of Echo Park, where the water is flat, the rocks golden sandstone.
The Uinta Mountain Group rocks are somber, sheer to the water. The
waves are high and fast and lurch upstream."[9] As Manly entered Whirlpool Canyon, his account becomes sparse on details. From that point
until he prepared to leave the river, he reported only the following in
Death Valley in '49:

> We kept pushing down the river. The rapids were still dangerous
> in many places, but not so frequent nor so bad as the part we
> had gone over, and we could see that the river gradually grew
> smoother as we progressed.
>
> After a day or two we began to get out of the canyons, but
> the mountains and hills on each side were barren and a pale yel-
> low caste, with no chance for us to climb up and take a look to
> see if there were any chances for us further along. We had now
> been obliged to follow the cañon for many miles.[10]

This is the biggest challenge to the conclusion that Manly traveled
all the way to present-day Green River, Utah, in the San Rafael Desert.
If Manly got off the Green River in the Uinta Basin in what is now
Duchesne County, he passed only through Whirlpool Canyon and Split
Mountain Canyon, which fit with the description "after a day or two we
began to get out of the canyons." If instead he traveled another 125 miles
to the area of Green River, Utah, he failed to account for Desolation

Canyon and Gray Canyon, the latter of which river historian Roy Webb describes as "the deepest and longest of the canyons of the Green."[11] Similarly, scholar James Aton writes in *The River Knows Everything*: "In Desolation Canyon, the Green River cuts a 118-mile, serpentine swath through a larger geomorphic unit called the Tavaputs Plateau. The region's massively crumpled topography of steep canyons and deep ravines has eroded out of hundreds of square miles of forested plateaus. At its nadir at Rock Creek, Desolation measures deeper than the Grand Canyon. Its 'gorgeous layered geology' and sharp-lined, castellated ridges are unique in canyon-country geology."[12] How could Manly have missed describing these canyons entirely?

To help understand the terrain below Echo Park, I asked for a description from Clint Goode, the professional river guide who accompanied me down the Green River to re-create Manly's voyage. Goode has spent twenty-six years leading river trips in Utah, Colorado, Wyoming, Idaho, and Arizona, and has taken hundreds of trips through the area from Lodore to Green River, Utah. He writes:

> Leaving Echo Park, the first canyon that you enter is called Whirlpool Canyon. Whirlpool Canyon's length is 11 miles. The first 4 miles are made up predominantly of the Uinta sandstone. Dark red throughout and takes 2 hours to get through when it's a windy day with an upstream breeze. Easy walks out can be had at the beginning and the end of the canyon. . . . Shortly after the dark red sandstone of Whirlpool Canyon you come to Jones Creek flowing into the Green. Again, an easy walk along a crystal-clear creek with shade the majority of the way. Pass Jones Creek and you float 7 miles to Island Park. Current throughout the 7 miles. Again, a few hours float in the wind and into Island Park. Once in Island Park you could pick many directions to walk. West, north and east are all an easy walk for miles. Island park is 7 miles in length. After leaving Island Park you enter Split Mountain Canyon. It also is a short run canyon that is 7 miles in length.[13]

Together, these canyons fit the first description that Manly left: "After a day or two we began to get out of the canyons."

Clint Goode continues his professional review below Split Mountain Canyon:

> Traveling through Desolation/Gray you enter a world of much more barren and steep landscape.... Possibly you could hike out but with much more demanding uphill travel vs. walking out flat land at multiple spots through Whirlpool/Split area. With 84 miles of floating through Deso/Gray and rough steeper side canyons, compared to roughly 25 miles through Whirlpool/Split broken up in 4 to 8 mile stretches with flat walks out between each stretch. These two canyons that rise up to 6,000' are much more challenging than Whirlpool and Split Mountain Canyons.[14]

My conclusion that Manly floated all the way to what is now Green River, Utah, means he missed or forgot the important details of these memorable stretches of river. In contrast to his thorough descriptions of Flaming Gorge, Browns Park, and Lodore Canyon, where men encountered the wonders of nature and risked their lives to pass through, Manly's pen is silent here, as it is in not describing other geological formations that followed. With his own brief reporting, Manly begins to show a trend that he also exhibited on the emigrant trail—omitting details and generalizing. Hundreds of miles were crossed by wagon with little or no mention of events or geological descriptions. One could be led to conclude that since Manly did not record a given event or geological detail, he therefore was never at a given location. But absence is not necessarily evidence, and Manly's accounts of other points along the way help establish his route along the Green. The absence of detail is understandable given that, as discussed in the introduction, Manly's original notes of the voyage were destroyed. By the time he composed his later works, "From Vermont to California" (1887) and *Death Valley in '49* (1894), many decades had passed since his 1849 journey, and he may have forgotten details.

It seems entirely possible that in his memory Manly combined Desolation and Gray Canyons, and that after describing his earlier, more memorable adventures in more detail, he reduced so many later canyon miles to a brief sentence. If, as so much other evidence from Manly's travels leads me to conclude, Manly did in fact travel through Desolation Canyon on his way to the San Rafael Desert, that could be accounted for by reading his two statements in *Death Valley in '49* as describing subsequent canyons. So "after a day or two we began to get out of the canyons" would be describing Whirlpool and Split Mountain Canyons, while "now been obliged to follow the cañon for many miles" and mountains providing "no chance to for us to climb up" would be describing the much longer Desolation and Gray Canyons.

In the end, Manly's failure to report Desolation and Gray Canyons in any detail is a stark incongruity to my conclusion that Manly ran the river hundreds of miles beyond the Uinta Basin. It is possible to account for this lapse, however, as I have done here, and combined with the remaining evidence—particularly the details of Manly's overland travel after leaving the Green, which I cover in subsequent chapters—the picture becomes clearer.

In the absence of details from Manly, we can better understand what Manly's party would have encountered below Echo Park using the accounts of Powell's exploration down to the San Rafael Desert and the Old Spanish Trail. John C. Sumner in Powell's crew of 1869 wrote of the transition from Steamboat Rock in Echo Park to the awaiting Whirlpool Canyon: "Off at seven o'clock and row down for one mile and a half along the base of Echo Wall, a nearly south course; passed the point of it, turned and ran due north for about five miles; back into the hard, red sandstone again, through a narrow, dangerous canyon full of whirlpools, through which it is very hard to keep a boat from being driven on a rock; if a boat should be wrecked in it her crew would have a rather slim chance to get out, as the walls are perpendicular on both sides and from 50 to 500 feet high."[15] Powell himself recorded,

When we left Echo Park on the 21st [of June] we soon ran into a cañon very narrow, with high vertical walls. Here and there

In his writings, Manly did not recount Desolation (top) or Gray Canyon (bottom), a fact that must be accounted for if he followed the river all the way to Gunnison Valley.

huge rocks jutted into the water from the walls, and the cañon made frequent sharp curves. The waters of the Green are greatly increased since the Yampa came in, as that has more water than the Green above. All this volume of water, confined as it is in a narrow channel, is set eddying and spinning by the projecting rocks and points, and curves into whirlpools, and the waters waltz their way through the cañon, making their own rippling, rushing, roaring music. It was a difficult task to get our boats through here, as the whirlpools would set them spinning about the cañon, and we found it impossible to keep them headed down stream.[16]

After deliberating between Whirlpool and Craggy as their name for the latest canyon ("neither of which is strictly appropriate for both parts of it," noted the major), Powell and his men ultimately picked Whirlpool Canyon.[17] With Whirlpool Canyon giving way to Island Park, Powell wonderfully described the change of scenery: "One, two, three, four miles we go, rearing and plunging with the waves, until we wheel to the right into a beautiful park and land on an island. . . . The broad, deep river meanders through the park, interrupted by many wooded islands; so I name it Island Park."[18] Of Island Park, Dellenbaugh wrote that although the canyon had been "exceedingly beautiful, nevertheless we did not mourn when late in the afternoon, just after running the last rapid, the magnificent cliffs fell back and we saw more sky than at any time since leaving Browns Park."[19] Dellenbaugh also noted that Powell deliberated between "Island Park" and "Rainbow Park" (for the colorful rocks all around) before settling on the former. All too soon, he continued, "our meanderings terminated at the foot of a valley where the river once more entered the rocks, in a gateway as abrupt, though not as imposing as that of Lodore."[20] These observations by Powell and his crew from their later expeditions help fill in the vague picture Manly left of the day or two he spent in Whirlpool Canyon and Island Park.

9/5/2006, Tuesday, Day 18, River Day 16

Jones Hole to Island Park

We are camped at Jones Hole. It is a beautiful campground with a stream named Jones Creek running clear and cool by our tents. Yesterday was so exhausting we have decided to slow down a little today. We will only be traveling about four or five miles on the river. It is good to have a day like this to rest and recover from Triplet and Hells Half Mile. There is a waterfall several miles up Jones Creek. Two of us have decided to hike up and see what it looks like.

Around 10:00 a.m. Greg and Brian, two friends who had joined us, along with the Dinosaur River Expeditions people and I hiked two miles up Jones Creek, behind Jones Hole to the waterfall, which was beautiful. Below the waterfall was a large pool of water. I got in and cooled off. It felt good to be away from all the hustle of the river crew and take a break. Hiking back down, I thought about Manly once again. His travels from the river's edge were predominantly for hunting purposes. There would likely have been security in having the other men close as well as the boats and supplies. After lunch we left our campsite for Island Park. The wind blew hard most of the time as we oared through the flat water. We arrived around 5:00 p.m. and are in a valley used for cattle grazing.

As we leave the canyons and enter Island Park, the rapids have become less frequent and not as large. Manly observed the same about the diminishing rapids. . . . The river widens in Island Park and, rather than canyon walls, we are looking at open plateaus and rolling hills. Tomorrow we will float through Split Mountain, a canyon with some rapids but nothing serious at this water level. After Split Mountain, the Green flows for more than 150 miles of open, flat water.

Leaving Lodore, the intensity of rapids and beauty of the canyons surrounding the Green become noticeably absent. Manly's entries about his observations and experiences on the river also become noticeably absent. With this lack of detail, determining his location and involvement on the river becomes even more difficult. Because of this literary omission, some believe he floated only as far as the Uinta Basin, which begins a day's float from here. Manly left us with only two references while floating the lower waters, helping to accurately determine the river miles traveled after exiting Lodore: canyons opening up and yellow soil. . . .

Emerging from Lodore and Dinosaur National Monument with these clues, we observed that the canyons do end and open, flowing, flatlands begin. Pinpointing the pale yellow soil is an opportunity to accurately locate Manly's exit from the river. From here to Green River, Utah, a distance of two hundred miles, I will continue to look for deposits of yellow soil.

The documented accounts of Manly over the previous 230 miles we have traveled have been surprisingly accurate, considering his forty-year delay in completing his account. Minor changes in the chronological order and directions of river flows have been noted, but there were no claims by Manly of seeing geological formations or river rapids that do not currently exist.

A secondary yet equally important observation is noting the time spent by Manly as he floated down the Green River. His recollections at three weeks seem inaccurate: "And for three weeks, over rocks and rapids, we floated and tumbled down the deep cañon of Green River." Several years later, Manly located his friend and traveling partner, Morgan S. McMahon, and asked him to write a chapter about his recollections of the journey west once they parted company after floating the Green. This McMahon did, more accurately accounting for the number of days spent on the river. With the help of McMahon's daily accounting, we were able to determine the river trip took close to thirty-nine days. Clint and I speculated that at the end of Lodore National Monument or at the Split Mountain "take-out" by Vernal, Utah, Manly and crew would have been on the river close to twenty-three days, which would leave sixteen days to reach the area where Green River, Utah, is currently located. Understanding this timeline helps to verify Manly's distance. Each day accounts for miles traveled. If Manly was on the river for a limited number of days, his distance traveled would be shorter. However, with a time line of [about] thirty-nine days, Manly would have been able to travel considerably farther downriver than many estimate.[21]

Traveling from the Gates of Lodore to Split Mountain took us five days. Two of those days we traveled only four to five miles. Before the river trip began, we planned to have two short days of river travel in these canyons. Manly had trouble in Lodore and mentioned that he floated only a short distance because of the rapids: "Some days we did not go more than four or five miles, and that was serious work, loading and unloading our canoes." Trying to duplicate his timeline, we purposely shortened these days.

It is late, and I will close for now.

The meandering waters in Island Park quietly give way to Split Mountain and its canyon below—an unforgettable and dramatic geological wonder on the Green River. O. G. Howland of Powell's first expedition provided insight into this spectacular arena. "On the 24th [of June] we climbed a cliff about four miles south of here, at the head of our next cañon [Split Mountain] . . . . Its hight [*sic*] is 2,800 feet. Back east as far as the eye can compass, from the hights on our left, is an elevated plateau of rolling country, covered with artemisia, a fine pasturage for game of all kinds [Island Park] . . . . On our right is a various-colored broken country, running and rising gradually back to the Uintah range of mountains."[22] Dellenbaugh sounded relieved when he reported that this section of river "differs from [Lodore] in that the descent is more continuous and not broken into short, violent stretches."[23] Nonetheless, he was taken by the rugged scenery: "The view . . . into the canyon was something wonderful to behold. . . . A wild and ragged wilderness stretched out in all directions, while down in the canyon more of a narrow valley than a canyon after the entrance was passed. . . . Crags and pinnacles shot up from every hand, and from this circumstance it was at first uncertain whether to call the canyon Craggy or Split-Mountain. The latter was decided on, as the river has sawed in two a huge fold of strata—a mountain split in twain. Hence we entered it with our boats to again descend, we had gone but a little distance before massive beds of solid rock came up straight out of the water on both sides and we were instantly sailing in a deep, narrow canyon, the beds at length arching over, downstream, high above our heads. It was an extraordinary sight."[24]

9/6/2006, Wednesday, Day 19, River Day 17

Island Park to Split Mountain Campground

The morning came early today. In the middle of the night, a storm blew through. I awoke to put up my tent; because of that, it did not rain. I slept fairly well. Currently, I am writing beneath some massive cottonwood trees, which tower over me. They are so large their trunks bend over to the ground with the weight of the tree. I wonder how old they are. My guess would be well over one hundred years. Today, we will run close to seventeen miles and take out at Split Mountain, which marks the end of the upper stretch of the Green. After today, the waters will be flat and calm and that stretch fairly uneventful. We are on River Day 17 as compared with Manly's estimated River Day 23. As we steadily paddle through these waters, I do not believe Manly moved as fast as he estimated; this becomes yet another difference between what was perceived by Manly and what really happened. So far on the upper stretch, the noticeable differences are as follows:

1. Manly moved more slowly than originally thought. The exaggeration of floating thirty miles in one day or the total distance in three weeks is difficult to substantiate.
2. He identified Ham's Fork incorrectly; it was actually Black's Fork.
3. He recorded Red Creek coming in from the west rather than the east.
4. He combined Triplet and Hells Half Mile as one rapid.

Manly's entries about the river and surrounding characteristics diminish drastically, but I will be looking for the yellow-cast soil he mentioned, for it was near such soil he met Chief Wákara and left the river. One other observation Manly made before his river voyage came to a close is the fact that a large cottonwood tree was lying in the water and covered almost the entire river. . . . I will also look for a narrowing of the river area where cottonwood trees grow. It is not possible that a cottonwood tree would almost cover the width of the Green. However, with numerous islands throughout the river's length, it is possible that Manly floated alongside an island in a narrow channel where the cottonwood tree would have fallen, blocking or obstructing the river flow. These clues are not much but the only ones given. I will write more after we get off the river today.

— ◦ —

Going through the last canyon in Dinosaur National Monument was fun. The rock formation can be easily identified as Split Mountain, as it looks like it splits, allowing the Green to flow through. Numerous rapids were not large but fun to run. Again, Manly did not record any experiences or identify land formations throughout these or the waters to come. His reasoning for this will remain a mystery as I contemplate why he did not record anything for such a long distance. Did he just forget years later in remembering the expedition, or are the waters below Split Mountain insignificant or not life-threatening enough to leave a lasting impression? As the day ends, all has gone well. We arrived at the boat ramp at 3:00 in the afternoon with increasing gusts of winds. With Lodore, Whirlpool, and Split Mountain Canyons having been successfully run, we will move on to slower water. My sense of accomplishment is high with having run these whitewater sections of the Green in the log canoes. This experience will never be forgotten. We will be staying in a campground in Vernal tonight. I am looking forward to a warm shower.[25]

8/15/2006, Tuesday, Day 21, River Day 19

Ashley Creek to Horseshoe Bend

Awakening today was glorious. In the distance, I can still see Split Mountain where the Green emerges from Lodore. The sun beginning to rise over Split Mountain and the sounds and sight of trumpeter swans and Canada geese flying gracefully overhead give this day a wonderful start. This valley is alive with wildlife. Last evening I watched a deer carefully choose its path, fording the Green. All that could be seen was her head as she crossed with ease. Manly recounted using his skills with a rifle to provide food. In these open lands I can see firsthand how finding game was not a problem. With humans' limited presence in 1849, wildlife would have been even more abundant, and yet today, in 2006, wildlife is all around. Today, we will try to float another twenty miles and camp in Horseshoe Bend. The log canoes are continuing to float well. Dallas and Clint have been constant throughout the journey, each doing his own part as we move farther down the Green.

As we begin floating on the water at 8:00 a.m., the air is clean and crisp. I think of Manly traveling at this same time of year. The bugs and mosquitoes I had been worried about are not present. Manly never mentions them, so I am assuming that in August these bugs will not be a problem for us either. We are prepared for them, but as of the second day on these calm waters, we have been spared.

I have mentioned before the beauty of the river. It flows quietly and has places in the Uinta Basin where it is very wide. Watermarks on the shore indicate it was a foot higher earlier in the year. I am happy with the water level and believe the boats will make it through this slow section. Floating around a silent bend, I can see an old log cabin fifty feet from the river's edge. Interested, I pull over and hike through the tamarisk to see what remains.

These early pioneers worked hard to survive. Arriving at the small log home, I first notice the chinked logs holding up the roof that was withered and sagging from years of erosion. Entering what was once the door, I spy an inscription: the homesteader's name. Carved in the logs, chiseled and fit with utmost care, I read "Dan." Seeing that name, where his only window looked out over the Green, personalized the experience for me. Dan, a man who worked hard in an unforgiving land, trying to make the best for family and self, left the only thing that he could for me to read: his name. My respect cannot be measured, nor will I ever forget his name.

Ahead of us is Horseshoe Bend, a ten-mile section in which the river makes nearly a complete circle. I will enjoy paddling through this. I have seen it overhead from an airplane and have looked forward for several years to floating around it.

It is now late in the afternoon and we have traveled twenty-two miles. Horseshoe Bend was a geological wonder. Just before the first turn, the wind kicked up. My canoe was blown right out of the water. As we progressed farther down the river, the wind changed directions, blow-ing at our backs. With that, we were pushed downriver at a fast pace.

As we traveled today, my thoughts were on the demand on the river by the farmers. Everywhere, irrigation pumps suck water from the river for the alfalfa fields. Increasingly abundant litter can be seen along the bank as we float. What a sight Manly would have had as he floated through without one piece of debris. A major effort to clean up the trashed areas should be undertaken.

The wildlife continues to be abundant. As I was quietly floating along, two antelope came over the ridge and down to the river to drink. I thought of Manly when he shot an antelope for food. Ducks and geese are everywhere.

At the end of this day, I sat on a ridge overlooking the land. No longer peaceful and quiet, the oil rigs in the background pump gas and oil night and day. Their diesel-powered engines run nonstop in a monotonous cadence. Even with this annoyance, the desert lands of the Green are a wonderful sight.

John Wesley Powell wrote of abundant plant life and potential settle-ment areas after leaving Split Mountain Canyon and floating through the northern Uinta Basin north to the mouths of the White and Duchesne (Uinta) Rivers:

> A mile and three quarters from here is the junction of the White River with the Green.... Excepting these little valleys, the region is one of great desolation; arid, almost treeless, with bluffs, hills, ledges of rock, and drifting sands. Along the course of the Green, however, from the foot of Split Mountain Canyon to a point some distance below the mouth of the Uinta, there are many groves of cottonwood, natural meadows, and rich lands. This arable belt extends some distance up the White River on the east and the Uinta on the west, and the time must soon come when settlers will penetrate this country and make homes.[26]

O. G. Howland in the same Powell expedition similarly described the Uinta Basin as "very fine for agricultural purposes and for grazing," noting that "the Indians of Uintah Agency have fine looking crops of corn, wheat and potatoes, which they put in this spring, on the sod."[27] John Sumner and George Bradley of the 1869 Powell expedition also wrote of the upper Uinta Basin being relatively fertile,[28] and Dellenbaugh in 1871 described areas along the river "carpeted with grass and surrounded by thickets of oak."[29] As I detail in part III, these observations by Powell and his men in 1869 and 1871 do not fit Manly's description of the vast, barren valley he entered on the Green, supporting the conclusion that he traveled beyond the upper Uinta Basin.

As the Green continues to wind south from the White and Duchesne Rivers into Desolation and Gray Canyons, it does in fact become desolate, as noted by these same early river explorers. William Ashley first described this land below the Uinta Valley as barren in 1825 when he recounted,

> I concluded to ascend this river [Uinta River] on my route returning, therefore deposited the cargoes of my boats in the ground near it, and continued my descent of the main river fifty miles to the point marked 5 on the topographical sketch sent you [United States War Department]. The whole of that distance the river is bounded by lofty mountains heaped together in the greatest disorder, exhibiting a surface as barren as can be imagined. This part of the country is almost entirely without game. We saw a few mountain-sheep and some elk, but they were so wild, and the country so rugged that we found it impossible to approach them. On my way returning to Tewinty [Uinta] River, I met a part of the Eutau [Ute] tribe of Indians, who appeared very glad to see us and treated us in the most respectful and friendly manner. . . . They also informed me that all the country known to them from South to West from the Tewinty River was almost entirely destitute of game.[30]

Ashley's note about game matches Manly's observation that he and his crew "had begun to get a little desperate at the lack of game."[31]

Powell then commented at length on what he named the Canyon of Desolation, below the southern Uinta Basin: "After dinner we pass through a region of the wildest desolation. The canyon is very tortuous, the river very rapid, and many lateral canyons enter on either side. These usually have their branches, so that the region is cut into a wilderness of gray and brown cliffs. . . . The walls are almost without vegetation; a few dwarf bushes are seen here and there clinging to the rocks, and cedars grow from the crevices—not like the cedars of a land refreshed with rains, great cones bedecked with spray, but ugly clumps, like war clubs beset with spines."[32] Dellenbaugh reported that Desolation Canyon "is ninety-seven miles long, and immediately at its foot is Gray Canyon, thirty-six miles long. Then comes Gunnison Valley," or the San Rafael Desert.[33] John Sumner of the Powell expedition summed up this stretch rather tersely: "Country worthless, though imposing."[34]

9/9/2006, Saturday, Day 27, River Day 24

Sand Wash to Gold Hole

The morning came early. I had to be up by 6:00 a.m. for another radio interview, but the satellite phone did not work. I was looking forward to it. Any time I am able to discuss Manly with other people is a plus. The weather is warm and calm. We are loading the boats and should be out by 10:00 a.m. All is well. Floating through Desolation will be enjoyable. I cannot believe we have been on the river for twenty-four days and have floated more than three hundred miles. I will write later.

As we begin to float down Desolation, the river continues to be wide, approximately 350 yards, and slow moving. The color is silty brown, the third change of color since we started. When we began, the water was clear and I could see the riverbed. As we entered Red Creek Canyon below the Flaming Gorge Dam, the water was still clear, but with the green moss growing in the riverbed, the water took on a beautiful, bright green tint. Now that many tributaries have deposited their waters into the Green, the water is brown. The walls of Desolation Canyon are a light tan. The rock is limestone and layered. The only vegetation growing is by the riverbank. . . . Farther down, we will stop and view some supplies explorers left in the early 1900s. These river travelers were miners looking for gold.

We are now at camp. We started at mile marker 96 and went to mile marker 82. Fourteen miles on slow water is good progress. We looked at a prospector's cache under a ledge this afternoon. I remember seeing it more than twenty years ago. It was enjoyable to visit the site again. While floating down the river, not only am I aware of what Manly was doing but also the many individuals who tried to find their fortunes on the river. Tomorrow we will visit a wooden skiff at Gold Hole, abandoned sometime in the 1900s.

I have seen more wild horses today than in all previous days. They look strong and healthy. Without man's intervention, Mother Nature seems to do just fine. Aside from the horses, the sight of other animals is rare and wild game has diminished, just as Manly noted.

Throughout the trip I have been rowing daily. With the amount of physical exercise that I have been doing, my weight has been dropping. My pants easily slide on or off and I have to cinch my belt two additional notches. If I am losing weight, Manly's men probably lost even more, for without adequate game always available, they would not have had enough food. Manly never mentions starving as he did in Death Valley two months later; nonetheless, he and the men must have been hungry much of the time.

As the river continually wound mile after mile southward, the men may have been second-guessing their choice to float the river as days seemed never to end. Was there bickering and criticizing of Manly? Quite possibly; Manly, however, did not write of it. It was his idea to float the river. He was elected captain of the voyage as well as acting to provide game to eat; in short, Manly seems to make all the decisions and the men prospered. If the journey began to sour after multiple days of river miles logged, Manly failed to write of it, which could be one possible reason for his not documenting the running of Desolation and Gray Canyons.

Tomorrow will be the last day of slow water. Since leaving Split Mountain, we have traveled close to one hundred miles in flat, slow water. . . . In 1911 the US government was considering placing a dam called Buell Dam in this canyon. Once again, as with Lodore, I am happy such ideas were not carried out.

The night is fast approaching and I need to get some sleep for tomorrow.

CHAPTER EIGHT

Beyond the Uinta Basin

PREDICTABLY, DELLENBAUGH'S DESCRIPTION OF DESOLATION CANYON is vivid: "The Canyon of Desolation pushes its rock walls around one so diplomatically that it is some little time before the traveler realizes that he is caught. The walls were ragged, barren, and dreary, yet majestic. We missed the numerous trees which in the upper canyons had been so ornamental wherever they could find a footing on the rocks. . . . Climbed out to study the contiguous region which was found to be not a mountain range but a bleak and desolate plateau thorough which we were cutting along Green River toward a still higher portion."[1] The specific point that Dellenbaugh makes about the barren nature and lack of vegetation in these lower canyons is the same observance made by Manly. Writing of the color in Gray Canyon, Dellenbaugh called it an "unusual feature." He continued his summary: "The work here was similar to that in Desolation. . . . The descent through Desolation and Gray had been nearly six hundred feet."[2]

9/13/2006, Wednesday, Day 31, River Day 27

Lion Hollow to Range Creek

It is cold this morning, which is a change in the weather. Not having access to weather reports, I am always looking at the horizons to the west and watching the clouds. I think a storm is coming.

125

Today was the hardest day of the whole expedition. The wind blew against us all day on the river. Without oaring, the wind would have blown the boats to the shoreline. With all that work, we still logged seventeen miles today and are camped below Range Creek. I am exhausted.

Winding down the river, we encountered rapids every mile or so. Three Fords Rapid was the best. It had some large rolling waves that were unexpected. As I dropped into them and crested over each wave, I realized Manly, between his limited experience and the difficulty in guiding the logs, would have had problems in this rapid.

We stopped in the middle of the day at McPherson Ranch. Jim McPherson was a rancher in the 1890s who was friends with various outlaw bands who roamed the area. He provided them with horses and supplies. The outlaws, in turn, paid him for his services. He said the outlaws treated him better than the lawmen.

I constantly wonder how people survived out here with what little they had. The lands are so unforgiving and harsh. It was a hard life for anyone living in this environment.

In the late afternoon, we left Desolation Canyon and entered Gray Canyon. These canyons are very different: Desolation Canyon has high canyon walls of red rock; in contrast, Gray Canyon's colors are brown, white, and yellow. The rocks and dirt are not as high and cedar trees as well as other brush grow on the sides and ridges of Gray Canyon. Now, I am intently looking for the yellow soil I have spoken of so many times. I am excited because the rocks and soil in Gray Canyon are a more earthy tone than the reds of Desolation Canyon.

We are thirty-one miles from the town of Green River. Tomorrow we will try to run twenty miles and finish the rest on Friday. Saturday we have the Green River celebration called "Watermelon Days" and the meeting with Lakota John. He is playing the part of Chief Wákara and I will be Lewis Manly, which should be fun. I hope the community of Green River is ready for the reenactment of Manly meeting Wákara.

George Bradley of the first Powell expedition used the by-now familiar word "barren" to describe the land as he entered the Gunnison Valley or San Rafael Desert. On July 13, 1869, he wrote: "Have now come out of Coal Cañon (the name given to the last part of the Cañon of Desolation because we found some coal beds) into a valley [Gunnison Valley] which seems very extensive, that is, it seems to be long but on each side is a barren parched dessert. The winds that sweep it are hot and sultry indicating that it is quite wide."[3]

One detail that further suggests Manly traveled all the way to where the Old Spanish Trail crosses the Green River is his recollection of "yellow caste soil."[4] On September 13, 1776, the Dominguez-Escalante party crossed the Green River and traveled through the Uinta Basin. In doing so, Escalante made note of yellow soil there: "According to our guide, one cannot cross anywhere else than by the single ford it has in this vicinity, which lies on the side west of the hogback on the north, very near to a chain of small bluffs of loose dirt, some lead colored and others of a yellow hue."[5] Yellow soil, then, cannot definitively prove Manly's location. Still, my journal entry describes my observation of predominantly yellow hills in the Gunnison Valley.

9/14/2006, Thursday, Day 32, River Day 28

Range Creek to Price River

We are now in Gray Canyon, which is much different than Desolation Canyon. This morning I am observing the rock wall across the river. Light tans and brown are the main colors. As I am continually looking for the yellows Manly spoke of, these colors are the closest I have seen to his description. Coming from the reds and maroons of Lodore and Desolation, this change is noticeable.

We will travel another fifteen to seventeen miles today. I hope the wind does not blow. My body is tired. All seem to be in good spirits, although it is obvious the weather is changing for the worse. Clouds are beginning to fill the skies. I hope the rain holds off until we get off the river. Today is the last full day of river miles. Tomorrow we will be close to Green River, Utah, and the celebration to follow on Saturday. I will write this evening.

We traveled fourteen miles today. We wanted to travel a few more, but large, dark clouds moved in and so did the cold rain and wind. We found a good camping spot by some cottonwood trees on the left

side of the river and set up camp. I got my tent up just in time. It is now raining very hard. I am satisfied and comfortable knowing I will stay warm and dry. Manly did not have the luxury of such modern-day camping equipment.

As we floated down the river today, I kept thinking about the yellow-cast soil. The soil that I see is a light brown or tan color. With the grasses and other vegetation growing out of the soil, all are yellow because of the seasonal change of fall. This vegetation makes the soils look yellow. Although not entirely satisfied with this, it might be the soil I am looking for. We are about seventeen miles from Green River, Utah, and should be just north of the town for Saturday's festivities. We have traveled more than four hundred miles on the river.

The canoe logs have floated well. They are running deeper in the water because they are becoming water logged but are still maneuverable. They have withstood the physical test to determine whether someone could float wood canoes for this distance, one of the main factors in taking them on our journey. To show Manly's claims are accurate concerning the log canoes, we needed to prove the logs' ability to endure the constant pounding and punishment. In rapids, they bounce off the rocks, sending dense, echoing sounds up and down the river. Their strength and durability have surprised me. They have exceeded all my expectations.

I will close for now and hope tomorrow goes well. The weather is changing and a cold front is moving in. This is the coldest weather we have seen on the river. My wife and children are going to meet me in Green River, Utah. I cannot wait to give them all hugs and kisses.

9/15/2006, Friday, Day 33, River Day 29

Price River to Green River, Utah

I am writing at the end of the day rather than the traditional opening at sunrise, and what a day it has been. It rained all night. We arose and got on the river about 8:30 a.m. Knowing the river expedition would be ending today, we were anxious to push on and finish the journey.

As we floated along, my vigil for the yellow soil became more intense. As we neared Gunnison Butte where the Green empties out of Gray Canyon, the dry summer grasses that have turned yellow because of the fall weather remain as I observed them yesterday. Is this possibly what Manly was trying to describe? The hills, buttes, and mountain sides are covered with yellow. Although still questionable, the soil and grasses growing are the best explanations of Manly's descriptions of yellow in this region. I have not seen yellow like this anywhere on the 430-mile expedition.

As we floated next to Gunnison Butte, the weather worsened. Lightning continually struck the canyon walls as loud claps of thunder rolled down to the river. I have never heard thunder so loud. The driving rain and hail pelted us as we continually tried to find our way out of Gray Canyon. I felt as if the heavens were trying to stop us from leaving. Of all 430 miles of river we have floated over the last month, these last few miles were the most dramatic. I was not afraid for my life or for the others, but having never experienced such strength and power from changing weather thundering over the canyon walls, this was an event I will never forget. I saw lightning strike the same canyon wall three times, sending rocks tumbling down thousands of feet to the river floor. I was almost overcome with this display of nature that matched nothing I had ever witnessed before.

We arrived at the boat ramp in the midst of hailstones pelting everything in sight. Finding cover, we waited for the storm to pass, then began to derig the support boats. The log canoes continued downriver with Clint and Dallas for the anticipated reunion tomorrow with Lakota John at the John Wesley Powell Museum.

After all boats and supplies were loaded, we headed to town, where the whole community was buzzing about tomorrow's Watermelon Days and the reenactment of Manly meeting Wákara. What a joyous reunion with our families and friends. Seeing my family was heaven-sent. I am so lucky to have a family that supports me in this adventure. Tomorrow will be gratifying. The community sponsors a morning breakfast, then a parade at 9:30 in the morning. Lakota John, who is playing the part of Wákara, and I, as Manly, will be on a float in the parade. The reenactment will be at 2:00 in the afternoon. We will float the log canoes down to the John Wesley Powell Museum and have the celebration on the front lawn.

I will write later this evening about our day. I am excited and glad the river expedition is complete. I learned so much by retracing Manly's trip on the river and have a better appreciation of what he encountered and how he survived those [. . .] days on the Green.

Knowing that an evaluation needed to be made of the two valleys and comparing their soil consistencies, I did not see "yellow caste" soils in the Uinta Basin. Floating along the river the lands adjacent were now heavily irrigated and used for growing endless fields of green alfalfa. Understanding through time the lands that Manly viewed were not the same because of the modernization of agriculture and farming techniques used for crop production. Nonetheless, I constantly looked for other colors of soils from cliff areas along the riverbanks that might show yellow soils. With this constant vigil as I passed through the Basin, I did not see what Manly described as a yellow hue. This project, however, changed noticeably when I entered the Gunnison Valley. Through all of my speculations on soils and their contents, standing on a hill overlooking the river, the untouched landscape unfolded the "yellow caste" soils that Manly would have noticed.

When he began his voyage on August 20, Manly felt confident that they could run the river to the Pacific Ocean within several weeks' time. Then, just before describing his encounter with Indians, Manly wrote, "We had now passed the troublesome part of our journey, and would be able to reach the sea coast in a few more days."[6] Manly thought his river expedition was in the last stages of floating due to the length of time he had already spent on the Green. It is clear Manly did not understand or realize the immensity of river travel that lay ahead of him. Surely he did not comprehend the deep canyons of the Colorado that he would soon enter. He incorrectly remembered in both *Death Valley in '49* and "From Vermont to California" that his time spent on the river is three weeks.[7] As I show later, however, after leaving the river Manly's overland journey lasted ten days and ended on September 30, 1849. His expedition on the Green, therefore, ended on September 21 and lasted thirty-three days, or four weeks and five days, and not three weeks as he remembered.

Of the final valley Manly encountered on the river, he wrote, "The new valley, which grew wider all the time, gave us hope again, if it was quite barren everywhere except back of the willow trees." In Ann Zwinger's words: "Gunnison Butte rises on the right skyline a reminder that Green River, Utah, was once called Gunnison's Crossing, after Captain John W. Gunnison. The original crossing was one of the few places for miles in either direction where there was a stable bottom and easy access to the river."[8]

Manly concluded his account of the river voyage by reporting,

> We were floating along very silently one day, for none of us felt very much in the mood for talking, when we heard a distant sound which we thought was very much like the firing of a gun. . . . We were pretty sure there were no white people ahead of us, and we did not suppose the Indians in this far-off land had any firearms. It might be barely possible that we were coming now to some wagon train taking a southern course, for we had never heard that there were any settlements in this direction and the barren country would preclude any such thing, as we viewed it now.[9]

Continuing to float a short distance downriver, he quickly realized where the gunshots came from. "We saw some person walking along down the river with something which looked like a gun upon his shoulder," he wrote, "and in a moment more we could see, farther down the stream, the tops of some Indian lodges, and it was not long before the inmates discovered us. I was about two hundred yards in advance of the other canoe, and the Indians motioned to us to come on shore, and made signs indicating that they would shoot if we did not come."[10] The situation had unfolded very quickly, and Manly had little time to weigh his options of floating by and risk being fired upon or pulling over and risk encountering hostile Indians in close proximity. He decided to go ashore, noting that pulling over to the riverbank was difficult because there was a cottonwood tree that has fallen over and was blocking part of the river.[11]

With some caution and yet desperately needing direction, Manly's party decided to approach the Indian camp. Climbing up the riverbank through the willows toward the Indian lodges, the seven California-bound forty-niners came face to face with Wákara.

9/17/2006, Sunday, Day 35

Green River, Utah

Today is Sunday, and we are staying in Green River, Utah, to pre-pare for the start of tomorrow's ten-day trek to "Mormonee." We have gone to the store and purchased all food items. The change from the river to the excursion across the Utah desert and moun-tains is anxiously anticipated. All went extremely well on the river and now it is time to start the land journey. My family is here with me, helping to organize.

Clint and I went to a high bluff by the river overlooking all the vantage points Manly writes about. It was rewarding to see where the Santa Fe Trail crosses the Green and where Wákara would have been camped on the west bank. The spur of the mountain Manly mentions as well as the valley opening up were both in view. To the distance in a northwest direction, the canyon Wákara pointed out and told Manly to go through can be seen. As we were about to film this part of the documentary showing all the important locations mentioned by Manly, Clint said to look behind me. When I turned around, there, in plain view, was a horizon full of yellow-cast soil, the soil I have been searching for ever since the Duchesne River confluence. I was finally satisfied and reassured with all the descrip-tions of land and river, fitting cleanly in correct chronological order, surrounded by the yellow soil.

After filming all the sites Manly defined, Dallas and I visited the John Wesley Powell Museum. It was enjoyable to look at all the historical and informative displays, but when we read about Manly's contribution, . . . so much information about his achievements and involvement had been omitted. . . . I explained to Dallas that in the near future the documentation in several places would change. . . .

When all the work of preparing for tomorrow was completed, we headed to a local pizza place and had dinner. It was different not having to cook our own dinner.

Part III

Overland

CHAPTER NINE

Encounter with Wákara

IN THE RUGGED AND UNFORGIVING LANDS ON THE WESTERN BORDERS of the United States in the 1840s and 1850s lived an equally rugged and powerful chief in the Western Ute Indian territory. Wákara, "Hawk of the Mountains," lived and roamed throughout what are now the states of Utah, Nevada, California, Arizona, Wyoming, Colorado, and New Mexico. Though not a chief of any of the major Ute bands, Wákara loomed large in the western lands as a popular leader of a band of roving Utes who traded and raided to gain economic prosperity. He was the most prominent Indian in the minds of Mormon settlers in the territory, and he often conversed and brokered alliances with Brigham Young, head of the Church of Jesus Christ of Latter-day Saints.

Wákara's name is sometimes given as Walker, Walkara, or Wakara, and in his own language it was "Oaqari" or "Rucca." According to some sources he also received another name in a dream vision: "Iron Twister, or Pan-a-karry Quin-ker *(Panaqari Kwin'wayke)*, words that carry the meaning of shining metal, money, golden and twisted, or one who twists gold."[1] He was born near the Spanish Fork River between 1808 and 1815 in the canyons south of what is now Provo, Utah. The name of his father, another Ute leader, is not recorded, but Wákara was part of a large family.[2] He was born into the Timpanogos Ute band but left amid conflict and formed his own separate group. Wákara grew fast and strong in the Western Ute Indian territory, which by the 1810s had acquired horses and become a powerful band.[3] In this era, Wákara learned the essential ways of trade, migration, and food sources for his people. Colonel Thomas L. Kane, a non-Mormon who had previously met the Ute chief in his travels in the West, spoke about Wákara in a discourse to the Pennsylvania Historical Society on March 25, 1850, using language that was common for the time but striking to the modern ear for its degrading tone:

> The Soldan [Sultan] of these red Paynims [pagans], too, their great war chief, is not without his knightly graces. According to some of the Mormons, he is the paragon of Indians. His name, translated to diminish its excellence as an exercise in Prosody, is Walker. He is a fine figure of a man, in the prime of life. He excels in various manly exercises; is a crack shot, a rough rider, and a great judge of horse-flesh.
>
> He is, besides, very clever in our sense of the word. He is a peculiarly eloquent master of the graceful alphabet of pantomime, which stranger tribes employ to communicate with one another. He has picked up some English, and is familiar with Spanish and several Indian tongues. He rather affects the fine gentleman.[4]

Standing uncommonly tall at six feet, six inches, with a countenance of intimidation, Wákara drew attention wherever he and his party traveled.[5] With his commanding presence and physical prowess, this "burly chieftain" provoked fear in others, often because of his notoriety as a horse thief and reputation as an aggressive trader.[6] Solomon Nunes Carvalho, a photographer and artist from North Carolina, met Wákara in 1854, in the area of Nephi, Utah, and found the opportunity to paint his portrait.[7] Dated May 8, 1854, the artist's work captured Wákara's physical qualities. The chief's dark eyes seem to see all as he moved swiftly through the corridors of human life and wilderness on the western frontier.

Historians William B. and Donna T. Smart wrote of Wákara as "proud, jealous, avaricious."[8] One can readily imagine the respect given in the vast openness of the western frontier of the 1800s to a man of strong stature, intelligence, and power. Author Paul Bailey wrote that "it was his personal deeds ... which set Walkara into the remembrance circle of

Indian renown. He was proud, irascible, fearless and unique. . . . Walkara was not stupid, nor was he weak. He knew when to fight, when to seek peace, and when to trade."[9]

In step with his leadership manner, the Ute chief arrived and departed all occasions in the finest of style. Kane spoke of Wákara's fashionable clothing: "His dress is a full suit of the richest broadcloth, generally brown and cut in European fashion, with a shining beaver hat and fine cambric shirt. To these he adds his own gaudy Indian trimmings, and in this way contrives, they say, to look superbly, when he rides at the head of his troop whose richly caparisoned horses, with their embroidered saddles and harness, shine and tinkle as they prance under their weight of gay metal ornaments."[10] On one occasion, a western traveler who met Chief Wákara on the Old Spanish Trail simply stated that he was the "Napoleon of the Desert."[11]

Wákara's Western Utes had positioned themselves for success in the nineteenth-century Great Basin, using the available options to their advantage and securing valuable homelands. As Sondra Jones explains, "Western Utes had been fortunate in claiming and holding the more fertile regions of the Wasatch Mountains, especially in the San Pete Valley and near the lush wetlands of 'Utaw' Lake." They were also adaptable to new free-enterprise opportunities made available by white settlement—trading along the trails and even outfitting travelers through livestock rustling. "The Utes," Jones writes, "were quick to adapt to new situations and exploit new resources or replace or augment the old."[12]

Leadership among Utes was often a flexible, collective affair, with councils and elders and subchiefs. If a leader fell out of favor, people simply stopped listening and started associating with another leader. Again according to Jones, Ute chiefs "won and held their positions by dint of their physical prowess, personality, assertion of authority, and . . . the prosperity they brought to their followers."[13] With the recent introduction of large-scale immigration to the area by white settlers, the Utes' traditional subsistence patterns had to change, and it was in this time of disruption that Wákara's focus on exploiting trade markets along the migrant trails proved successful.[14] Though he is sometimes best known for conflict, Wákara valued and sought out peaceful solutions—and he recognized that it was in peacetime that he could successfully trade and his people prosper. There was a strong tradition of peace among the Utes; as a news article from the period described, they "were among the most peaceable Indians in the United States and had been defrauded in the most shameless manner by government traders and contractors."[15] However, as diplomatic as Wákara was, he was not always able to work successfully with Indian, Spanish, and American peoples.

Wákara's relationship with the largest group of Euro-American settlers in the area, the Mormons, demonstrates the complexity and calculation necessary to ensure his own survival and interests and those of his people. With the cunning that Wákara possessed, he quickly realized that the Mormons' settlement and use of Indian lands was irreversible. So he positioned himself and his band to solicit and accept gifts such as horses, make trades (or take bribes) for peace, and share land to encourage trade. Wákara clearly understood that with the Mormon "invasion," survival depended on successful negotiation. Perhaps because of his willingness to take initiative, writes Sondra Jones, "the Mormons mistakenly assumed that Wákara held authority over all Utes."[16] In a meeting with Brigham Young, Wákara clearly stated his position for living among the Mormons, which showed both generosity and judiciousness: "Walkara talk with Great Spirit; Great Spirit say—'Make peace.' Walkara love Mormon chief; he is good man."[17] Jones gives a following summary of Wákara's business acumen: "Even after conflict erupted between Mormons and Western Utes, Wákara would explain that he never wanted to expel the Mormons, because if they left he would have no more herds to plunder or partners with whom to trade."[18]

Though other Ute leaders had differing feelings of acceptance toward the Mormon settlers,[19] Wákara placed himself in position of negotiator with Brigham Young, and Young felt he had an ally and something of a kindred spirit in Wákara. In 1853, the Latter-day Saint leader explained some of the chief's actions, stating: "Walker will not kill a white man, nor go on a stealing expedition to California until he offers sacrifices to his God, then he thinks he is doing right; and the reason he has not done more in his war on the southern settlements is because he could get no answer from his God. Had it not been for this, and the faith of this people, he would have destroyed those settlements before this time."[20] The next year, during a time of conflict between Latter-day Saints and Utes, he told his people,

> Allow me to say a word in behalf of Walker. I tell this congregation and the world, that 'Indian Walker,' as he is called, has not been at the foundation of the difficulties we have had. He has had nothing to do with them.... Has he done no wrong? I did not say he has done no wrong. He has been angry and felt at times that he would like to destroy this people; but I do know that he has been held by a superior power. At the very commencement of the fuss, he was not in favor of killing the whites.[21]

Young's characterization of Wákara recognized him as negotiating for his own and his peoples' security, sometimes with both fists.

Editorializing on the relationship between the two peoples, and likely influenced by statements from Wákara about his own professed motives, non-Mormon Thomas Kane stated,

> With all his wild cat fierceness, Walker is perfectly velvet-pawed to the Mormons. There is a queer story about his being influenced in their favour by a dream. It is the fact, that from the first he has received the Mormon exiles into his kingdom, with a generosity that in its limited sphere transcends that of the Grand Monarch of the English Jacobites. He rejoices to give them the information they want about the character of the country under his rule; advises with them as to the advantages of particular localities, and wherever they choose to make their settlements, guarantees them personal safety and immunity from depredation.[22]

With Wákara's calculations to always protect members of his Ute band while using the Mormon settlements for economic gain, there was doubtless an underlying current of frustration and anger as his dominance over his guarded lands gradually weakened. These feelings rose to the surface in a personal interview with Wákara conducted by M. S. Martinez prior to a peace conference with the Mormons on July 6, 1853.

Though Wákara's perspective is doubtless obscured by Martinez's, it is as close to Wákara's own feelings as we may get:

> At the request of Maj. [Jacob] Holeman Ind. Agent for U. Ter. [Utah Territory] I held a conversation with Indian Chief Walker respecting his feelings and wishes relative to the whites set[t]ling on his lands, and on the lands of the Indians generally.
>
> He said that he had always been opposed to the whites set[t]ling on the Indian lands, particularly that portion which he claims; and on which his band resides and on which they have resided since his childhood, and his parents before him—that the Mormons when they first commenced the settlement of Salt Lake Valley, was friendly, and promised them many comforts, and lasting friendship—that they continued friendly for a short time, until they became strong in numbers, then their conduct and treatment towards the Indians changed—they were not only treated unkindly, but many were much abused and this course has been pursued up to the present—sometimes they have been treated with much severity—they have been driven by this population from place to place—settlements have been made on all their hunting grounds in the valleys, and the graves of their fathers have been torn up by the whites. He said he wished to keep the valley of the San Pete, and desired to leave the valley of Salt Lake, as he could not live in peace with the whites—but that the Whites had taken possession of this valley also—and the Indians were forced to leave their homes, or submit to the constant abuse of the whites. He said the Gosoke Utes [Goshutes] who formerly lived in the Salt Lake valley had been killed and driven away, and that now they wished to drive him and his band away also—he said he had always wished to be friendly with the whites—but they seemed never to be satisfied—the Indians had moved time after time, and yet they could have no peace—that his heart was sick—that his heart felt very bad. He desired me very earnestly to communicate the situation of the Indians in this neighborhood to the Great Father, and ask his protection and friendship—that whatever the great father wished he would

do. He said he has always been opposed to the whites settling on his lands, but the whites were strong and he was weak, and he could not help it—that if his great father did not do something to relieve them, he could not tell what they would do.

I have had sincere talks with Sou-we-reats [Sowiette], (the man that picks fish from the water) Toe-kah-boo [Ticaboo] (Black belly) who have always expressed themselves in the strongest terms against the whites setling on their lands. Sow-we-reats in Uwinty Valley and Too ke boos, on the river of the same name—it is a fine valley, well watered, and has plenty of game. These Indians and their ancestors have long occupied this country—they very much dislike to leave it—they say they cannot live with the whites, for they cannot live in peace—the whites want every thing, and will give the Indians nothing—that they shoot the Indians if they walk over their grounds.

I have been acquainted with his country, and these Indians for upwards of thirty years. I have known Walker, Sou wah reats, and Tookeboos since they were children—I have always been on friendly terms with them—they talk freely with me—and express their feelings and wishes without reserve. One prominent cause of the present excitement is the interference of the Mormons with their long established Spanish trade, and the killing of an Indian trader by the name of Bowman, from Santa Fee [*sic*], and charging the murder to the Indians. I greatly fear that much difficulty will grow out of the present excited condition of the Indians,—should the Mormons continue their unkind treatment. I have just had a long conversation with the Chief Walker and make the above statement of his feelings with his expressions fresh in my mind.[23]

Wákara frequented the area of the Old Spanish Trail, where Lewis Manly and his men encountered him, because of its trade possibilities—particularly the slave trade. "The period from 1830 to mid-1840s was the height of the Great Basin slave trade," noted historian Lynn Bailey. "Age and sex of Indian captives seemed to have been the prime factors in all transactions."[24] Wákara would raid neighboring Indian bands, killing the warrior men and taking the women and children as slaves and selling them to the Mexicans, Californians, and Mormons for financial gain—about $100 for a boy, and between $150 and $200 for girls in good health, "who were in greater demand as house servants."[25] This trade resulted in a strong economic gain for Wákara's band.[26]

With the Mormon followers continually arriving in the Salt Lake Valley and expanding beyond the valley throughout the Utah Territory, Wákara saw an opportunity to increase his business of slave trading. Though he preferred trading with Mexicans, who paid more, he would frequently bring slaves he had captured or traded to remote Mormon communities in the hopes of trading or selling these captives for a financial reward. Initially, bringing enslaved women and children to these communities would invoke pity from the Mormons, who would purchase them to keep them from a worse fate. Brigham Young himself initially provided for redeemed Indian captives in his home. But at a special Utah Territorial legislative session, an act was passed on January 31, 1852, outlawing Indian slavery and resulting in escalating tensions between Utes and Mormons.[27] The decade after Manly encountered Wákara saw the "Walker War," followed by a treaty Wákara entered with Brigham Young and Wákara's baptism in the Mormon faith.[28]

Key to knowing where Lewis Manly got off the Green River is deducing where Wákara was when the two men met. As previously noted, several written accounts have indicated that Manly and Wákara met in the Uinta Basin of northeastern Utah, meaning he floated 290 miles and got out where Escalante and Dominguez crossed the Green in 1776. By referencing other historical documents, however, Wákara's travels in fall 1849 can be traced, and my conclusions presented here place him in southeastern Utah near the present-day town of Green River, meaning that Manly floated 415 miles to the Old Spanish Trail in the San Rafael Desert or Gunnison Valley.

Wákara was famous for stealing horses and trading along the Old Spanish Trail. Sondra Jones writes: "The San Pete and Sevier valleys became the apex of a major Spanish trade trail where buyers rendezvoused with Western Utes at least as early as the 1830s, and probably earlier. By this time Western Utes were also exploiting the web of Spanish trade trails as they exacted tolls, gifts, and barter from traders and explorers; ventured southeast along the trails to trade and raid in Navajo and Spanish borderlands; and by 1835, headed southwest to raid California horse herds." The trail became an Indian mode of travel as much as a Euro-American one.[29]

Jones goes on to describe the importance of horses to the Ute people: "Horses became *the* symbol of wealth and prestige. A man with many horses could travel, hunt, trade, or raid more easily and was free to be generous with his goods, which in turn elevated his status and influence. Horses were also an important medium of exchange, including as fee payments for shamans, bride-price gifts, or ceremonial gift exchanges." Historian Robert Foster indicates that over the course of his career, Wákara stole thousands of horses, from New Mexico to California.[30] He would sometimes catch other groups of Ute raiders by surprise, stealing the horses they themselves had just stolen.[31]

Three months before he encountered Manly's river expedition, Wákara met with Brigham Young to discuss the future of their respective people. On that day, June 13, 1849, Wákara and twelve other Ute leaders talked about future settlements and land issues with Young and other Mormon leaders. William Huntington, the Mormon interpreter for Wákara, told Young that "Walker wants us to go down to his land and make settlements."[32] Wákara indicated that he wished the Mormons to teach his people there to cultivate the soil, and he offered to guide the party south and show where the Mormon settlement would be. After the meeting, the peace pipe was passed, uniting the thoughts and words that were spoken. Jones helps clarify the event from the Utes' perspective: "Now Wákara was exploiting the new situation, hoping to raise his influence with the white settlers while cultivating potential trade advantages. . . . Wákara met with Young and claimed 'he don't care about the Land but wants the Mormons to go & settle it.'"[33]

Wákara led a party of Mormon explorers to the Sanpete Valley, arriving on August 20, 1849.[34] In October of that year, Utes brought a group of Latter-day Saint settlers to the same valley, where they settled the town of Manti.[35] After granting the land of Manti to the Mormons, Wákara and his entourage headed north back through the Sevier Valley to the Hobble Creek/Fort Provo area. Mormon settler William Lorton recorded his impressions of the man on August 22 and 23: "Indian Walker, the Utah chief & hawk of the mountain, came in town with his brother on horses. He is a famous horse stealer & the terror of the Spanard & Piede [Paiute Indians]. If a Spanard cheats him he will some times levy on a 1000 horses for pay[.] Walker is a man they say of good principles when treated kindly & says he wants to live like white people & dont want to live on buffalo meat all the time. He is intellegent & carries the various traditions that have been carried down to his tribe."[36]

With the winter months fast approaching, Wákara then left the Hobble Creek area and, I conclude, traveled southeast to the San Rafael Desert and the Green River, roughly 110 miles from Manti. Traveling by horseback and being familiar with the terrain, Wákara could have traveled this distance in several days. The two main objectives for his travels were to collect tolls from the autumn travelers on the Old Spanish Trail and to hunt buffalo in his familiar hunting grounds east of the desert,

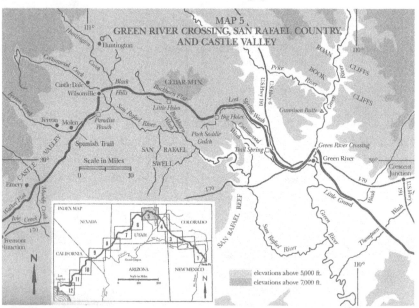

The route of the Old Spanish Trail crosses the Green River near present-day Green River, Utah; the route west from the Green River matches Manly's description of crossing the trail twice before ascending the Wasatch Plateau. COURTESY OF STEVEN K. MADSEN; PUBLISHED IN CRAMPTON AND MADSEN, *IN SEARCH OF THE SPANISH TRAIL*, 54

where the headwaters of the Colorado River originate.[37] On the west side of the Green River, where the Old Spanish Trail crossed the Green River, Wákara set up camp, "some four or five lodges in all."[38] Wákara's total party consisted of twenty-two Indians, among whom were at least two little children, mothers, young men, and Wákara's son, along with a herd of cattle and fifteen or more horses.[39]

Wákara's encounter with Manly on the Old Spanish Trail near the Green River was not the only meeting between Ute Indians and Euro-Americans at this site. One of the first documented encounters occurred in May 1844, when John C. Frémont met Wákara as they passed each other on the trail—the Ute chief traveling the trail "to exact his annual tax from the Los Angeles caravan."[40] A year before Manly's travels, in 1848, two travelers recorded references to Wákara and Utes at the Green and dependency on the Old Spanish Trail. The first, B. Choteau, noted in August 1848: "No grass on Green riv. Thickly timbered. Brush 14m. to camp on this side to make raft. 300 yds wide. There may be some Eutes here. Diff. bands, but friendly. Wak-Kuh-rai [Wákara] is a principal Chief."[41] Similarly, George Douglass Brewerton noted while traveling with Kit Carson in 1848, "In this labor [crossing the Green River] we were assisted by a party of Eutaw Indians who did the greater portion of the work."[42] Four years after Manly, on July 25, 1853, Gwinn Harris Heap recorded his experience at the same location: "At sunset, the crossing of Green River was effected, and we gladly gave the boat to the Indians, who ripped it to pieces to make moccasin soles of the hides. We proceeded a mile up the stream, and encamped in the midst of luxuriant grass. A band of twenty-five mounted Utahs accompanied us and passed the night in our camp; we gave them to eat, and they seemed quite friendly."[43]

Besides Wákara's frequenting the Spanish Trail, there is additional geographical evidence that Manly and the Ute chief met where the trail crosses the Green River. As previously mentioned, Manly had to maneuver his canoe around a downed cottonwood tree lying in the river to reach the west riverbank. Because the river is wide at this point (approximately 250 yards today), it appears Manly must be mistaken in his recollection. However, at the exact location where the Old Spanish Trail crosses the Green, it traverses an island or land bridge. On the west bank of the river, where Manly pulled over to meet Wákara, he would have floated down a very narrow channel between the island and the west shoreline. This narrow channel could certainly have been partially blocked by a downed cottonwood tree, giving the impression that a cottonwood tree was blocking the entire river. Several travelers on the Old Spanish Trail in the 1800s referred to this island as they crossed the Green. For example, John W. Gunnison's party of topographical engineers crossed on October 1, 1853, and observed, "We crossed the river by an excellent ford, which we had observed the Indians crossing, from a few yards below our camp (on the Spanish trail) to an island opposite, and from its upper end to the shore. The river is 300 yards wide, with a pebbly bottom."[44] Traveler Randolph Barnes Marcy recounted in 1858: "Crossed Green River today. . . . Upon striking the river you go to the lower end of a small pebbly island near the center of the river, slightly against the current, then with the current diagonally for the opposite side, where there is a good shore to come out, the crossing is little over the ¼ of a mile, camped on elevated ground."[45]

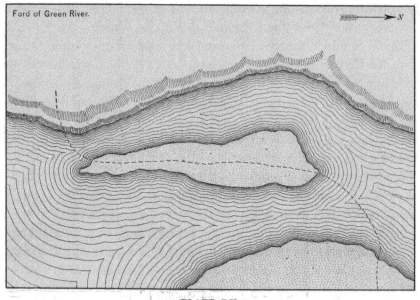

Ford of Green River.

N

PLATE LII

In 1877 the U.S. Geological Survey printed a diagram of the Old Spanish Trail crossing the Green River, showing a narrow channel formed by an island.

F. V. HAYDEN, *NINTH ANNUAL REPORT OF THE UNITED STATES GEOLOGICAL AND GEOGRAPHICAL SURVEY . . . FOR THE YEAR 1875* (WASHINGTON, DC: GOVERNMENT PRINTING OFFICE, 1877), 350

When Lewis Manly entered the Ute camp on September 21, 1849, he was immediately impressed with Wákara and felt he could help direct the river runners to safety. As the men stood face to face, they appear to have established a respect and mutual admiration—one for having traveled hundreds of miles on an unknown river, the other for having command of so much of an unforgiving land. The two men had similar experiences surviving and thriving in hostile lands, and Manly seems to have recognized their commonalities. "The Indian in the back part of the lodge looked very pleasant and his countenance showed a good deal of intelligence for a man of the mountains," he wrote, being of course a man of the mountains himself.[46] At the same time, it is difficult to overstate how very different the two men were, bringing to their meeting diverging agendas, cultures, ethnicities, and religious beliefs. Yet as they stood near each other on an ornate Ute Indian rug, their lives too were woven in solidarity on some level. They shook hands and sought to understand each other. There is a lesson in their bold declaration as they stood at the crossroads of the West—an enduring lesson of shared brotherhood and mutual respect despite differences.

On September 21, 1849, Manly had a fateful encounter with Ute warrior Wákara on the banks of the Green River. COURTESY OF DORIS HOLLOWAY SLEATH, AND LEROY AND JEAN JOHNSON

Portrait of Wákara by Solomon Nunes Caravalho, 1854. COURTESY OF GILCREASE MUSEUM, TULSA, OKLAHOMA

One reason Wákara and his group accepted Manly and his men with open arms was related to the Mormons that Manly had sought so desperately to avoid: "We went with them down to the tepee, and there we heard the first word that was at all like English and that was 'Mormonee,' with a sort of questioning tone." Manly did not hesitate: "I now told the boys that we were in a position where we were dependent on some one, and that I had seen enough to convince me that these Indians were perfectly friendly with the Mormons, and that for our own benefit we had better pass ourselves off for Mormons also." The others played along. "So we put our right hand to our breast and said 'Mormonee,'" he wrote, "with a cheerful countenance, and that act conveyed to them the belief that we were chosen disciples of the great and only Brigham and we became friends at once, as all acknowledged."[47] The meeting between Wákara and Manly on that remarkable day on September 21, 1849, carries with it, then, the historical significance of Wákara's respect for the Mormon settlers.

Manly found he was able to communicate fairly well with Wákara. "We became acquainted pretty fast now," he noted, "and I believe I could understand the sign language pretty well. They wanted to know where we [were] going, and I soon made them understand that the big water toward the setting sun was the point we were marching, or rather, sailing for, and the Chief seemed quite astonished, and seemed to wish to give us all the knowledge he had upon the matter, and seeming in order that I might have faith in his knowledge."[48]

Perhaps surprised by both what Manly had already undergone and his intentions of continuing so far, Wákara led him to the riverbank and stood on smooth sand. The chief then did his best to draw a map in the sand, detailing where Manly had traveled from and the canyons that he had encountered. He "began making out a map of the country, about Salt Lake, and marked out the roads that led to California."[49] The detail and accuracy of his map gave Manly confidence in Wákara's knowledge: "I understood him all right. It was all correct, as I very well know and assured me that he knew all about the country."[50]

As he continued mapping the territory, Wákara was very direct in warning Manly of the impassable river conditions that he would soon encounter: "Placing both fists on [a pile of stones] he raised them higher than the top of his head, and saying e-e-e-e-e-e and looking still higher and shaking his head as if to say: 'Awful bad canon' and thus he went on describing the river till we understood that we were near the place where we now were. . . . I understood perfectly plain from this that below the valley where we now were was a terrible cañon, much higher than any we had passed, and the rapids were not navigable with safety."[51] Manly's earlier account in "From Vermont to California" is even more vivid and detailed: "He went on to explain that we could ride to the mouth of the next big river in one day, and we supposed this was the Grand [or Colorado] River. Then he went on to explain to us that below this the river ran through a canyon with such high walls that no one could climb them to get out, and he showed us how the canoe would pitch about and finally turn over and drown us all."[52]

Wákara's description is evidence that Manly encountered him at the Old Spanish Trail, not in the Uinta Basin. First, Wákara was very clear that directly below the valley they were in, one day's travel would bring them to the Colorado River. In *Death Valley in '49*, Manly recalled that Wákara told him they would encounter the Colorado and a "great impassable" canyon two days ahead.[53] In fact, Powell's 1869 expedition reached the Colorado River from the Old Spanish Trail in three days.[54] Although Wákara's estimate was off, it is much closer to accurate assuming his meeting with Manly occurred at the Old Spanish Trail, rather than hundreds of miles north in the Uinta Basin. When William Lorton met Manly after his ordeals on the river, he noted in his journal, "I went to meet them and learned they were Green River floaters that had left Dallas, made canoes, and floated down Green River to the Colorado,"[55] meaning Manly told Lorton he had floated as far as the Colorado River, a much more accurate statement if he traveled as far as the Spanish Trail. The final reference to Manly floating all the way to the Colorado River came from one of his own men, Morgan S. McMahon. McMahon, whose account will be reviewed in detail in chapter 12, wrote, "[Manly] left us at the camp of the generous old chief Walker on the west bank of the river near the mouth of the 'great seven days cañon.'"[56]

Besides explaining that the canyon became impassable downriver, Wákara warned Manly of other Indians that lived farther down the river:

"Then Walker shook his head more than once and looked very sober, and said 'Indiano' and reaching for his bow and arrows he drew the bow back to its utmost length and put the arrow close to my breast, showing how I would get shot. Then he would draw his hand across his throat and shut his eyes as if in death to make us understand that this was a hostile country before us, as well as rough and dangerous."[57]

The lands of Wákara's Western Ute people covered lands surrounding the Green River from the upper stretches of the Green and Yampa River confluence to below the confluence of the Green and Colorado, but within that territory, different Ute bands had different relationships with Euro-Americans.[58] Just as Wákara indicated, south and east of the Old Spanish Trail was the territory of a more hostile band, the Sheberetch or Elk Mountain Utes.[59] And farther down the Colorado River were other indigenous people, including Paiutes and Navajos, whom Wákara would have viewed with suspicion and who were regularly the victims of his raiding and kidnapping.[60] Placing Manly at the Old Spanish Trail, nearer the confluence with the Colorado River, helps explain the urgency of Wákara's warning of hostile people downriver.

After his conversation with Wákara, who painstakingly tried to persuade the river runner to change his course of travel to safer horizons, Manly began to rethink his route. "I now had a description of the country ahead and believed it to be reliable," he wrote.[61] "It seemed perfectly plain to me and I believed him, for he had made so perfect a map of the country we had passed over, I did not doubt his knowledge and description of the country we had not seen."[62] With his life-saving advice, Wákara extended a true hand of friendship across the lines between Indian and settler, to aid these men of the mountains. "As soon as I could conveniently after this, I had a council with the boys," Manly continued, "who had looked on in silence while I was holding the silent confab with the chief. I told them where we were and what chances there were of getting to California by this route, and that for my part I had as soon be killed by Mormons as by savage Indians, and that I believed the best way for us to do was to make the best of our way to Salt Lake. 'Now,' I said, 'Those of you who agree with me can follow—and I hope all will.'"[63]

Once again, Manly took charge as he discussed with Wákara the risks of river travel and decided to abandon the water route for safer travel on land. One can only imagine the intense discussion Manly and his men had in forecasting their future and hopes of survival. For his part, Morgan S. McMahon did not understand the sign language of Wákara and felt that continuing down the river was much safer than "wandering across a dry and desolate country which we knew nothing of." Responding, Manly stood strong in his decision to leave the river and walk back to Salt Lake City: "I know this sign language pretty well. It is used by almost all the Indians and is just as plain and certain to me as my talk is to you. Chief Walker and his forefathers were born here and know the country as well as you know your father's farm, and for my part, I think I shall take one of his trails and go to Salt Lake and take the chances that way." Still, McMahon and Richard Field held firm: They would not try the land route but would stick to the river.[64]

After these intense decisions were made, a sense of relief must have followed for both forty-niner and Indian as both began to enjoy each other's company in a festive atmosphere. Manly recounted, "When our plans were settled we felt in pretty good spirits again, and one of the boys got up a sort of corn-stalk fiddle which made a squeaking noise and in a little while there was a sort of mixed American and Indian dance going on in which the squaws joined in and we had a pretty jolly time till quite late at night." He noted that these Utes "proved themselves to be true friends to us."[65] Manly and his crew then spent the night in Wákara's camp, "as they considered us good mormons now." The men were given "some meat to eat and we felt safe in their camp."[66] When they awoke the next day, Manly began preparations for the journey to Salt Lake City, or "Mormonee."

According to Manly's account in "From Vermont to California," it was not until morning that everyone made their final decision about which route to pursue. He wrote, "The next morning we talked over our prospects, and discussed fully the information we had just obtained from the chief, and as a result five of us concluded to take Walker's advice a go across the mountains to Salt Lake."[67] As the day progressed, Wákara helped Manly prepare for the journey on land: "When the Chief got up I made signs that I wanted to start for 'Mormonee,' and pointing to the horses, and to some clothes, needles, and other trinkets we had with us, gave him to understand I was 'on the swap.'"[68] Realizing he needed supplies that were necessary for survival across the desert lands, Manly "gave them to understand that we would swap (narawaup) with them for some horses so he brought up a pair of nice two year-old colts for us. I offered him some money for them, he did not want that, but would take clothing of almost any kind. We let them have some that we could get along without, and some one let Walker have a coat. . . . We let them have some needles and thread and some odd notions we had to spare."[69]

It is significant that Wákara parted with horses, which as previously reviewed were the Indians' main source of travel and security as well as a show of wealth. Never did Wákara demand any payment or participate in posturing that put Manly or his fellow travelers in jeopardy or acted as a threat to their lives. In the spirit of friendship and respect, these two men stood on common ground, seeming to appreciate and understand each other's will to live.

With Manly's preparations made and supplies in order, Wákara pointed the men toward Salt Lake. "I then went to Chief Walker and had him point out the trail to 'Mormonie' as well as he could," Manly wrote. "He told me where to enter the mountains leading north and when we got part way he told me we would come to an Indian camp, when I must follow some horse tracks newly made; he made me know this by using his hands like horse's forefeet, and pointed the way."[70] As the morning progressed and the time neared for the forty-niners to separate into two parties, a final council was held to review their respective decisions. With emotions at their peak, the seven that braved the dangerous waters of the Green stood in a circle: "We shook hands with quivering lips as we each hoped the other would meet good luck, and find enough to eat and all sort of friendly talk, and then with my little party on the one side and McMahon and Field, whom we were to leave behind, on the other, we bowed to each other and bared heads, and then we started out of the little young cottonwoods into the broad plain that seemed to get wider and wider as we went west."[71]

Encounter with Wákara

Then Lewis Manly, John Rogers, Alfred Walton, and Charles and Joseph Hazelrig slowly started in a northwest direction on foot, leaving Morgan S. McMahon and Richard Field behind. In doing so, there must have been a deep sense of sadness and some apprehension as their dream of reaching California together ended.[72]

Author's Note: Just as I followed Manly's path down the Green River, I retraced his ten-day trek from the Green River to Hobble Creek or Fort Provo. Unlike the Green River journals, which were written in August and September 2006 while floating down the Green, the land travel was accomplished in stages over several years of research and visitations. I did parallel the same dates of Manly's trek of September 22 through October 1 to give credibility of traveling at the same time and experiencing the changing of the summer season to fall. However, the stages of travel occurred over the period 2006 to 2014. The dates for each journal entry are listed at the beginning of each day's accounts.

CHAPTER TEN

Desert and Plateau

As Manly prepared for his land journey to Salt Lake City on the morning of September 22, 1849, his direction of travel was to the northwest. As he wrote, "Walker had explained to us that we must follow some horse tracks and enter a cañon some miles to the northwest."[1] Such a direction of travel fits much better with Manly departing from the San Rafael Desert than the Uinta Basin, which is directly east of the Mormon settlements where Manly ended up.

With the Ute chief's blessing and direction, Manly and his men set out in that direction, only to be followed by Wákara a short distance later. He pointed out the party's mistake and underscored the importance of following the right trail:

> We were not much more than a mile away when on looking back, we saw Chief Walker coming towards us on a horse at full speed; and motioning for us to stop. This we did, though some of the boys said we would surely be marched back and scalped. But it was not for that he came. He had been watching us and saw that we had failed to notice the track of the horses he told us about so he rode after us, and now took us off some little distance to the right, got off his horse and showed us the faint horse tracks which we were to follow and said 'Mormonee. . . .' He then bade us good-bye again and galloped back to his own camp.[2]

The "faint trail" Wákara indicated was likely one he had recently traveled on to reach the Old Spanish Trail. He had come from the area of what is now Manti, Utah, after guiding a group of Mormons there and giving the land to them as a gift. As historian Wade Allinson concludes, "The only reasonable explanation as to why Chief Walker would have known of the Indian camp and the fresh horse tracks is because he made the tracks himself on the way back from Manti a few days earlier."[3]

It is fair to say that Wákara's acts of friendship and respect made the difference between success and disaster for Manly and his men as they navigated an unforgiving land. The encounter was so dramatic and welcome that many years later Manly recorded these words:

> The Indians here have the reputation of being blood thirsty savages who took delight in murder and torture, but here, in the very midst of this wild and desolate country we found a Chief and his tribe, Walker and his followers who were as humane and kind to White people as could be expected of any one. I have often wondered at the knowledge of this man respecting the country, of which he was able to make us a good map in the sand, point out to us the impassable cañons, locate the hostile Indians, and many points which were not accurately known by our own explorers for many years afterward. He undoubtedly saved our little band from a watery grave, for without his advice we had gone on and on, far into the great Colorado cañon, from which escape would have been impossible and securing food another impossibility, while destruction by hostile indians was among the strong probabilities of the case. So in a threefold way I have for these more than forty years credited the lives of myself and comrades to the thoughtful interest and humane consideration of old Chief Walker.[4]

Wákara's and Manly's paths would never cross again. For his part, the Ute chief continued his travels and trade throughout the southeastern lands of the Utah Territory. As Mormon pioneers, gold seekers, and other emigrants streamed across the Western Ute territorial lands to cross and/or settle, Wákara found himself in a battle to preserve his nation's traditions and values while accepting and adapting to the realities of a rapidly changing American West. Unfortunately, as historian Sondra

Jones writes, "The next decades would be filled with increasing hardship, exposure, hunger, degradation, and death."[5]

A little more than five years after directing Manly to safety, Wákara came down with a severe cold, followed by pneumonia. He died on January 29, 1855, and was buried high on a mountainside near Meadow, in central Utah.[6]

In recounting the first days of land travel, Manly recorded other important details that help identify his location and direction of travel. First is his characterization of the nearby mountain formation. "We now resumed our journey," he wrote, "keeping watch of the tracks more closely, and . . . we came near the spurs of the mountain which projected out into the barren valley."[7] Such a description matches precisely with what travelers would experience as they traveled northwest from the banks of the Green River at the Old Spanish Trail. From that vantage point, the most prominent geological feature is the towering Book Cliffs, rising two thousand feet from the valley floor on the southern and western end of the Tavaputs Plateau. These cliffs clearly extend like spurs out into the barren San Rafael Desert, just as Manly described.

Even more telling is Manly's description of the prominent system of roads he encountered, which he himself identifies as the Old Spanish

The end of the Book Cliffs in Gunnison Valley matches Manly's description of "the spurs of the mountain, which projected out into the barren valley."

Trail. "We crossed several well marked trails," he wrote, "running along the foot hills, at right angles to our own. This we afterwards learned was the regular trail from Santa Fe to Los Angeles."[8] This is unmistakably the Old Spanish Trail, which had its two ending points in Santa Fe and Los Angeles and which indeed had "several well marked trails" because it was used for travel by both people and livestock. The fact that Manly crossed the trail at "right angles to our own" shows that he had left the Green River in the San Rafael Desert and was then traveling northwest, since the Old Spanish Trail turns south-southwest at that point.[9]

It is a vital point that Manly himself identifies the Old Spanish Trail as the place he departed from the river, and it is one other writers have noted. In *Colorado River Country*, David Lavender writes of Manly's journey and concludes, "Since the trail ran south of Tavaputs Plateau, the boaters evidently crossed not only Lodore but Desolation and Gray as well." He adds in a footnote, "I assume Green River town because Manly later speaks of gaining 'the regular trail from Santa Fe to Los Angeles.'" Wade Allinson arrives at the same conclusion: "Walker and Manly encounter each other at or near the traditional crossing of the Green River near the City of Green River in September."[10]

As Manly moved northwest from the Green River, he found himself in an extremely desolate valley, "a level country to go through for about ten miles from camp."[11] In describing these flatlands, Manly again used a word to illustrate his surroundings that he had used when he neared the end of his river voyage: barren. "The country off to the west of us now seemed an open, barren plain," he noted of his land travel. "The plain itself was black and barren and for a hundred miles at least ahead of us seemed to have no end . . . as we came near the spurs of the mountain, which projected out into the barren valley."[12] Others who traveled before and after Manly on the Old Spanish Trail, west of the Green River, write similar descriptions of the barren lands in the Gunnison Valley, or San Rafael Desert. Orville Pratt wrote in September 1848, "Made a fine march today of 30 m. & camped on the St. Rafell [Huntington branch of the San Rafael River]. . . . The country continues as almost all the way heretofore, sandy, hilly & utterly barren. Water is also scarce."[13] Gwinn Harris Heap recorded in his journal in July 1853, "The character of the country and soil continued unchanged, rocky ridges worn into fantastic shapes, and soil loose, dry, and barren. . . . The trail led us over low hills much cut up by dry and rocky ravines, and on our right were sandstone bluffs. Vegetation was scanty, principally dwarf cedars, Artemisia, and cactus, and occasionally patches of grama grass. We found no water from camp to camp."[14] The dry, barren lands of the San Rafael Desert were also documented by Old Spanish Trail travelers on the east side of the Green River looking west. In August 1853, Jacob Heinrich Schiel of the Gunnison party wrote, "From the elevation of the taller hills lying east of the Green River one can look for great distances over the barren, wasted land. As far as the distant Wasatch Range [looking west] one sees only a series of open, parallel ravines and fantastically shaped sandstone ridges without a trace of vegetation. . . . It is a region where, according to the quotes of Kit Carson, the well known mountaineer and guide, 'not a wolf could make a living.'"[15]

Manly made no mention of crossing any streams or water sources on their first day as they traversed the San Rafael Desert. This would have greatly concerned the men as their water supplies diminished and their dependency increased in the dry land. Continuing to travel northwest, on the faint trail Wákara had shown them, it was not until the end of the day that the men discovered a water source. "At some big rocks further on we camped for the night," Manly noted, "and found water in some pools or holes in the flat rocks which held the rain." At one of the pools, he shot a small duck for food.[16]

This pool and others close by were natural water tanks that had formed from rain washing down open lands or small gullies into nonporous rock formations. Finding these natural water tanks in such a remote location—within a day's walk northwest from where the Old Spanish Trail crosses the Green—raises the possibility that other travelers in the mid-1800s also mentioned similar water tanks. In fact, Orville Pratt wrote in his diary of 1848, "Stopped & nooned at the Green riv. Sp. [spring, 17 miles from Green River] & went on from there to some dry grass on the route about 10 pm. from the sp. & camped. Found water in a canion [Lost Spring Wash] to the left of road about 400 yards."[17] Traveling in the same westward direction as Manly, Pratt's description matches Manly's identification of a canyon, four hundred yards to the

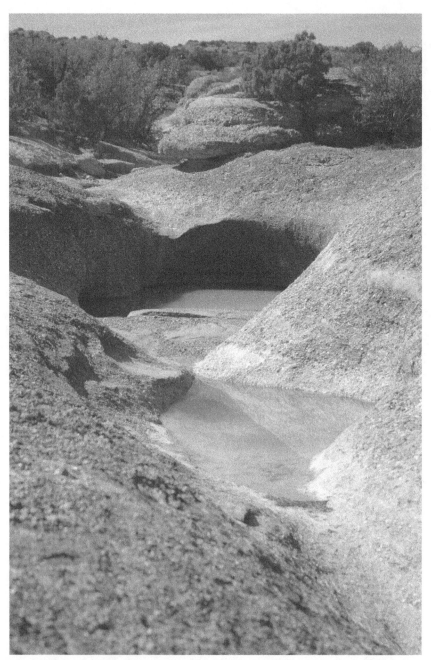

Manly found little water as he traveled overland and noted relying on occasional pools of rainwater carved out of the rocks, like the ones found by the author in Gunnison Valley.

left. Likewise, Oliver Huntington, traveling east off the Wasatch Plateau, wrote an extensive account of an identical feature in his 1855 diary:

> May 31st left the wagon trail and took the old Spanish Trail being led by some Indians from Huntington Creek who said we could save three days travel in going to Green River. . . . Traveled hard that day and found no water until near night and that was in a perpendicular rock canyon in holes and puddles at the bottom. . . . Some brought up water in buckets for their stock by traveling over one fourth of a mile or rather climbing while others clambered down to an overhanging rock and drawed up water with lassos and then passed it from hand to hand until it reached the top. This was very dangerous work, occupied ten men. . . . Nine o'clock at night we hitched up and started travel until daylight when we came to more similar holes whair we watered everything to their fill & stayed until noon.[18]

For weary travelers following the Old Spanish Trail north past the San Rafael Swell—an "enormous, jagged, inclined ridge . . . seventy miles long by thirty miles wide" that "remains remote and impassable"[19]—water held in these natural tanks northwest of the Green and Old Spanish Trail was a welcome discovery. Randolph Barnes Marcy in 1858 described these water-holding rocks: "Left camp without water 9 a.m. In two miles came to water in a rocky tank formed in the bed of an arroya. . . . A good ridge road for about six miles, heavy sand 3 miles."[20] All three of these documented travels, by Pratt, Huntington, and Marcy, support Manly's description of defining land characteristics: no rivers or streams available for water sources; rainwater being held by rock formations; rock tanks in a canyon; traveling northwest, within one day's journey on the west side of the Green River.

Spending their first night at the natural water tanks, now called "Big Holes," Manly wrote: "Our party consisted of five men and two small ponies only two years old, with a stock of provisions very small including that the old chief had given us."[21] With water, sagebrush to fuel a warm fire, and the duck Manly shot, the men's morale again soared. "We felt in pretty good spirits," he noted, "and congratulated ourselves on being good mormons, and fortunate indeed we were in espousing the cause as we did. At first we thought McMahon and Fields [*sic*] had made a grand mistake in the course they had taken."[22] The circumstances offered a welcome relief for these tired men, a chance to dream of brighter days to come.

9/18/2006, Monday, Day 36, Trek Day 1

Green River, Utah, to Dry Mesa

I was up at 5:00 a.m. getting everything ready for the beginning of the trek to "Mormonee." The trek across desert lands is much different than the trip down the Green River. The Green usually gave us a more accurate course for Manly's travels. The problem of documenting or wondering if we were on the same water course Manly used was nonexistent. The Green was our guide. However, the land trek of ten days from the Green River to Hobble Creek/Fort Provo will be a constant challenge of correctly identifying the probable route taken by Manly and his men. To accomplish this, my research included many trips, prior to this journey, across the Utah lands to identify and locate Manly's possible routes. By documenting the correct starting point at Green River, Utah, and the ending point in Utah Valley, the challenge became identifying the middle trails through Manly's written descriptions, which was accomplished with several years of study, research, and on-site analysis. With the logical paths determined, our journey became one of enduring the hardships Manly encountered by walking those same distances.

By 7:00, Clint and Dallas were on the trail headed to the distant canyon northwest from Green River. The start went well. I am not able to walk this section because I have to shuttle the vehicle. I am the only one who knows the path that must be followed, so for this stretch, I am running support for the rest of the team.

Cody, the wrangler from Zion Ponderosa Ranch Resort, brought the horses yesterday. He will accompany me to a designated meeting place where Clint and Dallas will join us for lunch. At the noon break, we plan to be thirteen or fourteen miles into the trek. It is within this day's hike we will encounter the water-laden rocks that saved Manly

---

and his men. We will film and take still pictures of that area. Today is the longest section of the trek. It is also the most dangerous. We will be without support vehicles in a remote area for the afternoon and will take the essential supplies with us on horse or all-terrain vehicle. Safety is of the utmost concern, and I will be driving the all-terrain vehicle with the safety gear, food, and other supplies. The trek over Dry Wash, located a little northeast of the San Rafael Swell, is estimated at ten miles. I believe we can cover the distance in five hours. Hopefully, we will start about 12:00 or right after lunch. I will close for now and write later tonight about our progress.

The afternoon and evening across the desert and up Lost Spring Wash was one to remember. Clint and Dallas came to the lunch stop on time. Trekking around the spur of the mountain, as Wákara had instructed Manly to do, was the first goal achieved in the land journey. Arriving at 11:30 a.m., we ate and then started for the water holes up Lost Spring Wash. Cody had the horses ready for anyone who needed to ride. Dallas chose to walk while Clint rode. Clint's feet are becoming increasingly blistered and sore. It took us about an hour and thirty minutes to arrive at the water holes. It was exciting to look at these natural tanks of water and reflect on how they saved Manly's life. . . .

After reviewing with everyone the events that happened there from these natural tanks, we climbed up to the ridge. It was gratifying to look east and see the Book Cliff Mountain Range and where we had traveled around the end spur as Manly did. After a short rest, I showed the boys the trail that continued northwest towards Cedar Mountain and then left them to shuttle the truck around to an arranged meeting place by Cedar Mountain. I rode the all-terrain vehicle back down the wash, loaded it on the trailer, and drove to our meeting place.

It was 5:30 p.m. when I arrived, and I could not locate the boys. I knew that nightfall would come within one and a half hours. My worries increased as I searched. It was starting to get dark, and if I did not find them, they would not have dinner or sleeping bags to stay warm throughout the night. Finally, just before dark, they came in sight on an old dirt road seldom used. What a relief!

Dallas walked every step. I felt bad. He was exhausted and looked discouraged, but I knew he was dedicated to walk the whole distance, and today was the first test of his commitment. I am so proud of him. I quickly made dinner and all were in bed by 8:30. I estimate that we traveled thirty miles today. Looking back at where we had come from, I was happy with today's accomplishments.

We are now north of Lost Spring Wash and on flat ground. Tomorrow will be much easier. We will turn in a more westerly direction and follow a dirt road by Chimney Rock towards Furniture Draw. I estimated that today would be the hardest walking day.

My thoughts are of Manly and how his men would have accepted this trek. They had just traveled 415 miles on the river and were now walking 175 miles to Mormonee, when they could have stayed on the original wagon trail and been in Mormonee within 175 miles. Although Manly does not write about any desertion or ill feelings about their efforts, distances traveled, and time lost, this would have been the time. If any of the men were upset, Manly did not record those thoughts.

I have seen how difficult traveling is and the toll it can take on a group's attitudes. Even on our trip, I have to be careful about what is said and try to make it comfortable for all. Manly may also have experienced difficulties with the social aspects of traveling such long distances together.

I am relieved we all arrived safely tonight and hope the remainder of the trip goes smoothly. I am very tired and will close. Tomorrow we will try to reach our goal of twenty miles.

Starting out on their second day of land travel (September 23), Manly made mention of other significant land descriptions and very important related trail crossings. "The next morning we started on," he recounted, "and crossed three or four old trails going southwards, at right angles to our own, and along the foot of the mountain. It seemed to be a level plain down south, as far as the eye could reach, but we had no knowledge of where these trails led to, so we followed our little new trail, and soon entered the canyon exactly as it had been described to us, and as we had been directed to do."[23] This describes their trek across the desert through Furniture Draw on to Buckhorn Flat and ending in Castle Valley, an estimated distance of sixty miles. Given the distance, Manly apparently misnumbered the days of travel. The distance to travel from the Green River to the natural water tanks or Big Holes would have been an estimated seventeen miles. This Manly accomplished on his first day. Traveling from Big Holes to Castle Valley, where Manly would begin his ascent up a canyon traveled by Wákara, would have taken two more days of travel, not just one. The trail, traversing the flat barren lands of Furniture Draw and Buckhorn Flat, would have been over thirty-five miles, a distance Manly could not have traveled in a single day, the second day of travel as he accounts: "We started on in the morning, following our faint trail till we came to the cañon we had in view, and up this we turned as we had been directed, finding in the bottom a little running stream."[24] I conclude that Manly simply omitted the second day of travel on the flatlands, as he had done describing sections of the Green River. Manly's estimated distance of land travel in the first three days, therefore, would have been sixty miles.

Traveling across these barren lands, it becomes clear that there is one distinct difference between the San Rafael Desert and the Uinta Basin, where some have concluded Manly traveled. From the Green River traveling northwest to the mountains of the Wasatch Plateau, Manly did not report crossing any streams or waters. These lands are graphically described as flat and dry with little or no potential future for agricultural use. John C. Sumner of the Powell party recorded his impression of the San Rafael Desert: "The valley, or rather desert, first passed is of little use to anyone; the upland is burned to death"; he later called the area "as desolate a country as anyone need wish to see."[25] In contrast, the Uinta Basin had long been described by other early travelers as having ample water for development and crop production. In 1776, the Dominguez and Escalante party crossed from east to west through the Uinta Basin and the Duchesne and Strawberry Valleys in the hopes of establishing a domestic trade and travel route. They were also seeking "a more or less direct route from Santa Fe to the recently established garrison and town of Monterey on the California coast."[26] In their book *Journals of Forty-Niners*, LeRoy and Ann Hafen describe the direction of travel of the Dominguez-Escalante party as "northwestward to cross the Green near present Jensen, Utah. Moving westward up the Duchesne and Strawberry valleys, they crossed the Wasatch Mountain to Utah Lake."[27] The journals kept by Dominguez and Escalante reporting the undeveloped Uinta Basin and Duchesne and Strawberry Valleys describe a landscape very different from Manly's descriptions, since he was traveling a different course—across dry lands of the San Rafael Desert to Castle Valley. Approaching the Green River some 150 miles above where Manly left it, the Dominguez-Escalante journal reads, "From here downstream there is a lot of good pasturage in its box channel bed, which is wide and level . . . after going two leagues northwest came to a large river which we named San Buenaventura [Green]."[28] Here the Uinta Basin began to show its agricultural promise to the Spanish fathers. Crossing the Green and traveling west on a Ute Indian trail, the fathers detail traveling a wholly different direction than Manly, as well as describing water flowing from the southern slopes of the Uinta Mountains and abundant plant life. Their three days of travel from September 16 to 18, 1776, differ starkly from Manly's three days of northwest travel from the Green:

September 16: Crossed the river [Green]. We took to the west and, after going one league along the northern side and meadow of the river, crossed another smaller one [Brush Creek] turned west, which comes down from the northwest. . . . Over the same meadow we turned south-southwest for a league and crossed another rivulet [Ashley Creek] a little larger than the first, which comes down from the same northwesterly direction and enters the river. From both of them irrigation ditches can be dug for watering the land on this side . . . which is likewise good for farming. . . . We continued exactly where the tracks led, descended once more to El Rio de San Buenaventura [Green River]. . . . We kept on following it over the meadow by the river's edge . . . after having gone over the broken hills and slopes, and the meadow mentioned, six leagues to the southwest, and in the whole day's march eight leagues.[29]

In this day of traveling, the Dominguez-Escalante expedition crossed the Green River north of present-day Jensen, Utah, and east of what is now Vernal. The party crossed Brush and Ashley Creeks and then camped in a meadow just west of the river called "The Stirrup."

> September 17: We set out from the meadow for Las Llagas de Nuestro Padre San Francisco toward the southwest, went up some low hills, and after going a league left the path we were following, the one on which the racks of horses and people continued. . . . We crossed a dry arroyo, climbed up a hill, and after going west a league and a half over good terrain, almost flat and arid, arrived at a high ridge from which the guide pointed out to us the junction of the rivers San Clemente [White River] and San Buenaventura [Green River], which, now joined together [at present-day Ouray, Utah], flowed to the south with respect to where we stood.

At this point the guide, Silvestre, led them away from the Ute Trail they had been following.

> We descended to a plain and another river's large meadow, and, after going west another league and a half, arrived at the juncture of two medium-sized rivers which come down from the sierra which lies near here and to the north of El Rio de San Buenaventura. The one more to the east before the juncture runs to the southeast, and we named it Rio de San Damian [Uinta River]; the other to the east, and we named it Rio de San Cosme [Duchesne River]. We continued upstream along the latter. . . . We turned southwest over a plain which lies between the two rivers, went up some hills of loose stone, and very troublesome to the already hoofsore mounts; we went down another meadow of El Rio de San Cosme, and, having gone southwest for half a league and one-half toward the west over the meadow, we halted on La Ribera de San Cosme.[30]

By the end of September 17, then, the Dominguez-Escalante expedition had crossed or encountered six rivers since they had crossed the

Green the day before. Their camping location for this night's stay was just east of Myton, Utah. Their directions of travel were west and southwest.

> September 18: We set out from La Ribera de San Cosme, and because the guide wanted to cross over to the river's other side and follow it, he stuck us through an almost impenetrable willow bosque, or thicket, and into marshy estuaries which made us back-track and cross the river thrice while making many useless detours. Then over a plain next to its meadows we went three leagues west, turned west-southwest one league, crossed the river [Lake Fork River] a fifth time, and again took to the west, in which direction we traveled three leagues and a quarter, now over the river's meadow, now over the plain next to it. We climbed up to a not very high mesa, flat on top and very stone, traveled for about three quarters of a league, which includes the ascent and descent, crossed another small river [Duchesne River] which close to hear flows into the San Cosme and which we named Santa Catarina de Sena [Duchesne], and halted by its edge. Today nine leagues. . . .
>
> There is good land along these three rivers [Lower Duch-esne, Lake Fork, Upper Duchesne] that we crossed today, and plenty of it for farming with the aid of irrigation—beautiful pop-lar groves, fine pastures, timber and firewood not too far away, for three good settlements. . . . Tomorrow we shall begin climbing it and going across where it appears less lofty.[31]

In the three days of travel by the Dominguez-Escalante party after crossing the Green River in the Uinta Basin, they covered 65½ miles and identified eight rivers or streams.

In contrast, Manly's first three days after leaving the Green River involve traveling northwest, not southwest. He did not record any sight-ing or crossing of rivers and only found rainwater in natural tanks or basins. Manly's travel distance on his first day is estimated at seventeen miles, which is within range of the twenty-one miles the Dominguez-Escalante party traveled on their first day. Manly's second and third days of traveling, which covered about forty miles, were described as barren and desolate, with no mention of rivers or streams, which were constantly on the travelers' minds. As previously reviewed, Manly erred in not accounting for his second day of land travel, but other Old Spanish Trail travelers crossing the same lands Manly did on his second day did not include in their diaries crossing any rivers or streams and reported instead the same dry, barren conditions that Manly experienced during three days in the San Rafael Desert. These other travelers' search for water was dramatic and required great effort to sustain life.[32]

On the fathers' third day of travel from the Green, water was again a constant, with reference to irrigable lands and the direction of travel. Ending their third day after the Green, the Dominguez-Escalante expedition had now traveled 65½ miles *west and southwest* of the Green and had crossed or identified eight rivers or streams. Manly, on the other hand, crossed about sixty miles *northwest* in his first three days of land travel, with no reference to streams or flowing waters. The contrast makes clear that Manly confronted and passed through lands much farther south of the Uinta Basin on his way to Salt Lake City. He must have left the Green River in the San Rafael Desert, not in the Uinta Basin.

9/19/2006, Tuesday, Day 37, Trek Day 2

Dry Mesa to Buckhorn Flat

The weather was clear as we awoke and prepared for our second day of the trek. Dallas and Clint were sore but ready to take on the upcoming twenty miles. With us traveling an estimated thirty miles on the first day, the next twenty miles should go more quickly. We had a filling breakfast and were ready to go by 8:15 a.m. Dallas, Clint, and I began walking towards the ridge line of Cedar Mountain that we have used for our guide since leaving Green River. Within the first five miles, we walked to the south of a distinctive butte called Chimney Rock. It is beautiful, standing by itself with Cedar Mountain directly behind. Manly made no mention of this butte but did recount how he and the men were increasingly becoming more concerned about the lack of food.

By noon we passed it and were coming down Furniture Draw into Buckhorn Flat. The canyon we will walk through is in view and will be reached by afternoon tomorrow. Manly remembered this canyon: "We started on in the morning, following our faint trail till we came to the cañon we had in view."

By late afternoon, I had shuttled the all-terrain vehicle by truck and walked ten miles. I am tired and can appreciate what Clint and Dallas have accomplished as well as Manly and his men. I cannot see Manly and the other four all walking together as they traveled towards Mormonee. Clint and Dallas walk at different paces. Clint walks faster while Dallas keeps a slower, more even pace. Manly's men would probably have walked in a similar fashion.

As I was walking, I thought of dinner and how enjoyable it would be. Manly recorded that food was not as plentiful; therefore, they must have gone hungry some evenings. That would be difficult, to work so hard and not eat well. Those men were hardy and strong willed, living on their dreams of reaching California and striking it rich.

We arrived at our evening camp by 5:00, enjoyed a wonderful dinner, and were ready for bed by 7:00. We traveled twenty miles today and have now logged fifty miles in two days—a wonderful start. Other than some sore muscles, all are doing well. Cody, who brought the horses, is a tremendous help. He is here in case someone needs to ride. I am glad he is willing to be a part of the expedition. The trip has many challenges and safety is of the utmost concern.

After dinner, we played some games, trying to hit targets with Frisbees made of uneaten tortillas. It keeps spirits up and takes thoughts off the upcoming miles. Tomorrow we will continue to walk westward to the canyon entrance of Rock Canyon. Then up on the Wasatch Plateau we will go. Walking and river running are different in their physical demands. The trek requires constant hydration from the exertion of walking long distances. However, the river carries everything along at a surprisingly equivalent pace. I am tired and happy that we are on schedule. The days are long but rewarding when we reach our goal of miles traveled. Tomorrow is another twenty-mile goal.

On September 24, 1849, Manly moved westward across the final barren lands of Castle Valley. For two days he had been approaching a high mountain range running north to south, and he knew he would soon have to climb these mountains. Wákara had previously explained "where to enter the mountains leading north."[33] Gwinn Harris Heap also described these same mountains and the Castle Valley floor extending southward much like Manly. In his travels on the Old Spanish Trail in 1853, Heap recorded, "The country opened to the north and northwest, showing a level plain to the foot of the Wasatch Mountains. These mountains extended north, west, and southwest as far as our sight could reach."[34] Before reaching the mountains, known today as the Wasatch Plateau, Manly crossed "three or four old trails going southward"[35] on the eastern slope. For the second time, Manly unknowingly but accurately described the Old Spanish Trail in its path southward to Los Angeles. In documenting the trail, historians Gregory Crampton and Steven Madsen report, "From Little Holes, the trail advances westward, threading its way through Furniture Draw, and then crosses Buckhorn Flat to reach the Black Hills and its northernmost point—approximately 39°12' north latitude. From the Black Hills, the trail drops down [heading south] to Huntington Creek in Castle Valley."[36] The Gunnison party found themselves in the same location in 1855, as E. G. Beckwith reported: "The Spanish trial, though but seldom used of late years, is still very distinct where the soil washes but slightly. On some such spaces to-day we counted from fourteen to twenty parallel trails, of the ordinary size of Indian trails or horse-paths, on a way of barely fifty feet in width."[37] Manly remembered this unique landscape vividly, commenting, "It seemed to be a level plain down south, as far as the eye could reach, but we had no knowledge of where these trails led to."[38] Exactly as Manly remembered, the flatlands of Castle Valley do in fact give way to the majestic rising mountains of the Wasatch Plateau, which the band of forty-niners would soon traverse as they followed Wákara's faint trail.

Manly's description of the trail closely matches the location and nature of the Old Spanish Trail, which west of the Green River ran north and south, parallel to the east side of the Wasatch Plateau in Castle Valley and, as Beckwith pointed out, consisted of multiple parallel tracks. Manly continually demonstrates an attention to detail, even when recounting the ordeal decades later.

The question now arises: Which canyon did Manly ascend on his fourth day of travel? Viewing the high mountain peaks of the Wasatch Plateau from the Castle Valley floor, just southeast of present-day Castle Dale, Utah, one can readily see several canyons leading to the summit of the mountains. The northernmost canyon is called Straight Canyon. It is a wide-mouthed canyon, running northwest in direction, and is the source for Cottonwood Creek, which winds through Castle Dale on its way to confluence with the San Rafael River. As Straight Canyon gains in altitude, it narrows and becomes a very well-defined, steep, V-shaped canyon. Traveling up this canyon would have been extremely difficult. The river bed is very rocky and drops in altitude quickly, while the slope, length, and narrowness of the canyon walls would have made travel on foot or horseback very difficult.

Two canyons to the south is Ferron Canyon. Like Straight Canyon, it has a large mouth or open area, through which Ferron Creek flows freely. Also similar to Straight Canyon, Ferron Canyon narrows into a V-shaped canyon with very steep slopes that would have been extremely hard to climb.

Located between these two steep, narrow canyons lies Rock Canyon. Unlike Straight and Ferron Canyons, Rock Canyon is a much shorter

Rock Canyon rises from Castle Valley to the Wasatch Plateau.

canyon that is not as long nor as steep from the floor of Castle Valley to the top of the Wasatch Plateau. Its canyon walls are more open or U-shaped, allowing for easy access. Reviewing and researching the early maps of this region, a definitive clue points to this as the canyon Manly would have traveled.

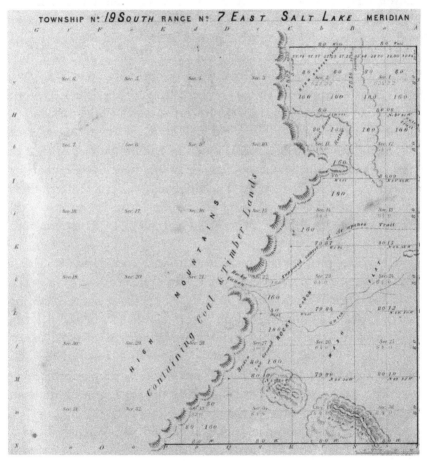

In 1873 A. D. Ferron was commissioned by the Surveyor General's Office in Salt Lake City to survey and map Township 19 South Range 7, East Salt Lake Meridian, Utah Territory; his map includes details matching Manly's description of his ascent of the Wasatch Plateau. COURTESY OF GENERAL LAND OFFICE RECORDS, BUREAU OF LAND MANAGEMENT, U.S. DEPARTMENT OF THE INTERIOR

On June 19, 1873, a cartographer, surveyor, and mapmaker named A. D. Ferron was commissioned by the Surveyor General's Office in Salt Lake City to survey and map Township 19 South Range 7, East Salt Lake Meridian, Utah Territory. This map was completed October 11, 1873. Ferron provided great detail in his map, including both a stream and an Indian trail exiting Rock Canyon (which he called "Rocky Canyon"). Ferron labeled the stream "West Gulch" and the Indian trail "Supposed Course of Arapene's Trail." Arapeen was Wákara's younger brother and was his constant companion as he moved throughout the western lands. An example of this was when Mormon explorer Parley P. Pratt came in contact with both men on December 6 and 7, 1849, during Pratt's expedition to the southern lands of the Utah Territory. As recorded by one of Pratt's men, Robert Campbell, "Capt Walker & another Indian rides into Camp and Glad to see us knew he would see us soon, for he dreamed he would, told us he had lots of trade, wished us to go back down the Sevier about a mile where there was good bottom with feed. . . . Parley reads letter from Brigham to Captn. Walker Dimic interprets it tells about the sack of Flour for him, he makes no answer till he sees Arrapin his Brother, all the band is coming & will encamp with us tells Parley."[39]

It is telling, then, that the Indian trail in Rock Canyon was associated with Arapeen, who traveled extensively with Wákara across the western lands and, upon Wákara's death in 1855, became chief himself until he died in 1860.[40] Additionally, Wákara was seen in the area of Manti, Utah, on the western slope of the Wasatch Plateau in Sanpete Valley, in August and in December of 1849. A direct line between Manti and the Old Spanish Trail crossing at the Green River passes directly over the high mountains of the Wasatch Plateau, making the Rock Canyon route an efficient way to travel between the two.

As Manly and his men began to ascend the Wasatch Plateau through Rock Canyon, Manly described the canyon where timber and grass appeared, as well as a small stream: "We started on in the morning, following our faint trail till we came to the cañon we had in view, and up this we turned as we had been directed, finding in the bottom a little running stream [West Gulch]. Timber began to appear as we ascended, and grass also."[41] In his earlier account in "From Vermont to California," Manly provided even more detail: "So we followed our little new trail, and soon entered the canyon exactly as it had been described to us, as we had been directed to do. Here we followed up a little running stream. The mountain had some pine timber on them, there were plenty of grapes [grass?] and we go along very pleasantly."[42]

Manly was not the only Euro-American to use the Indian trail through Rock Canyon in this period. John McEwan, a Mormon living in Manti, was assigned to help establish and settle the Elk Mountain Mission, where Moab, Utah, now stands. In September of 1855, McEwan found himself separated from his traveling party as they returned from the mission and were attempting to cross over the Wasatch Plateau from Castle Valley to Manti. In his diary, McEwan reviewed his ordeal and gave valuable insight into the Rock Canyon trail. "I started at day light taking the indian trail," he recorded. "I came across our trail in Castle Valley. . . . I proceeded along our trail up a creek, water brackish, thence up a Kanyon, thence up the mountain . . . this trail is not traveled as a general thing by the indians, only by Arraphere and his band, and only a person [that] was acquainted with the trail."[43]

McEwan ultimately had to be rescued, and the Indians in the rescue party provide more corroboration connecting the trail to Arapeen. "[Rescuers] being 5 in number 3 whites and 2 indians belonging to Arra-penes Band . . . they said Arra-pene and 1 of the indians along felt very bad also. . . . These boys left Manti City on Tuesday evening at ½ past 10 o'clock P.M. to go in pursuit of me. Wednesday about noon they overtook me on the trail as stated above."[44]

Climbing up Rock Canyon on their fourth day of land travel, they surely would have felt renewed hope as the landscape began to change dramatically. The barren desert valley now gave way to a small creek of running water with an abundance of trees and grass. Wákara had told Manly "where to enter the mountains leading north, and when we got part way he told me we would come to an Indian camp."[45] The description "leading north" fits with the Wasatch Plateau; if Manly had started in the Uinta Basin, in contrast, the only mountains of considerable length and size he would have reached walking in a northwest direction from the Uinta Basin are the Uinta Mountains. These mountains, unlike the Wasatch Plateau that stretches north to south, have the unique geological characteristic of running east and west.

Other major differences between the Wasatch Plateau and the Uinta Mountains are their topography and vegetation. Manly describes the range he encountered as "rolling hills, high on the mountain side"; elsewhere reports that his party "slept and ate and plodded on again," all the while "at a great elevation."[46] These rolling hills do not fit the defining characteristics of the Uinta Mountains, with their high peaks and heavily forested lands.[47] Climbing Rock Canyon, Manly is not descriptive of the distances traveled or uniqueness of the canyon itself other than the small running stream, timber, and grass that he observes.

Manly is quite descriptive, however, about what he found at the top: "Sometimes we were near big snowbanks, which told us that we were at a great elevation."[48] On top of Rock Canyon, in fact, they would have been at quite a height; the highest point on the plateau is South Tent Mountain, elevation 11,285 feet. Snowbanks located in the alpine biomes above 10,000 feet often last year-round and would have been preserved

Snowbanks perch along the summit of the Wasatch Plateau.

throughout the entire year. If Manly had started his land journey from the Uinta Basin, rather than the San Rafael Desert, he would have not encountered such high elevations throughout the entire journey. The highest point of his journey would have been Strawberry Summit, at 8,020 feet, which is not high enough to feature snowbanks in September.

As previously reviewed, seventy-three years before Manly traveled across central Utah, the famed Dominguez-Escalante expedition was traveling across the territory from east to west. From September 19 to 23, 1776, Dominguez and Escalante journeyed from the Uinta Basin to Spanish Fork Canyon, at exactly the same time of year as Manly's journey. The dramatic contrast between their report and Manly's helps establish that the latter was not traveling from the Uinta Basin, but rather from the San Rafael Desert.

Significantly, the only mention of snow the Dominguez-Escalante party made was far in the distance to the north, where the "Sierra Blanca de los Lagunas," or Uinta Mountains, "displayed its tallest shoulders and peaks covered with snow."[49] As the Escalante party steadily traveled in a west-southwest direction to Spanish Fork Canyon, their observations and encounters over the next five days were of open grasslands, pastures, and sagebrush. On September 19, 1776, three days after crossing the Green River, they recorded "going up a gradual hill with some tree growth . . . to the water source which we named San Eustaquio [Red Creek, elevation 6,600 feet], having traveled two and a half leagues west. This water source is perennial and copious, and there is a abundant pasturage by it."[50] The next day, September 20, they traveled "southwest up a long but gradual incline, then swung west for a little less than three leagues and a quarter over a stretch of sagebrush" before coming to "a short, narrow valley, ample and gently sloping," followed by "a very pretty and pleasant narrow valley with the most abundant pastures." They camped at the top of what is now called Deep Creek, a half mile from Summit, elevation 8,020 feet."[51] Again traveling southwest the next day, in contrast to Manly's north-northwest direction, the Dominguez-Escalante party passed on September 21 through intermittent stretches of sagebrush and groves of trees, which were near water. It was on this day that they topped out at "a very lofty ridge," which was Strawberry Summit.[52]

On September 22, 1776, the Dominguez-Escalante company followed what is now called Upper Diamond Creek and climbed around the north flank of Red Mountain, descending its western side and camping at the junction of Wanrhodes Canyon and Diamond Creek, about five miles above where Upper Diamond enters Spanish Fork Canyon, which they reached the next day, September 23, 1776, seven days after crossing the Green River in the Uinta Basin.[53]

Comparing the journal of the Dominguez-Escalante expedition to Manly's accounts reveals three additional differences that make it clear the two parties journeyed from different locations on the Green River. First is the dramatic difference in altitudes. The Dominguez-Escalante journals record the group traveling through open plains, good terrain, gently sloping narrow valleys, hills, and meadows that are very flat and suitable for farming. Though they do travel down some steep narrow valleys, their land descriptions are not at all what Manly experienced: towering summits and high mountain plateaus of "rolling hills high on the mountain side" and exposed northern slopes.[54] Manly ascended the Wasatch Plateau to an elevation of over 10,000 feet on his third day of travel and remained at that high altitude for five consecutive days, eventually finding his way northwest to the Spanish Fork Canyon on day

View atop the Wasatch Plateau; Manly described "rolling hills high on the mountain side."

nine. The Escalante party in comparable travel time journeyed across the Uinta Basin to Red Creek, then past where Strawberry Reservoir is now located and down Diamond Fork Canyon to Spanish Fork Canyon. They found themselves traveling in altitudes ranging from 4,900 feet to 8,020 feet, where they crossed over the Strawberry Summit.

The second difference is the plant life observed. At their lower elevations, the Dominguez-Escalante party encountered sagebrush, heavily forested valleys, groves of white poplar trees, and prickly pear cactus.[55] Manly, meanwhile, encountered high plateaus, grasslands, and mountains that "had some timber on them." He saw bare stretches as they passed above the timberline—around 11,000 or 12,000 feet.[56]

The third differentiating factor, as outlined previously, is the direction of travel. Manly is clear that he changed direction on the evening of day four or morning of day five, leaving the faint trail and turning northward to "follow some horse tracks over rolling hills, high on the mountain side."[57] Manly kept up this northward direction until the eighth day, and he came to Spanish Fork Canyon as he traveled northerly.[58] In the Dominguez-Escalante journals, the direction of travel from day four through day seven, when they reach Spanish Fork Canyon, is unmistakably west and southwest.[59] Though the Manly party of 1849 and the Dominguez-Escalante party of 1776 both converged at Spanish Fork Canyon, they arrived from very different directions.

When Manly reached the top of the mountain, he made a significant change in the direction of his travels towards Salt Lake City: "Following the Chief's instructions we left the trail and followed some horse tracks over rolling hills, high on the mountain side."[60] The Wasatch Plateau is unique in its open grasslands that roll across the high plateaus at over 10,000 feet in altitude. As Manly traveled up Rock Canyon onto the Wasatch Plateau, he traveled east to west. Upon reaching the summit after a 1,700-foot climb, Wákara's Indian trail continued in that same direction of east-west, crossing over the plateau where Wagon Ridge Road is now located and descending the west side of the plateau through Manti Canyon to the newly established Mormon community of Manti. Manly, however, "following the Chiefs instructions," began to walk to the north, where he soon encountered a Ute camp.[61] It was a pivotal instruction to follow. Had Manly's party not remembered Wákara's words to leave the trail once on the top of the mountains, they would have crossed over the Wasatch Plateau and headed toward the Sevier Valley, not the Mormon settlements to the north.

At the top of Rock Canyon, there is a naturally formed stairway of impressive rock ledges, showcasing thousands of years of erosion's smoothing of rocks as water flows from the plateau. On the upper tier of one of the top-right shelves stands a rock that is sheltered from the water flow. And engraved on this rock, about three feet from its base, are the names of several people who passed the spot sometime in the past. Though the engravings have only partially survived, the following can be deciphered: MANLY, AL, RO.

The first inscription is unmistakable. As he had done at Ashley Falls on the Green River, Manly appears to have again recorded his name on a rock as his written declaration of where he had traveled.[62] The second identifying rock inscription of "AL" could be the first name of Alfred Walton, while "RO" could be the first two letters of John Rogers's last name. It seems beyond coincidence that these three inscriptions are found at the top of Rock Canyon where, I argue, these men passed on September 24, 1849.

Wákara had informed Manly that he would meet a group of Utes camping on the Wasatch Plateau; Manly recounted that the chief "said after three 'sleeps' we would find an Indian camp on top of the mountain." Sure enough, on the fourth day, "we found the Indian camp exactly as the Chief had described, consisting of two or three lodges."[63] At this point in the story, a few questions need to be answered. Who were the Indians camped on the top of the mountain and what relationship did they have to Wákara? Why was the Indian camp located here, and what were the Indians doing at this high altitude?

When Manly first arrived at the camp, an Indian woman immediately recognized his mode of transportation. "The woman pointed to our horses," he noted, "and said 'Walker' so we knew they were aware that we got them of him."[64] This observation indicates that the Indians Manly encountered were not only Ute but part of Wákara's own entourage. Further, the fact that Wákara detailed to Manly the exact location of the camp indicates that Wákara had recently been with them on top of the mountain, where he had presumably set up the camp for gathering and preparing food for the coming winter, before heading to the Old Spanish Trail and Green River where he encountered Manly.

"The men were all absent hunting," Manly wrote, "but the women were gathering and baking some sort of a root which looked like a carrot." In traditional Ute culture, while men primarily hunted, women and children were "generally responsible for gathering non-meat items and preserving them for storage."[65] Manly observed their work with the unidentified root: "When sufficiently cooked they beat them up and make the material into small cakes which were dried in the sun . . . intended for winter use." The raw root "contained a sort of acid juice that would make the tongue smart and very sore but there was a very good rich taste when cooked."[66] The Wasatch Plateau had been used for thousands of years by the Native Americans in hunting, planting, and gathering of food supplies. According to David B. Madsen, between 1,500 and 2,000 years ago, "the production and use of . . . tools, in addition to the growing of corn, beans, and squash, appears to have spread to other hunting and gathering groups to the north as well as to both the east and west of the central Wasatch Plateau region."[67] The plateau had been prime land for hunting and gathering for the Fremont people. In the book *The Fremont Culture*, James Gunnerson writes about the Fremont population and their dependency on Ferron Canyon, located five miles south of Rock Canyon. "The Fremont people occupied about 20,000 square miles of territory, but only a small percentage of it was usable for farming. . . . A few of the most favorable areas [were] Ivie Creek, Nine Mile canyon and Ferron Creek."[68] The United States Forest Service published a report that also detailed the importance of the Wasatch Plateau for Native American cultures:

Evidence of thousands of years of occupation by both native peoples and early pioneers can be found in ruins, rock-art, and abandoned working landscapes throughout the Forest [that is, the Manti-La Sal Forest, which encompasses the Wasatch Plateau]. American Indians have a long history of using the Forest for sustenance and sacred activities. . . . Another important ancient cultural landscape is found on the Ferron/Price Ranger District on the Manti Division. This landscape consists of a concentration of alcove or rock shelter sites in the Quitchipa/Pines area. These sites occur in the outcropping Castlegate Sandstone formation and frequently possess well-preserved cultural deposits, potentially dating back to the earliest periods of human occupation in the Intermountain Region (ca. 10,000 B.P. [before present]).[69]

As these reports detail, the plants and animals of the Wasatch Plateau were a critical food source for native people.

Further research helps establish that the "some sort of a root which looked like a carrot" was wild potato. Virginia Simmons writes in *The Ute Indians of Utah, Colorado, and New Mexico*: "The largest part of women's time was occupied with harvesting and preparing food. . . . Among the staples were Indian ricegrass and sunflower seeds; sego and mariposa lily bulbs and wild onions; all the tender parts of bulrushes and cattails; roots of wild potatoes and yampa; cactus and yucca fruits; chokecherries, serviceberries, buffaloberries, squawberries, and currants."[70] The habitat of the wild potato is at high elevations such as those found on the Wasatch Plateau, as explained by botanists David M. Spooner and Robert J. Hijmans: "Wild potatoes occur between 388°N and 418°S, with more species in the southern hemisphere. Species richness is highest between 88 and 208°S and around 208°N. Wild potatoes typically occur between 2000 and 4000 m altitude [6,562 to 13,124 feet]. . . . There are 199 wild potato species. These wild species all grow in the Americas, from the southwestern United States to central Argentina and Chile."[71]

Piecing together the available information, one can reconstruct a timeline for Wákara's travels in August through September of 1849. After suggesting to the Mormons that they build a settlement in Manti in mid-August, Wákara traveled to Salt Lake City. Since he met Manly thirty days later, the Ute chief then would have had to travel in a southeast direction and would have had to cross the Wasatch Plateau to reach the Spanish Trail. En route, Wákara left part of his traveling party on the plateau for fall food gathering and hunting. He then continued on down the east slope of the plateau in Rock Canyon and followed his "faint trail" to the banks of the Green River and the Old Spanish Trail. He would point out the same faint trail to Manly three weeks later.

Though Manly gave a fairly detailed description of the encampment of the Ute Indians and his interaction with them, he did not say how many people he encountered. He did note the presence of "two or three lodges," which gives a rough idea of the size of the group camped there.[72] Manly also described the geographical location of the Ute encampment as being at "the summit at a low pass." This description matches the location of a small valley where North Dragon Creek flows northward into what is now Joe's Valley Reservoir. The valley is a low point near the summit of the Wasatch Plateau, and it would have had water for growing crops like wild potatoes.

After Manly's brief encounter with the Western Ute Indians, and observing that they were busy in gathering food supplies, Manly decided to move away from the camp to spend the fourth night of their trek apart from the Indians. He did not give a reason for doing so, but since he knew the Utes recognized his horses as Wákara's, "and might have taken us for horse thieves for aught I know," Manly likely considered it safer to keep a distance. The travelers set up camp early, before sunset, near a stream and a stand of pine trees, about a mile past the Indian encampment.[73]

The evening soon became eventful as some Indians from the camp visited them to trade and have a shooting contest. Manly's company gave "some needles and a few other trinkets" in trade for venison, and Manly noted with apparent pride, "I beat these fellows shooting at a mark, and then they wanted to trade guns, which I declined."[74] After the capsizing and other mishaps on the Green, Manly's rifle was the only gun among his company, and they had depended heavily on it for survival as they traveled west.[75] The venison was much needed, as the men's food supplies were becoming very limited; Manly wrote, "This piece of meat helped us along considerably with our provisions."[76] The visitors then left Manly's camp, which would be his last association with Wákara's band—or any other Utes. Manly readily understood the importance of his fortuitous encounter with Wákara and maintained a deep appreciation for the chief, as evidenced in William Lorton's journal account of meeting Manly in September 1849: Manly reported that he and his men "would have starved to death but for Indian Walker who gave them as much as they could eat, & traded the horses to them for ammunition The Indians were very kind to them."[77] Manly's own writings decades later signal that his admiration for Wákara and the Utes continued to the end of his life.

9/20/2011, Tuesday, Day 38, Trek Day 3

Buckhorn Flat to Top of Rock Canyon

Today is day three of our trek across Buckhorn Wash and up Rock Canyon onto the Wasatch Plateau. The morning breaks and the day is clear and cool. Our campsite is positioned perfectly to view where we have been and where we are going. Looking back to the east, Cedar Mountain is in full view. I estimate with the miles we have walked that it is almost twenty miles distant. Cedar Mountain is a great geological positioning point. I am sure the Ute Indians used it for a directional point in coming or going to the Green River and Old Spanish Trail.

Looking to the west and the path we will be taking today, our canyon that we will be going up (Rock Canyon) is in view. . . . I am anxious to climb the canyon today and see how hard it will be. From the maps the mouth of the canyon is roughly fifteen miles away from us and will be seven miles to climb up. That distance of seven miles is another reason that the Ute Indians used Rock Canyon. It is much shorter, not as steep, and in the ideal location for fast travel. We will leave at 8:00 a.m. and should be at the canyon by noon or shortly after. The topography of the mouth of the canyon is open rolling hills with little vegetation. Very similar to what we have been walking through. It is very dry. There is a stream bed to our left that is dry, but some vegetation growing along the banks. The maps show this stream bed as Ferron Creek. Manly makes no mention of water from a creek until he comes to Rock Canyon.

Walking due west on a dirt road and across farming fields, we have our sights set to enter the mouth or water drainage of Rock Canyon. It is light brown or tan in soils and rocks. It continues to be very dry throughout the whole region. This is a pivotal place in the land journey for Manly. As Wákara advised, Manly is right on schedule as he enters Rock Canyon on his third day of the trek. Like Manly, our expedition is running exactly as many days as Manly traveled. Our expedition will travel up Rock Canyon on our third day just like Manly. Entering the canyon on September 20, we are only four calendar days behind Manly, who entered the canyon on September 24. I purposely have done this to match the weather patterns that Manly might have encountered. The weather is very comfortable, and I expect Manly experienced the same, for he does not make mention of poor weather conditions. The canyon is a wide canyon at the bottom and narrows quickly towards the top. It is not like the canyons to the north or south that are very narrow, steep, and long. Arriving at Rock Canyon by noon, we eat a light lunch and prepare to move up onto the Wasatch Plateau.

As we begin walking up the canyon, it is 1:30 in the afternoon. The sun is warm and a breeze is blowing comfortably. Beginning our upward ascent, it became readily apparent why this canyon was frequently used by Wákara and his Ute band. The canyon is a short canyon, estimated at seven miles of ascent onto the Wasatch Plateau. Though a steady climb upwards, there are not any places that are so difficult that man or horse or cattle could not travel. Manly mentions a small stream flowing from the canyon; however, as we walk up there is no water flowing in the stream bed. There is evidence that water once flowed down this canyon but no longer on a regular basis. It must have rained here in past days because the stream bed is still wet and muddy. Local farmers have told me that due to water drilling on the plateau for the grazing cattle, the small creeks and streams have dried up and no longer carry water. What a shame.

Following the trail on the left side of the canyon, halfway up the canyon or approximately four miles, the ATV trail we are following turns to the left, exposing the original Ute Indian trail that continues straight. What a delight to walk over a mile on the original Ute Indian trail that Manly walked. This trail is much rockier with bends and turns to avoid the larger rocks, but very evident that it was cut or developed by the early peoples that lived in North America. Turning back to the east, I can look down Rock Canyon and over the terrain that we as well as Manly had covered in the last two days. The San Rafael Swell is clearly in view to the distant southeast. It is easy to see how the Old Spanish Trail as well as Wákara's faint trail had to swing northward around these impassable lands of the Swell.

We continued to move steadily upward and arrived at the top of Rock Canyon at 3:30, taking just two hours. I am sure Manly made just as good of time, even with his two horses, supplies, and men.

Arriving at the top of the canyon, we had an unexpected excitement when we viewed old etched signatures on sandstone rocks. Looking at the etchings closely, we had a discussion that these initials carved in the sandstone rocks could be signatures of Manly and his party. The signatures are much worn and very old. One signature or initial is GR. Possible John Rogers?

Another closely reviewed pictograph or etched initial looks like M N, possibly an L after the N. Could it have been Manley, the spelling he used in 1849 as he spelled his name then? It cannot be determined for certain, but who knows? Another initial on two letters are etched in the rock as AL. Maybe this is short for Alfred Walton? Other initials are: V, C, and L.

In reviewing these inscriptions from a professional standpoint, as much as I would like to see a Manly or Rogers's inscription, I do not think these inscriptions are from these men.

Carved in stone near the top of Rock Canyon are three separate names, one of which almost certainly spells out "Manly."

Author's Note: As noted previously in the chapter, further research and verification provided more conclusive evidence that the rock inscriptions were in fact the work of Manly and his company.

After spending an hour at the top of Rock Canyon, we continued to follow a dirt road west-northwest. Knowing that Manly is on his third day of his land journey as we are and that he meets or encounters Wákara's Ute band, my mind is full of thoughts as to where this encounter might have been. Manly writes that he encounters Wákara's band as soon as he is on top of the plateau. My answers to these questions are quickly found. We had walked northwestward only two miles when we came to a ridge that overlooked a beautiful valley to the north. This valley is now Joe's Valley Reservoir. It is here that Manly would have encountered Wákara's Utes. The valley is protected from strong winds and has a stream flowing through it, which is now part reservoir. Manly mentions that the Indians are farming and gathering a yellow root (wild potatoes). This location would have been ideal for farming and preparing for the cold winter season.

I have previously scouted the area and know this road will lead us to a higher pass that will put us on top of the Wasatch Plateau. It is now late in the afternoon, around 5:00. The day is drawing to a close, and we have decided to camp in the cottonwood trees in a secluded area where we are sheltered from the wind. All is well, and we look forward to a good night's sleep and starting out on our fourth day of walking to Mormonee.

After the rendezvous with Wákara's Western Utes on the afternoon of the fourth day of land travel, Manly's account becomes quite vague and generalized for the next four days of travel. While moving northward on Days 4 through 7, Manly remarks in a few short sentences about how he and his men are not finding wild game to shoot and eat: "One day I scared a hawk off the ground, and we took the sage hen he had caught and was eating, and made some soup of it. After being on this trail six or seven days we began to think of killing one of our colts for food for we had put ourselves on two meals a day and the work was very hard; so that hunger was all the time increasing."[78] In his earlier "From Vermont to California," Manly also recorded his concerns about the lack of food: "Occasionally we saw a sage-hen but no other game, although signs of deer were quite often met with, and we would have greeted the sight of the animals themselves with a good deal of pleasure and satisfaction, for our provisions were getting pretty short and we did not feel like stopping long to hunt, with only one gun to hunt with."[79]

This is the first time in all of Manly's writings as he travels west that he speaks of a lack of food. With his hunting abilities, Manly never before encountered an area where he could not provide food from wild game. On the Wasatch Plateau, there were deer and other game present, but time spent hunting, the shortage of firearms, and the increasing length of the expedition were important factors dissuading the men as they began to weaken in strength and determination.

With limited information given about this portion of his journey, it is difficult to pinpoint Manly's location on the Wasatch Plateau for Days 4 to 7. One detail Manly gave contradicted an earlier statement he made. As he continued north-northwest after meeting the Ute camp, Manly wrote, "We thought this was a pretty long road for Walker to ride over in three sleeps as he said he could."[80] But as Manly himself wrote several pages back, it would be after three days that they would reach the Ute encampment, which they had already done.[81]

9/21/2011, Wednesday, Day 39, Trek Day 4

Wasatch Plateau

Dallas and I rise early and prepare for our first full day's journey on the Wasatch Plateau. We continued walking at a comfortable pace in a northwest direction and came to a higher ridge. Rising off of the ridge was an old, abandoned road that found its way to the top. Through research, I learned that this old road was called Wagon

---

Ridge Road. It was made by the early Mormon settlers who brought their wagons over the Wasatch Plateau from Manti heading east. These early settlers would have followed the trail of the Ute Indians in making their wagon road. . . .

Reaching the top of the ridge, the whole world was below us. Looking east back to where we have been walking, I can see the start of Rock Canyon and across Buckhorn Flat, Cedar Mountain, and on to where we started by the Green River. It looks so far away and yet here we are on the fourth day of walking. Turning to the west I can see where the Wasatch Plateau drops down into Sanpete Valley. I know if we were to follow the trail westward, we would drop down into Manti within the day. . . . Like Manly, we turn north and follow the ridgeline. I imagine one of the reasons that Manly turned north is, he knows that SLC is northward and water and game or food will be more abundant than what they had experienced in the valleys. The view is unbelievable. The pine trees are deep green, the aspen trees are turning various colors of yellow, and the open areas are full of wild grasses. Indeed, the hills are rolling like Manly described.

We continued to walk northwest at a very comfortable walk. Some of the upper ridgelines are bare of vegetation. What a view and spectacle of wonder! While walking we see several water springs. Water on the Wasatch Plateau would not have been a problem for Manly and his men. I don't see as many deer as I would have expected. Maybe because of the upcoming annual deer hunt season, they're not as readily seen. We have four days of walking in this high altitude ahead of us. I am very comfortable and enjoying the dramatic change of scenery and cooler temperatures. The Wasatch Plateau continues to stretch northward and gives us no indication where it will end. After walking an estimated twelve to fifteen miles, we decide to end the day a little earlier than normal. Dallas and I go our different directions to explore and enjoy time alone.

The day is closing and I feel renewed after walking four days to the spectacular sights on top of the Wasatch Plateau. I will close for now.

9/22/2011, Thursday, Day 40, Trek Day 5

Wasatch Plateau

Morning frost greets us as we rise early and begin the usual day of breakfast and taking down camp. Dallas and I are ready to go at 8:30 a.m. Walking along the ridgeline, we continue in a northwest direction. My map details that we will continue in this direction for several miles and then we will make the dramatic turn to the north, following the ridgelines of the Wasatch Plateau. We pass several springs that give plenty of water and would have been welcomed by Manly and his horses. Again the view of walking on top of the Wasatch Plateau is spectacular.

At noon we reach the junction where the trail or road called the Skyline Drive turns north. . . . Manly writes that the mountains that he is on are ones that have rolling hills and abundant grass. I truly look out over rolling hills full of abundant grass, all at an elevation of over 10,000 feet. As unique in descriptions as Manly was on the Green, verifying that he was on the Wasatch Plateau stands strong as one of the definitive locations Manly describes. There is no mistake that the Wasatch Plateau was the mountain range Lewis Manly described as he traveled north towards Salt Lake City.

Like yesterday, walking is comfortable and not much change in elevation. I do know we are close to 10,000 feet in elevation. The air is cool and crisp. We have comfortable clothing that keeps us warm at this altitude. With the limited and well-worn clothing that Manly had, he would have been much colder than we have experienced. As we continue to head north, the westward trail that leads off of the Wasatch Plateau to the town of Manti falls behind our view. At this location, it is easy to see how Wákara would have traveled up the eastern slope of the Wasatch Plateau from Manti, crossed the plateau and down Rock Canyon. It would have been quick and much easier than traveling other canyons. Towards the end of the day Dallas and I decide to camp in an area called Horseshoe Flat. It is a large flat area on the high point of the plateau. Spirits are good and we realize that within a couple of days our journey will end. That knowledge is comforting, but Manly would not have known this as he prepared for an evening of sleep and uncertainty.

9/23/2011, Friday, Day 41, Trek Day 6

Wasatch Plateau

Mornings always come early due to the cooler temperatures. Dallas and I seem anxious to continue to move northward along the Wasatch Plateau. The air is still and sky blue with some white, billowy clouds. Looking to the southeast where we have walked for the past two days, I can still see the San Rafael Mountains in the far distance. They are very distinguishable due to the ruggedness and rough, uneven tops or peaks of the mountains. Directly in front of the Swell is a large, open plateau that we crossed over. The entrance that leads down Rock Canyon is no longer visible since it is several hundred feet below the plateau. The rim or plateau that I am looking at is called North Horn Mountain. Mahogany Point, overlooking the town of Castle Dale, is in clear view.

The aspen trees are changing colors every day. Their golden-yellow leaves are a sign that winter is soon to arrive. Manly must have felt this concern in seeing and feeling the changing of the weather, for he was at this location in the same week of September that we are here. I am sure there were disappointing moments for him and his men, knowing that winter was closing in and the gold mines of California were so far away.

Walking our normal pace of fifteen miles per day, we continue to make good progress across the plateau. We are fortunate to have good weather to help us in our trek. Manly does not mention poor weather in his journey over the plateau either. He was lucky, as we are. However, in the journals of William Lorton, he records Manly's appearance after leaving the Wasatch Plateau and alludes to the fact that Manly and his men had been very cold while on the mountain.

Overlooking the vast Wasatch Plateau, most of the pine trees throughout the landscape are brown and dead. There has been a bark beetle blight that has destroyed over 80 percent of all pine trees. If a forest fire ever were to break out in this area, it would devastate the entire Wasatch Plateau. As mentioned in past journal entries on the Wasatch Plateau, there is plenty of water. Springs are everywhere. It is easy to realize why the Ute Indians would have farmed and traveled on the plateau, because there is so much fresh water available.

We are at camp now and all is fine. Each day we become more tired of the walking but have kept our spirits. Tomorrow I anticipate better views of the northern part of the Wasatch Plateau. I will close for now.

9/24/2011, Saturday, Day 42, Trek Day 7

Wasatch Plateau

We rise and off we go again. After walking a couple of miles on a steady increase in altitude, we come to a ridgeline that exposes the northern part of the Wasatch Plateau. Wow! Looking north, the plateau begins to narrow, bending in the far distance towards the left or west. I can see Spanish Fork Canyon that we will be walking down on Day 9, only two days from now. From this distance it is easy to see how Manly would have stayed on the plateau until it ends and then walked into Spanish Fork Canyon. I am excited to see Spanish Fork Canyon and know this journey is fast ending. So many emotions of challenges and accomplishments swell within me. Though Manly did not know his route like we do, he must have seen and realized the plateau was narrowing and he would be coming down to the valley floor very soon. Looking more to the west, the Sanpete Valley is in full view. Across the valley lies Salt Creek Canyon. This is the canyon that the Mormon pioneers traveled through with Chief Wákara on their way to finding the location of Manti on August 20, 1849. It was just thirty-eight days later, on September 27, that Manly would have stood in this general location overlooking the Wasatch Plateau and Sanpete Valley floor.

I have seen several deer today. Manly mentions the lack of game as he travels. That surprises me, since the area would not have been hunted like it is today. Maybe with the cooler temperatures the deer had started to move to lower ground. The ridge that I am on has a lot of bare rock on the tops of the ridge. Light brown in color. The wind is whistling through the pine trees. So many are dead.

Tomorrow will be a day of determining the logical place that Manly begins to come down off the plateau. He gives us some clues in his writings in that he heads in a north direction once he is on the valley floor then turns and goes westward down Spanish Fork Canyon. It is also important to remember that he has to be very close to Spanish Fork Canyon when he comes down from the Wasatch Plateau, since he travels from the valley floor to Hobble Creek in one day and can only travel an estimated twenty miles per day. So the exiting point of the Wasatch Plateau has to be within a twenty-mile radius of Hobble Creek. With this timetable, he has to come down off the Wasatch Plateau on the eighth day and walk out to Hobble Creek, which is located just right of the mouth of Spanish Fork Canyon, on the ninth day. Dallas and I are currently averaging between fifteen and twenty miles of walking per day. We have traveled a little faster or covered more distance on the valley floor than on the Wasatch Plateau. We have been walking on dirt roads that have made it easier. Manly would have been following an Indian trail that would have been much harder to travel over.

We have two very exciting days ahead of us. Camp is set and I look forward to coming down off the plateau soon. Retracing the Manly journey is coming to an end very fast.

As the Manly expedition continued into its eighth day of travel, the survival of the party became a growing concern due to the length of the expedition, lack of food, and cold weather conditions in the high altitudes of the Wasatch Plateau. "The lack of provisions made us think very seriously of sacrificing one of our ponies for food, for we were on half rations, and felt every hour an increasing appetite," Manly wrote. It was on this eighth day of their land journey that a change of geography and trails followed gives the men renewed hope and encouragement that their remote journey would soon be coming to an end. In "From Vermont to California," Manly recorded that he and his men were high on the mountain above the timberline but soon find their way to lower elevations and a larger or wider trail to follow: "We now seemed to be on a northern slope, and the hills seemed destitute of timber. Soon our little trail merged into a larger one, and we thought we would be coming to some valley."[82]

The view north from the Wasatch Plateau stretches down to the top of Spanish Fork Canyon. Manly wrote, "On the eighth day our horse-tracks came out into a large trail which was on a down grade leading in a northward direction."

Manly also recorded an important directional observation: "On the eighth day our horse-tracks came out into a large trail which was on a down grade leading in a northward direction."[83] These three data points—traveling north, on a downgrade, finding a larger trail to follow—help pinpoint Manly's location. My reading of the source indicates he had come to the point where the Wasatch Plateau is bordered to the west by Sanpete Valley and to the north by Spanish Fork Canyon. At this northwestern point of the plateau, he would have needed to descend the plateau to continue his journey to safety. This he did on the western slope, close to the location of present-day Indianola, Utah. Arriving on the Sanpete Valley floor, Manly would have found the larger Indian trail on a downward slope leading north, as he explained. Here Manly would have camped for his eighth night. Little did he know that his journey to "Mormonee" would be ending the next day. Camping on the northern end of Sanpete Valley, approximately twenty miles from Hobble Creek, Manly's expedition needed only to continue north to Spanish Fork Canyon and then follow the canyon northwest to the Utah Valley and Hobble Creek.

If Manly had begun his land journey in the Uinta Basin, which is to the northeast of Spanish Fork Canyon, and then summited and traveled along the Uinta Mountains at "a great elevation" for days, this path could not have led him to the south end of Utah Valley, more than fifty miles south of Salt Lake City.

9/25/2011, Sunday, Day 43, Trek Day 8

Wasatch Plateau to Sanpete Valley

Today is a beautiful day with a cloudless sky of blue. This is the day that Dallas and I anticipate coming off of the plateau and down to the Sanpete Valley. We start early at 8:00 and begin walking in a north-northwest direction along the plateau. It is very evident that the plateau is gradually turning to the left or northwest direction. Ahead of us lies Spanish Fork Canyon that Manly travels down on his ninth day. We are right on track. It is so important that the miles and directions match to a tee what Manly experienced. The leaves on the trees have continually changed with the cold nights. More and more yellows and oranges appear on the aspens.

We are now stopping for an early 10:30 lunch and deciding what direction we are going to take in coming off of the plateau. We are looking in a northwest direction down a canyon that leads to Indianola, Utah. This location is a very probable spot for Manly to head down off of the mountain. From our lookout we can see straight down to the valley floor and on to the Spanish Fork Canyon. It is important to remember that Manly comes off of the mountain on his eighth day and arrives in Hobble Creek on his ninth day. We will determine the distance and see if it is possible to walk from where we are to Hobble Creek in two days. That is a very important fact to determine. There is no other mountain range in the area that allows for Manly to come off the mountain, walk north to Spanish Fork Canyon, and arrive at Hobble Creek in two days.

In researching Manly's route from the Green River to his land trek, this is the only location that is not clearly identified by factual

---

recording of Manly or researched by myself. This location is probable, but only that. His coming off the mountain could be a canyon to the north or south. However, we are close, and I know that if I were Manly or the Ute Indians, this canyon seems very likely to be where I would exit the Wasatch Plateau. I will write this evening as to the time it took us to reach the Sanpete Valley.

We are a day and a half from this tremendous journey ending. Before I start walking down, I look across the Sanpete Valley to Mount Nebo. It is dusted in snow and towers over the valley. Salt Canyon lies to the south and was the canyon Wákara traveled when he guided the Mormon leaders to Manti in August of 1849. So much history and wonder standing on top of the plateau. Many times I wish I could have been with Manly on this journey, to understand his personality and listen to his reason for the decisions that were made. Manly was truly a man that carried the fabric of American exploration and freedom throughout these western lands.

We have been walking for forty-five minutes and have already dropped in elevation several hundred feet. Walking downhill, we are covering ground much faster. I am looking over the Sanpete Valley, which is well defined. The valley floor is flat and grassy. To the south, I can see Manti. Weather is warmer as we drop down. I will close for now.

It is now 12:30 and we are well past halfway of reaching the valley floor. We have been walking for an hour and a half. Warmer weather greets us as we continue down the mountain. Manly would have welcomed this change in climate. His clothing and shoes were much worn, according to the journal description by Lorton, when they arrived at Hobble Creek. Dallas is enjoying the walk and is leading me down. The low-lying foothills are now beginning to rise over us. Looking back to the top of the plateau I have to look up on a forty-five-degree angle. All is very calm and quiet. We are not experiencing the wind like we did on top. This is a fun day.

We are now in the grasslands of Sanpete Valley. This would have been the first time Manly walked in Sanpete Valley. We have moved very fast due to the downgrade. It is 1:30 in the afternoon. It only took us 2½ hours to reach the valley floor. This is surprising to me, but in reviewing Manly's journal, his day 8 moves fast and he walked in a north direction on the valley floor. We have not reached Thistle Creek yet, but when we do, we will turn in a north direction towards Spanish Fork Canyon. I estimate that it will take forty-five minutes to reach the low point of the Sanpete Valley before we can turn north. I will update when we reach the turning point north.

We now have arrived at Highway 89 and will turn north like Manly did. It is 3:00 in the afternoon and we have traveled thirteen miles in 3½ hours. Dallas and I feel good with our progress. I have decided to take some time and write. Dallas has continued northward on Highway 89. I will just have to catch up to him. I am writing at a historical marker designating that in 1865 an Indian massacre occurred with a family that was farming the land. The 1800s provided adventures, new lands, and dangers all at the same time. We will walk an estimated two or three more hours and then camp.

I am now closing out one of the most enjoyable walking days of the journey. When we came to Highway 89 near the Sanpete River bottom, we turned northward, just as Manly remembered, and walked another three hours or nine miles. It is now 6:00 p.m. and we have finished our monumental day of coming off of the Wasatch Plateau and walking northward in Sanpete Valley. We walked past Birdseye, Utah, and are very close to Thistle, Utah, which is located at the mouth of Spanish Fork Canyon. Just like Manly, we are on track to arrive at Hobble Creek in the late afternoon or early evening of the ninth day. I estimate that we are seventeen to twenty miles away from Hobble Creek. As we are getting closer to Spanish Fork Canyon, the Sanpete Valley narrows into a small canyon that leads in a downward direction. We are right on the trail that Manly details. As the Sanpete Valley narrows, the looming mountains of Spanish Fork grow larger and larger. Manly and his men must have known with the well-worn trail they were following and the ending of Sanpete Valley, a change of finding help was close at hand. Little did they know it would be on the very next day.

The autumn colors are striking as the late afternoon sun plays off of the willows and cottonwood trees. Without the traffic of Highway 89, not a sound would be heard. The sun is making its way down over the western ridgeline of the valley, and the shadows seem magical as they race up the eastern slopes of the Wasatch Plateau. Tonight is a good night, with anticipation of the journey ending tomorrow at Hobble Creek. It is getting late and time to close for the day.

Good night.

CHAPTER ELEVEN

Arrival and Reunion in Utah Valley

ON MANLY'S NINTH DAY OF LAND TRAVEL, HE AND HIS MEN CONTINUED walking in a northern direction, passing where the current community of Birdseye, Utah, is located. Traveling on this larger trail, he makes mention that "soon our little trail merged into a larger one" for another five miles.[1] Manly would have turned in a northwest direction into Spanish Fork Canyon, following it down into Utah Valley and Hobble Creek. The men's spirits were high as the trail widened and elevations dropped. As the Spanish Fork Canyon ended and opened into the Utah Valley, Manly remarked, "We did come out into a wide valley with some appearance of fertility."[2] It was on this ninth day, in the late afternoon, that Manly's fortunes once again turned for the better when they encountered an emigrant camp in Utah Valley at Hobble Creek: "On the ninth day we came into a large valley, and near night came in sight of a few covered wagons, a part of a train that intended going on a little later over the southern route to Los Angeles but were waiting for the weather to get a little cooler, for a large part of the route was over almost barren deserts."[3]

As previously discussed, it was on this day that William Lorton, a California-bound emigrant, recorded in his journal the emergence of the Manly party from Spanish Fork Canyon. The entry bears reproducing in full:

> September 30th was the Sabbath. Mr [Lewis] Granger preached a sermon on profanity &c. The meeting was held under the trees, under which sat a large assemblage of emigrants, & a number of

Manly and his companions traveled down Spanish Fork Canyon and arrived at the Mormon settlements in Utah Valley on September 30, 1849. PHOTOGRAPH COURTESY LAYNE V. NAYLOR/SHUTTERSTOCK.COM

Indians with their rifles & arrows stood a little ways off listening to they knew not what. The ladies sat in the tent. While engaged in the discourse the team with my things arrived. Not long after I see 5 men with 2 horses packed coming down the big kanyon to the S. east. I went to meet them & learned they were Green River floaters that had left [Charles M.] Dallas, made canoes & floated down Green River to the Colerado. They said they had had a hard time of it & nearly all lost their lives dashing amonge the rocks & down rappids & over falls. They had all lost their fire arms except one, & would have starved to death but for Indian Walker who gave them as much as they could eat, & traded the horses to them for amunition & clothes, put them on a trail & told them it was 8 sleeps to the valley. The Indians were very kind to them. They had hardly any clothing & shoes on them. They said it had been very cold on the mounts, that they had seen mountains of every shape & form. Walker, who is named after the great mountaineer, gave them a map of the country in the sand. He would heap up the sand for mountains, the valleys in between & mark out the roads & rivers with a stick.[4]

For Manly's part, his record confirms that he and his men conveyed the details of their ordeal: "We camped here and told them of the hardships we had passed through."[5]

Lorton's journal entry verifies several important details of Manly's travel timeline. First, Manly and his men had just come off the mountain or mountains, and they reported how cold it had been. As discussed, traveling on the Wasatch Plateau put them at elevations that exceeded 10,000 feet, while they would not have encountered these high-altitude conditions if they had traveled across the Uinta Basin. Second, their clothing was extremely worn and in very poor condition. One can only imagine what state their shoes were in after traveling 415 miles down the waters of the Green and then walking 175 miles across the Utah Territory.[6] Third, Manly arrived at Hobble Creek on September 30. Though according to "From Vermont to California" Manly mentioned to the emigrant train that he and his men had been traveling for five weeks,[7] and according to *Death Valley in '49* he was on the river "for three weeks,"[8] previously reviewed research shows that he departed Lombard Crossing on August 20. Manly arrived at Hobble Creek on September 30, and, with my conclusion that his land trek took ten days, he would have met Wákara on the banks of the Green on September 21, making thirty-three days on the river. Subtracting two of the days for Manly's party to construct their canoes after Ashley Falls, the men spent thirty-one days, or four weeks and three days, traveling on the river. The average distance per day would have been just over thirteen miles a day, a much more reasonable pace than twenty miles a day, which they would have had to accomplish had they been on the river for only three weeks, as *Death Valley in '49* incorrectly reports.

Manly recorded his relief at finding the emigrant company and that they treated him and his men with hospitality. The train "seemed to have plenty of food" and gave the new arrivals a hearty meal, which "was the very thing we needed."[9] That evening, Manly's group realized the opportunity the wagon train presented them in their continued quest to reach California. They wanted to see if they might accompany the train as it took the southern route to California. They learned that two men could join with no difficulty; any more than that would require buying more supplies. "We went into our own camp," Manly recalled, "and between that time and morning we had a discussion over the situation, and could see no other way than to accept any place we could get, and if no better way could be found, we could go to Salt Lake and get some flour and bacon, and with our two ponies could follow along."[10]

The mood during these discussions between Manly, Rogers, Walton, and the Hazelrig brothers must have been very serious. These men together had endured unimagined trials, and they had relied upon each other for survival. Now, suddenly, the group of five began to fracture, each following his own instincts to reach California. Manly did not relate that these discussions were difficult, but the men doubtless felt a mixture of emotions: relief that their isolation had come to end, uncertainty as to what lay ahead, and concern for each other's safety and welfare.

The day Manly met the emigrant company, Sunday, September 30, was a consequential one for the wagon train. The emigrants were presented with a plan for their travels and a document outlining rules of government for the journey.[11] Company member Adonijah Welch recorded, "The emigrants from the various states have gathered on Hobble Creek to the number of two hundred with nearly seventy wagons. . . . At the close he [Welch] gave notice that a meeting would be held forthwith to take measures for obtaining a guide and such regulations as would be necessary for safely persuing the southern route to California. . . . At the appointed hour the emigrants again met to receive and act upon the reports of the com[m]ittees. . . . It also provides for the origination of the entire [company] into seven divisions and for the election of a captain over each division who shall hold the office of captain of the guard one night in the week."[12]

9/30/2012, Sunday Day 44, Trek Day 9

Sanpete Valley to Hobble Creek, Utah

The ninth day of following Manly's land route began with a wonderfully clear, crisp morning. Not a cloud in the sky. The sun is rising over the Wasatch Plateau and creeping down the mountains on the west side of the Sanpete Valley. Quietly standing by Thistle Creek, it was enjoyable to see the water babble and dance as it flows northward. Not a large creek, but plenty of clear, cold water for the livestock in the area. Our goal today is to walk twenty miles, at three miles per hour, arriving at Hobble Creek in the late afternoon. Looking north as I walk, the valley floor continues to narrow as the canyon walls are closer together. The soils in the canyon are a brown color with abundant cedar trees growing on both sides. After walking two miles, I begin to see a change in the canyon area that I am going through. Thistle Creek seems to be rushing by me more quickly as I continue to walk down. In the distance and to the north of me, I can see a large vertical rise of layered rock, light brown to yellow in color, pointing to the western sky. This is much different than the dirt-filled hills that surround me. Getting closer and having walked three miles, I know that I am leaving Sanpete Valley and entering Spanish Fork Canyon.

Following Thistle Creek on the east side, Dallas and I arrive at the confluence of Thistle Creek to the left and Soldier Creek to the right. There, both join to form Spanish Fork River. At this point it is very noticeable that the direction of travel will turn from a northern route to a northwestern direction. To officially enter Spanish Fork Canyon, I place all my clothes and belongings with me over my head and wade through Soldier Creek at the confluence. Dallas just swims through the water. The water is brisk but not bone-chilling. I laughed thinking how many times Manly would have done the same thing, trying to keep his clothes and supplies dry.

As we begin to turn left into Spanish Fork Canyon, we encounter a landmark that Manly would not have seen. In 1983, there was a very large landslide that occurred, in which a natural dam of mud, rock, and debris was created, blocking the Spanish Fork River. We found ourselves climbing up several hundred feet to cross over the large landslide. On top, Spanish Fork Canyon clearly came into view. Sweeping to the left, running northwest, the change of leaving Sanpete Valley and entering Spanish Fork Canyon is clear. The mountains bordering the canyon seem higher as the drop of elevation winds to the northwest. I am amazed at the beautiful fall colors that cover both sides of the canyon. Red, orange, and yellow are everywhere.

Continuing to follow the river's path downward, I estimate that we have covered over ten miles in four hours. Within a short distance from entering Spanish Fork Canyon, to my right or northeast, Diamond Fork Canyon enters or drops into Spanish Fork Canyon. This is the canyon and location where the Dominguez and Escalante party entered Spanish Fork Canyon in 1776. Many historians have thought Manly followed this course as well.

As we continue to travel down the canyon, the elevation drop is very noticeable. There are some winding turns but also several long straight sections. The canyon continues to open up and the view of the western sky is continually growing larger. On one of the final turns in the canyon, the Utah Valley comes into view. I can see across the valley to the Oquirrh Mountains. This change to open space, and leaving the mountains and freezing temperatures, would have been a welcomed relief. We are out of the canyon now and can see as far north as the Traverse Mountains that lead into Salt Lake Valley. Knowing the trail Manly was following turns to the right and leads to Hobble Creek, he would have had six more miles to travel to reach the safety of other emigrants waiting to travel to California. Walking three miles per hour, we will be at Hobble Creek in two hours or at 3:00 in the afternoon. Lorton records in his journal that he sees Manly and his men coming out the canyon in the afternoon. It is fun to know we took the same number of days as Manly did to walk this section of the expedition 163 years ago and are arriving at approximately the same time.

It is now 3:00 p.m. and we have arrived at the town of Springville, where Hobble Creek quietly runs through on its way to Utah Lake. My feet are in the cool, clear water of the creek. Dallas and I have traveled twenty miles today in seven hours. What an exciting feeling to have arrived after all the miles logged on the river and land. I keep thinking of what Manly would have thought as he came in contact with other emigrants for the first time in over

> a month and a half. Even though he knew that his journey to Cal-
> ifornia was not yet complete, the safety and security of being with
> others would have been comforting. This is such a milestone for me
> and my research. I am so thankful for everyone, especially Dallas,
> who has helped me along the way. I will end for now.

The next morning, October 1, 1849, Manly and his men learned more about their prospects for joining the wagon train. "Some of the boys next day arranged to work for their board," he wrote, "and the others would be taken along if they would furnish themselves with flour and bacon."[13] If they went, they would be expected to help with camp duties. Reviewing their financial situation, Manly found that "John Rogers had a dollar and a half and I had thirty dollars, which was all the money we had in our camp."[14] With the train not expected to leave for two or three more weeks, giving the deserts to the south a chance to cool off, Manly and one of the Hazelrig brothers set out with their ponies to acquire provisions. Manly wrote that he and Hazelrig intended to travel north to Salt Lake City, which they learned was some sixty miles north.[15] With this agreement, according to Lorton's journal, all of Manly's men except one (who is not specified) had decided to continue across the southern route to California.

On the night of October 1, at the end of their tenth day of land travel, Manly and Hazelrig reached "a Mormon fort," or Fort Utah. Manly incorrectly references its location on Hobble Creek, but they had left the emigrant train at Hobble Creek, seven miles back; Fort Utah was actually on the Provo River.[16] In his writings, Manly did not provide a description of the fort, but other sources fill in the picture of its unique characteristics and purpose. Brigham D. Madsen gives a brief history and description of Fort Utah in *A Forty-Niner in Utah*:

Brigham Young [sent] thirty-three men under John S. Higbee in March 1849 to make a settlement at Fort Utah. The party built their fort on the south side of Provo River at what today would be 1st North and 18th West in the city of Provo. It was 300 feet long, 150 feet wide, and was surrounded by a 14-foot high stockade with a bastion within, on which the settlers mounted a six-pound iron cannon for protection from their good friends, the Utes. Log cabins, built of split box elder logs with lumber and dirt roofs, were placed side by side around the perimeter of the fort, and a corral for night herding was situated in the southeast corner of the stockade. Each cabin has two cloth covered windows and a few could boast of split-log floors. In May, Isaac Higbee was appointed to replace John S. Higbee as leader of the settlement.

By summer there were about forty families engaged in farming 225 acres near the fort but there was a season of real privation somewhat ameliorated by the passage of groups of California gold-seekers through the valley who traded some goods to the destitute settlers. A successful harvest in the fall relieved the scarcity of food, but other goods were in short supply.

By November 27, 1849, there were 57 log houses occupying the 17½ acres of Fort Utah, a sawmill, and a tannery.[17]

When Manly and Hazelrig arrived at the fort they realized no men were there, but they found another emigrant train and approached the last wagon, where a shocked Manly received a welcome surprise: "As I rode around and looked into the front of the last wagon, a woman turned around to see who had come, and as she looked at me I was surprised and delighted to find it was Mrs. [Sarah] Bennett whom you remember we could not find at Council Bluffs. I was more than glad to see her face again I assure you."[18] Months ago, and hundreds of miles back, Manly had searched for the Bennetts so they could travel west together but had finally given up and set off with the Dallas company. One can only imagine the excitement and joyous reunion. Lewis and Sarah spent the next part of the day talking about their separate journeys and how each had survived the untamed lands of the west. Then Asabel Bennett arrived, having been out herding cattle, and Manly noted, with some understatement, that he "was glad enough to see me, I assure you."[19] In fact, the two men "had an all night story to tell each other of our separate adventures since we left Wisconsin."[20]

It was during this evening reunion that Manly finally figured out how they had missed each other back in Nebraska. Manly had searched for Bennett at the crossing of the Missouri River in Council Bluffs, since he "knew of no place where people crossed the river," but the Bennetts had "crossed farther up at a place called Kanesville, a Mormon crossing, and followed up the Platte river on the north side."[21] One consequence of this separation was that Manly had been low of supplies, since Bennett had had all his gear, including clothing, gun, and Winnebago pony.[22] Manly was disappointed to learn that the horse was gone, having broken free along the trail and followed a herd of bison.[23]

As the newly reunited friends enjoyed dinner together, Manly learned of the Bennetts' plans for completing their journey to California. After many discussions and arguments among their party, they had agreed to try "a new route for wagons," the "Southern route" to San Bernardino.[24] Like the wagon train at Hobble Creek, the group at Fort Utah was waiting a few weeks for temperatures to cool. Bennett further informed Manly that the wagon train had hired a Mormon named Jefferson Hunt to guide the group. Hunt "had more than one wife, but he had convinced them that he knew something about the road."[25] Each wagon would pay him ten dollars to guide their train.[26]

Manly's encounter with the Bennetts suddenly opened up another option for getting to California. When he explained that he was on his way to Salt Lake City to get supplies and join the wagon train at Hobble Creek, Bennett told him "I should go no farther after grub for he had plenty and I could go with him, and need not do any camp duty either."[27]

10/1/2013, Sunday, Day 45, Trek Day 10

Hobble Creek to Fort Utah

Today is the last day of retracing Manly's long journey from the emigrant trail crossing on the Green River to Fort Utah. One hundred and sixty-four years ago to the day, on October 1, 1849, Manly left Hobble Creek with Hazelrig heading north to Salt Lake City. As Dallas and I leave the quiet flowing waters of Hobble Creek, we travel north through Springville and, wanting to leave the busy part of the city, turn in a northwest direction. I wanted to walk on the open back roads that soon led to open grasslands and farming fields. It feels better to walk in open areas, as Manly would have done. The ground is flat and continually opens up to the Utah Valley ahead of us. Looking to the east, the same majestic Wasatch Mountains stand strong and tall as they did in Manly's day. I imagine Manly would have kept constant sight of them, knowing he was now leaving the mountains that he had spent the last week in and was now traveling in more open and easier terrain. Walking along, we passed an apple tree and I picked an apple. My new red companion lasted with me for about ten minutes before he disappeared in my mouth. I know Manly did not run into any fruit trees, but if he had, what a wonderful treat he would have had.

Dallas and I have been walking for an hour and a half and have covered four miles. We continue to walk in a northwest direction. Knowing that Fort Utah is only three and a half miles away, I can only imagine the wonderful surprise Manly would have had in meeting Sarah Bennett at Fort Utah for the first time since they were separated at the Missouri River months before. Dallas and I both continue to walk at a constant pace, realizing each step is one closer to finishing the journey. I will close for now and write again when I am closer to the fort.

～

Dallas and I are now approximately one mile from Fort Utah. Throughout the whole journey, I am constantly thinking what Manly would have felt or realized. Knowing I am so close to the fort, there must have been that moment that Manly first sees the fort from the distance. . . .

Walking for twenty minutes, I look across a vacant grassy field and see the replica of the old Fort Utah. Box-shaped walls standing over ten feet tall with two raised fortress corners become visible. I can see in the middle of the fort is a cannon placed on a raised platform looking over the walls. Dallas and I have made it! Walking up to the fort, I feel rewarded. All that surrounds me is quiet, clear, and calm. I touch the walls and once again place myself in 1849 and imagine the feelings and emotions that Manly would have had. Not only seeing the fort and the events surrounding it, but finding Mrs. Bennett standing by her wagon. What a complete feeling of relief and joy Manly would have had. Once again, I can only imagine that special time both shared as time stood still.

Finishing our journey in the early afternoon, Dallas and I have walked seven and a half miles from Hobble Creek to Fort Utah in three hours. I am so thankful for all the people that have helped me along the way. I can't list everyone because there are so many. Dallas has always believed in me and this project. I am so thankful for him and our strong love for each other. With the ending of retracing Manly and his journey, I now look forward to compiling all the materials and completing the book. Indeed, Manly said it best: "I am content."

I end for now.

After camping that night with the Bennetts, Manly arose the next morning to continue discussions about joining them. "After breakfast," he recounted, "Mr. Bennett said to me:—'Now Lewis I want you to go with me; I have two wagons and two drivers and four yoke of good oxen and plenty of provisions. I have your outfit yet, your gun and ammunition and your two good hickory shirts which are just in time for your present needs. You need not do any work. You just look around and kill what game you can for us, and this will help as much as anything, you can do.'"[28] Manly accepted the offer, reporting, "So it seemed to be well fixed." His concerns quickly refocus on his companion Hazelrig, as well as the others who were waiting at Hobble Creek. Food supplies still needed to be secured for the men. Inquiring with other emigrants camped at Fort Utah, Manly was able to find the necessary foodstuffs. Manly was the only one who had much money, including sixty dollars he got from Dallas for his pony, so he paid for all the supplies and sent Hazelrig back to Hobble Creek with the rest of his money, telling him the men could help themselves to all Manly's gear there, "as my own I had now nothing to fear, and gave all over to the other boys to help them along."[29] Manly's insistence on ensuring the safety of and provisions for his companions exemplifies his true character. He was elected captain of the expedition on the shores of the Green River as they began their float and steadily maintained that responsibility to the day they separated. No loss of life or tragedy occurred under his watch of 415 miles down the Green and 175-mile trek across the Utah Territory.

Time was short, and with his responsibility to his companions ful-filled, Manly focused on preparing for the final push to California with the Jefferson Hunt wagon train. William Lorton recorded that the group at Hobble Creek departed October 2, but Manly did not detail the date or time that the Bennett wagon or the other emigrants left from Fort Provo. Because the Hunt wagon train was at Election Creek on October 3 (where Payson, Utah, is now located),[30] there is a strong likelihood that Manly and the Bennetts left Fort Utah on the morning of October 2. If so, they would have traveled the approximately eighteen miles in one and a half days.

On October 3, the train of more than seventy wagons and "a big drove of horses and cattle, perhaps five hundred in all," was formed into divisions with elected officers and a schedule for departure south.[31] In his entry this day, Adonijah Welch called the wagon train the "San Joaquin Company,"[32] but in short time, as they traversed the desert, many started to call it instead the "Sand Walking Company," as Manly did.[33] By the time stragglers caught up and the various companies of the wagon train joined together, there were 104 to 107 wagons total.[34] Though Manly, Rogers, the Hazelrig brothers, and Walton ended up in the same wagon train, there is no record that they renewed their association on the trail. Manly did note that ultimately, much farther south, "of the Green River party only Rodgers [sic] and myself remained with this train."[35]

As Manly continued southward to California with the Hunt wagon train, he continued to have dramatic experiences. He had to make decisions that balanced life and death for all and gave new meaning to devoted friendship and dependability upon each other to survive.

These historical events are beyond the scope of the present book, but two other thoroughly researched books pick up the story. The first book, *Into the Jaws of Hell* by Tom Sutak, details the travels of the Jefferson Hunt wagon train generally. The second book, *Escape from Death Valley* by Leroy and Jean Johnson, details Manly and his companions' journey through the unknown lands of Death Valley on their way to the goldfields of California after leaving the Hunt wagon train. Both books bring Manly's adventures to life and give a better understanding of the struggles and deep devotions he carried for all whom he met. Readers may also be interested in Deborah A. Fox's *The Man Who Beat Death Valley, Based on the TRUE STORY of William Lewis Manly*, which presents Manly's adventures as a graphic novel.

Evidence that William Lewis Manly traveled as far as present-day Green River, Utah

1. Warning of the upcoming canyons of the Colorado River
2. Warning of hostile Indians downriver
3. Travel in a northwest direction
4. Directions for Manly to follow fresh horse tracks
5. Observations of the spurs of the mountain
6. Directions to cross trails that were later known as the Old Spanish Trail
7. Barren valley
8. Water holes
9. No water or streams
10. Crossing the Old Spanish Trail a second time
11. Mountains leading north
12. Canyon up into mountains leading north
13. Snowbanks
14. Left Wákara's trail
15. Three nights to top of mountain
16. Hunting, planting, and gathering roots
17. Cold on the mountains
18. Trail leading north
19. Spanish Fork Canyon

In the narrative, I provide a detailed explanation of each piece of evidence.

CHAPTER TWELVE

M. S. McMahon's Story

"It will be remembered that the author and his friends, after a perilous voyage down Green River, halted at the camp of the Indian chief, Walker, and there separated, the Author and four companions striking to Salt Lake, while McMahon and Field remained behind, fully determined to go on down the river."
—WILLIAM LEWIS MANLY, *DEATH VALLEY IN '49*, 279

AFTER WILLIAM LEWIS MANLY RECOUNTED HIS TALE IN *DEATH VALLEY in '49*, including the rest of his harrowing journey to California, he included at the end of the book a forty-page letter from Morgan S. McMahon. In his account, McMahon wrote his recollections of events and travels after he and Richard Field separated from Manly, and these details become pivotal in validating Manly's own story. Just as Manly did in his book, I have designated chapter 12 in my book as McMahon's story.

McMahon's references to himself in the letter are very limited, making definitive identification possible only through extensive research. He referred to himself only as M. S. McMahon and wrote that after he arrived in California in 1850, "I remained in the mines until July fourth, 1851, exactly one year from the time I entered Sacramento, when I started home by way of Niceragua [*sic*]. In due time after an interesting trip, I arrived home and again entered upon the study of my chosen profession, graduated from an honorable college, and am now, as you know, practicing my profession on the sea shore."[1]

Morgan S. McMahon was born in 1825 in Indiana.[2] On March 28, 1848, the year before his journey west, McMahon at age twenty-two married Rodah Ann Cooper, age seventeen, of Van Buren County, Iowa.[3] Knowing McMahon left his new wife to seek the goldfields of California, it becomes clear that one of the reasons he would return to Iowa after his one-year stay at Sacramento was to rejoin Rodah. Traveling back to Iowa in 1851 by sea from California to the isthmus of Panama, then overland to the Atlantic Ocean and then by sea again back to the United States, McMahon intended to enroll in and graduate from "an honorable college." Knowing that Morgan was married in Iowa, it seemed probable that he attended college in that same state. In fact, records of the Alumni College of Physicians and Surgeons at Keokuk Medical College indicate that McMahon and nineteen other graduates completed schooling there in 1858.[4] After graduation in 1858, McMahon continued to reside in Iowa until 1862; the census of 1860 lists his home as Union, Davis Co., Iowa. He and Rhoda had a son, John, born in 1855.[5]

The McMahons moved to California in 1862, and Morgan continued to practice medicine in the San Francisco Bay area, in the town of Fairfield. In 1867, he appeared on a voter registration list in Solano, California, and his middle name comes to light: Morgan Strange McMahon.[6] In 1870, he resided in San Jose, where he was presumably living when he wrote to Manly for *Death Valley in '49*.[7] In 1881 he was living in Oakland, then in Santa Cruz in 1889. Morgan S. McMahon died in Santa Cruz on March 26, 1898, at age 72.[8] His wife, Rhoda, died October 13, 1912, in Alameda, California.

Some forty years after their shared experiences, Manly contacted McMahon and asked him to give "a synopsis of the history of incidents, experience, and observations of our mutual friend, Richard Field and myself," after they separated from Manly at the Green River.[9] As he began doing so, McMahon echoed Manly's veneration for Wákara, speaking of "the generous old chief Walker." He also detailed his location "on the west bank of the river near the mouth of the 'great seven days cañon.'" Wákara earlier had indicated this canyon, "shaking his head as if to say:—'Awful bad canon.'"[10] To say the Colorado and Grand Canyon are close is much more feasible from the San Rafael Desert than the Uinta Basin. It should also be noted that five years later, Solomon Carvalho, traveling with the John C. Frémont party, wrote of an "Indian village" at the crossroads of the Green and the Spanish Trail, at "a fertile spot on the western bank of it."[11]

When Manly and his men left McMahon and Field at the Green River on September 22, it was their understanding that the two men would either continue down the Green with the hopes of floating to California or follow Wákara on his fall buffalo hunting trip east.[12] Manly recalled, "Mac, and Field still thought it a bad idea to follow the advice or act on the information of an ignorant Indian, whom they could not understand, and would rather follow the Indians, they here were going East instead of West."[13] Contemplating their options without the leadership of Manly, both McMahon and Field struggled to make the right choice. They worked on the boats, and then "after a day or two Field lost courage and finally determined to go no further down the river." Wákara "in the meantime had repeated his friendly warnings appertaining to the great danger in going further down the river." McMahon maintained something of a resolve to keep on the river, though he admitted, "You know that I was the biggest coward of the whole seven; but I assumed courage and told Field that I would go down the river alone; and, for a time, I thought I would do so; but after some reflection I concluded that, perhaps, discretion was the better part [of] valor, and reluctantly gave it up. We now decided to follow you, or to take some other unknown route and try to make our escape out of this most perilous condition." As both men began to prepare to follow Manly's path to safety and Salt Lake City, once again the uncertainty of direction and lack of confidence brought another change in the path they would follow: "After making pack-saddles, and getting almost ready to start," McMahon recalled, "we were, through Walker's kindness and persuasiveness, overcome, and consented to go with him, feeling confident that we would not starve to death while with him. We did not now have Manly with his long experience, and his old rusty, but always trusty, rifle as a sure defense against possible hunger and starvation. The old chief, and, in fact, the whole tribe, seemed pleased when we consented to go with them."[14] They decided that following Wákara and "the twenty-two Indians" gave them the best chance of survival.

With preparations made, Wákara and his band crossed the Green with McMahon and Field. When they reached the east bank, they camped for the night. The next morning, they were on their way, "Walker having informed us that he intended going up into the buffalo country on the head-waters of Grand [Colorado] river."[15] From the Old Spanish Trail crossing at the Green River, they would have had to travel east along the southern end of the Book Cliff Mountains to reach the headwaters of the Colorado River.

The records of early Euro-American explorers corroborate that the headwaters of the Colorado River in present-day Colorado were a place to hunt bison. Warren Angus Ferris, an explorer, mountain man, writer, and cartographer, detailed in writing and cartography that "the exact range of the Bison westward in the year 1835" passes directly through the area of the headwaters. Properly identifying the headwaters of the Colorado River as buffalo habitat, Ferris's observations are consistent with McMahon's detailed explanations of the buffalo fields on the headwaters of the Colorado River.[16] In an article written in the *Utah Historical Quarterly*, author Stephen P. Van Hoak explained the context for such long journeys by the Utes to hunt bison: "By 1841, nine thousand mounted Northern Shoshoni and Western Utes were in direct competition for a rapidly diminishing resource—the western buffalo. As western bison became increasingly scarce in the 1840s, buffalo hunting became far more problematic for Native Americans. Rather than searching nearby rivers for herds of buffalo, ever increasing numbers of Ute and Shoshoni now had to go on 'big hunts' in order to find significant herds of bison. They were compelled to travel longer distances to the east, where buffalo herds were larger, and consequently spent ever-greater periods of time on the hunt."[17]

McMahon and Field spent nine days with Wákara's band and apparently received special treatment, being considered Wákara's "honored guests."[18] McMahon remarked that the entire party was mounted on horseback, but it is unclear if Wákara would have had enough horses to carry twenty-four people, including the two guests. More likely, some were on foot, as was more traditional. If the party had traveled twelve to fifteen miles per day, they would have gone 120 miles east in nine days, far enough to reach the Colorado, but McMahon indicated they did not make it that far, suggesting a slower pace. Having women and children on foot, as well as a herd of livestock, would have slowed the party down, perhaps to something more like six or seven miles a day.[19]

McMahon observed that as they began to travel, "we set out across a not entirely barren plain, for there was much sage-brush, and several varieties of cactus."[20] Other explorers and emigrants traveling the same trail east of the Green River similarly commented on the sparseness, which they found to be relative but not entire. Gwinn Harris Heap wrote in July 1853 that east of the Green on the Spanish Trail had only "a scanty growth of stunted wild sage and cacti," while Solomon Carvalho commented the next year, "The divide between Grand River and the Green River is barren and sterile to a degree."[21]

As the first day of travel ended, the party camped "close up to the foot of a range of rugged, rocky mountains, where we found water." One spring along the foothills of the Book Cliffs, called Browns Wash Spring, is located nine miles from the Green River near Middle Horse Canyon, the approximate distance the Wákara party would have traveled per day. Two other springs within twenty miles of the Green River and Old Spanish Trail crossing are Trough Spring and Mud Spring, and these springs were very likely used in subsequent days of traveling.

On the second day of his journey with the hunting party, McMahon spoke again of the barren, open country and detailed the lack of food; in fact, he called it "the second day of starvation." Their hardship only worsened, McMahon wrote:

> All went well for four or five days, when we all got entirely out of food except a few ounces of flour which we had hidden away for a possible emergency. During the following two days and nights all were entirely without food except the two little children, whom you no doubt remember. We gave their mother a little flour now and then which she mixed with a little milk which one of the cows afforded, for the little ones. These Indians did not seem to suffer for want of food; even when we were starving, they appeared happy and contented; and one young fellow would sing all day long while we were starving.

Fortunately, some of the Indians found and killed a wild cat and two rabbits, while their traveling companions had no such luck in hunting: "We got nothing." Later that evening, in camp,

> one of the boys brought over to our tent a quarter of the cat, which was more than a fair share of the whole supply, as twenty-two of them had only the two little rabbits and three quarters of the unfortunate cat. We boiled and boiled the cat's hind leg, but never got it done. We waited as long as we possibly could, gave up in despair and put a little flour into the broth to thicken it, and drank it. It was not good but much better [than] the meat of the cat. That cat and the rabbits were all the twenty-four of us had to eat after fasting two days, until late in the evening of the next day.[22]

On estimated day three (McMahon was inconsistent in recording his days with Wákara, as evidenced by his recounting that "all went well for four or five days,"), the food situation improved a little. Wákara took "one son" with him and scouted ahead toward a nearby mountain range. When the main group caught up to them at a small canyon where "we found them with a fine mountain sheep which they had killed and brought down to the dim, little-used trail where we camped." Once again, the Utes shared with McMahon and Field, giving them a full quarter of the sheep, "while the twenty-two Indians had the rest."[23]

As the days wore on and Wákara's party continued east with little food, both McMahon and Field became increasingly discouraged, hoping to turn north toward the California Trail.[24] McMahon's travel to the east and desire to head north help us determine their location, and it is important to bear in mind that McMahon could be confident in directions because Field had a compass with him.[25]

On about the eighth day, they had no food, and late in the afternoon, "we crossed the fresh trail of some other band of roving red-skins." Wákara and two of his men left to investigate this other band of Indians, traveling southeast. Later that night, one of the men returned and informed them that the wandering band had been found and that the group was to accompany him back to "their new-found friends."[26]

Now McMahon and Field seriously reconsidered traveling with the hunting party. Wákara was changing his direction of travel from east to southeast, and both men understood they were traveling in an opposite direction from their goal of reaching the safety of the emigrant trail and Fort Bridger. "We were almost starved to death," McMahon recounted, "and had about come to the conclusion that we could be obliged to make some change." They decided to part company with Wákara's band and began making plans. McMahon realized they were a "considerable distance" from the Green River, though "probably not more than one hundred, or one hundred and twenty miles from the place where we parted" from Manly.[27] Such an estimate supposed a travel rate of eleven to thirteen miles per day, but as previously noted, the party likely would not have been able to cover that distance with tribal members on foot and herding cattle.

Author's Note: Morgan S. McMahon provided very limited details of his journey after leaving Manly at the Green River. He and fellow forty-niner Richard Field traveled east with Chief Wákara for about nine days and then proceeded northward for the next six days. Analyzing what little information was given by McMahon, I prepared to retrace his steps as I did Manly's. I mapped the approximate route and determined the closest water springs they would have had to utilize in order to survive the dry, desolate lands. Rather than re-create the journey in fifteen days, I drove a four-wheel-drive truck and an off-road vehicle and covered the miles over four days. This on-site review allowed me to assess possibilities of where they might have traveled.

10/13–10/14/2013, McMahon and Field Trek Days 1–9

Green River in the San Rafael Desert to Westwater Canyon

The morning is bright and beautiful as the sun's rays make their daily entrance into Gunnison Valley [which I also call the San Rafael Desert elsewhere]. White clouds are streaming by overhead as I stand on the east banks of the Green River where the Old Spanish Trail crossed the Green. I am looking at the island, choked in tamarisk bushes, that was so critical in aiding early travelers crossing both east and west on the Green. Standing on the eastern riverbank, I think of the makeshift camp Wákara had set up before all left to the buffalo fields at the headwaters of the Colorado. I am anxious to take the final steps of my retracing McMahon's journey with Wákara and finding the mysteries of where they went and camped as they continued to the buffalo fields. Walking up a steep incline to the east from the riverbanks, I am able to quickly look over the flat lands of the Gunnison Valley to the Roan/Book Cliffs that I will be heading toward. I am ready.

Crossing over the flatlands of Gunnison Valley, I quickly find myself in the middle of alfalfa fields. The farmers here are pumping water from the Green River to bring life to their irrigated fields. The green fields expand over three miles to the east and south before the natural sage and cactus flora reclaim the barren flat lands. McMahon stated that he camps the first night at a spring, and the closest one from the river is Browns Wash Spring. It is approximately ten miles from the river and located at the base of the Book Cliffs. After leaving the alfalfa fields, the lands turn quickly to yellow color or hue. Once again I wonder if this is the yellow color that Manly refers to as he leaves the Green River.

Arriving at the base of the Book Cliffs, I turn up Middle Horse Canyon. It is a canyon that runs northwest. At the base of this canyon, I find the small spring of Browns Wash. The spring is small and is protected by the gray, towering Book Cliffs that constantly stand guard over it.

Traveling back down Middle Horse Canyon, I turn and travel to the southeast towards Hatch Mesa. It is the southernmost point of the Book Cliff Mountains. All the spurs of the Book Cliffs are ash gray in color. The mesas are spectacular and overlook the Gunnison Valley. Traveling over the flat lands on many unmarked dirt roads or trails, I quickly find my way around Hatch Mesa to Floy Wash. Arriving at Floy Wash, I turn northward and follow the wash up to Trough Spring. It is located at the mouth of Floy Canyon. Unlike the small spring at Browns Wash, Trough Spring is very large. There has been considerable construction work completed there this spring. Dirt mounds or retaining walls have been constructed to allow more water to be held and not run off. I am sure this work was completed by the cattle ranchers in the area to water their livestock. The pool of water shows a spectacular reflection of the tan, soiled Book Cliff Mountains and foothills to the north. The land remains very dry and shows the dry, crusty surface of cracking soils where water erosion marks from past rain storms have freely traveled. The only real vegetation in this region is large thistle bushes growing on the banks of the spring. They too are brown with the fall season. No cottonwood trees are present. I have traveled seven miles and estimate that at Trough Spring, Wákara would have camped on the second night.

In taking the southern route around Hatch Mesa from Middle Horse Canyon, there is a shortcut mesa to Trough Spring. From Middle Horse Canyon I traveled east between Hatch Mesa and Horse Mesa. As I climbed the gradual incline, I kept thinking if Wákara with his band and animals would have climbed this ridge. Walking up the small ridge for fifteen minutes, it is not a hard ridge to access and would have cut off an estimated four miles of travel. Again, I cannot say for a certainty this shortcut would have been the way Wákara went. Certainly seems logical. Once on top of the ridge I could look down to the east and clearly see the path to Trough Spring.

I now have traveled an estimated seventeen miles around Hatch Mesa or thirteen miles over the shortcut called Green River Gap. I am ready to move farther east. The landscape does not change. Dry, flat, barren lands with a chalky light-brown color stretch as far as I can see. I cannot help but imagine the discouraging thoughts McMahon would have as he traveled across these dry lands. His dream was California, land of opportunity. These flat dry plains and towering desolate mountains offered no hope.

As I had chosen to travel to the south of Hatch Mesa, I also choose to drop down from Trough Spring and travel south around Christmas Ridge. It is a smaller ridge that runs into the valley. I just keep thinking the path might be longer but easier to walk with cattle and women with children. I am sure Wákara's Utes were a strong-minded people, though, and I should give them more credit for living in this inhospitable land. Once around the south end of Christmas Ridge I again head to the northwest, up Crescent Canyon to Mud Spring. This distance is nine miles. Like the shortcut at Green River Gap, there is another shortcut through Thompson Pass. I circle around and take Thompson Pass as well. Once again, the pass is not steep and could have been used to save miles. I remember

McMahon stating that they went through a pass and at times were in the mountains. McMahon just does not give the detailed directions that I found with Manly's accounts. The springs that I am finding are easy to locate. There is limited plant growth around them, which can be seen from a distance. I now have traveled twenty-six miles, which I estimate took three days for McMahon. Traveling at the same time of year as McMahon, I find the weather is comfortable during the day and slightly cool in the evening. I have not seen any other animals besides antelope and crows. There is just not much out here!

Leaving Mud Spring, I travel back down in a southwest direction and follow the Book Cliff Mountains. The landscape does not change and I continue to traverse across very barren, dry lands. As I move further to the southeast and toward my destination of Thompson Springs, I-70 is in full view. Watching the vehicle traffic pass so quickly, I smile to think how slow the Wákara party traveled and what a fast-paced life we all experience now! There are certainly times in my life that walking in the open lands, uninterrupted by cell phones and laptops, provides me a lifeline. Following these travelers of the 1800s certainly gives purpose to life.

I arrive at Thompson Springs to find a small community busy with daily life. At one home on a back road, the children are jumping on a trampoline in the backyard. How fun, to live in such an open area. From past travels I know that due north, up Thompson Canyon Road and merging with Sego Canyon Road, there are treasured petroglyphs of past Indian generations in Thompson Wash. With these fantastic petroglyphs so close to me, I decide to take time and explore. I see images of small animals, buffalo and horses, white shields painted red, along with Indian figures with triangular torsos. The art style is Fremont, Archaic, Barrier Canyon, and modern Ute. As I view these petroglyphs, I think of how strong these early Indian peoples were. This land is so desolate; they would have had to be so strong to survive. I remember Manly recognizing this strong side of Wákara and how he provided for his Ute nation.

At Thompson Springs, the approximate trail that I have been retracing reaches the most southern direction. From here, I begin to turn northeast and follow the Roan/Book Cliff Mountains. Leaving Thompson Springs, I estimate that Wákara's hunting party would be on their fifth day of travel, having gone seventy-one miles. As I crisscross over the open lands, I now am traveling onto Windy Mesa

Rock art of bison and other figures at Thompson Springs near the Book Cliffs. Morgan S. McMahon recounted traveling through this area with Wákara's group as they went to hunt bison.

in the Grand Valley. All the dry washes from the Roan/Book Cliffs drain to the southeast before turning northeast and passing Thompson Springs, after which the washes drain to the southwest. Small change, but out here it is noticeable. I do not have a spring location within the ten-mile-per-day travel time that I have estimated for Wákara. My next scheduled stop where I think the Wákara party camped for the evening will be at Cisco Springs.

I have continued throughout the day again, traveling in a northeast direction. The exposed gray rock strata in the Book Cliffs are incredible. The lines slant slightly upward to the west. This land is truly a land that time has forgotten. Towards the end of the day, I find the dirt road that leads to Cisco Springs. Following the road in a northwest direction, by Danish Wash, I come over a slight hill and find Cisco Springs, literally an oasis in the desert. . . .

Abundant plant life surrounds the larger-than-expected spring. Cottonwood trees line the spring as well. They are in their fall colors of bright yellow. I quickly go to the spring and put my hands in the cool water. What a great experience. Isolated, quiet, and life-saving are these springs. I can only imagine the countless times these spring waters saved the lives of both human and animal. It is here that I estimate the Wákara party camped on their seventh night. With no spring location between Thompson Springs and Cisco Springs, the welcomed relief that all made the two-day journey to these spring waters would have been rewarding. I camp for the night at the spring and prepare for the very cool evening. All is quiet and remote. I find myself sitting and looking out over the horizon imagining what these early travelers would have been thinking about. Though over 150 years have passed between McMahon's travels and my retracing his steps, the thoughts of survival and living in these open lands remain the same, a connection that I will always hold and enjoy.

Morning comes early as the sun greets an open sky. No clouds in sight. It is cool but I am prepared with warm clothes. I bet McMahon and Field did not have much as far as warm clothing. Continuing in a northwest direction, I travel up Cottonwood Wash to the base of the Book Cliffs. Here I find a faint dirt road that goes northeast along the foothills of the Book Cliffs. I cross through endless dry washes and thread my way along the Book Cliffs. This is a fun road to travel. Once again as I travel, I look to the south and can see endlessly over the open plains of the Grand Valley. It is in this long stretch that the next closest water for the Wákara party that I have located is an unnamed spring past Buck Canyon Wash. Reaching a dry creek bed where I estimate this unnamed spring would be located, I turn south and follow the dry stream bed. Within two miles I come to the spring. It is small, but a spring nonetheless. This distance from Cisco Spring is six miles. I would again theorize that the Wákara party would have spent their eighth night here. I stop for lunch and climb a small plateau just to get higher and see down on the Grand Valley. In the far distance I can see two cedar trees, and that's it! Blue-gray sagebrush is the only other plant life I can see growing. It is interesting that just past the Grand Valley is the mighty Colorado River. McMahon never saw this river. Such a desolate area, and yet within a day's walk you can be to one of the major rivers in the United States. The different hues of the soil from light tan to burnt orange cover the entire valley.

After my break, I continue to head towards Westwater Creek, which would have been McMahon's ninth day of travel. Westwater Creek is an important watering hole and stop in that it is here I feel McMahon leaves the Wákara party and heads out on his own with Field. In the afternoon, I rise over a small bend by Potato Hill and see Westwater Creek. It is a small, clear, free-flowing creek. Once again, I stop and touch the water. It is cool and I would like to take a drink but do not due to the impurities of giardia and other bacterial diseases. I decide to end my day's journey here, knowing that tomorrow, I will be exploring over the Roan/Book Cliff Mountains to the Green River at Ouray, Utah. Traveling this distance, I will need a lot of time to review and contemplate the routes taken. . . . The estimated travel distance from the Green River is sixty-nine miles. I will close for now and look forward to my journey over the Roan/ Book Cliff Mountains tomorrow.

Once McMahon and Field made their decision to leave the company of the Utes and depart north in search of Fort Bridger or some other settlement, they informed their "good friends" of their intentions. McMahon "requested the boys to bring in our mule and horse, which they did after failing to induce us to go with them."[28] On the morning of estimated day ten after leaving the east banks of the Green River (making it around October 3), the two men "started out on what then seemed, and afterwards proved, to be a perilous voyage through deserts, and over rough mountains." McMahon noted that they began traveling northeast, forced in that direction by a mountain range, then proceeded northwest when they were able. This is a convincing account, given that the Roan or Book Cliff Mountains recede in a northeast direction around the southernmost end of the Book Cliffs, sixty miles from the Green River, opening travel through the Grand Valley in a northeast direction. In the likely event that McMahon and Field parted with the Wákara party at this southern point of the Book Cliffs, they would have had two options available to them. They could travel in a northeast direction along the edge of the Book Cliffs and Grand Valley to avoid the Roan/Book Cliff Mountains towering above them to the north, or they could enter the canyons to the north-northeast, crossing directly over the Book Cliffs.

The exact location of the camp McMahon and Field departed from can only be estimated. With the mention of a trail running in a southeast direction, surrounded by dry lands and an estimated sixty miles from the Green River, one site becomes probable. Traveling east around the southern slopes of the Book Cliff Mountains and beginning to move in a northeast direction, the welcome Westwater Creek would have provided the necessary water and resting area for the party. In the book *Forgotten Pathfinders*, Jack Nelson describes a common trail in this vicinity, used by both Indians and mountain men. According to Nelson, "it would appear to be the one most used" in the area and matches the trail encountered by Wákara.[29]

The journey through a desolate wilderness that ensued after departing from the Utes was arduous for McMahon and Field. It is not known how far McMahon would have traveled before entering one of the many canyons leading through the Roan/Book Cliff Mountains. At this stage of travel, McMahon did not mention following any trails. When the men were traveling with Wákara, both rode horses, but now, McMahon wrote, "I put him [Field] on the old sore-backed mule, where he rode most of the time for the next four days, while the little horse carried our baggage, and I led the way as usual, on foot." With McMahon walking, their daily pace would have been similar to the distances covered while traveling with Wákara. On their first day alone, they killed a small rabbit and ate wild rosebud seeds. McMahon also commented that "the days were quite warm, but the nights were cold."[30]

McMahon did not provide any detail of their second day of isolated travel; however, on their third day McMahon recounted that their food and water supply became increasingly critical. That afternoon, they came upon "some small red berries, similar in appearance to what I, in my childhood, knew and relished as Solomon's seal berries." McMahon reported, with self-deprecation, "I being a natural coward, and fearing that they might poison me, did not eat any of them, but generously allowed my good friend to eat them all." That night Field "began to complain of pain in his stomach and bowels, and was soon vomiting at a fearful rate; so violently, indeed, that I was apprehensive that he might die." McMahon then recounted Field's agony and the partial relief that came from the heavens:

He suffered most intensely, and soon became very thirsty, and, there being no water within many miles of us, he appealed to me to bleed one of the animals and let him drink the blood. . . . At about eleven o'clock, when his pains were most severe, a dark cloud, the first we had seen for months, came over us, and a little rain began to fall, when I at once opened our little camp kettle and turned the lid upside down, and into both kettle and lid there fell perhaps two or three teaspoonfuls of pure water, every drop of which I gave to the sufferer.[31]

For the next four days, the men "did not have a drop of water except the two or three teaspoonfuls which the stingy cloud left to save the life of the 'berry-eater.'" These may be the same type of berry, squawbush or skunkbush berry, that Manly and his men had found on the river back in Browns Park.

The barren conditions of their surroundings did not improve, and the two men found themselves "traveling hard during the day, and burning up with fever [i]n the night." Finally, on the sixth day since leaving Wákara—fifteen days since leaving the Green River—they decided to turn straight west in hopes of reencountering the river. After traveling over a mountain "and down into a plain of sand, sage brush, and cactus" all day, the men found themselves in Wonsits Valley of the southern Uinta Basin. Soon they noticed a change in their pack animals: the "fast failing brute companions scented water, or that they instinctively knew that it was not far away." They made camp, arose before dawn, and "about ten o'clock, through the hot glimmer of the down-pouring rays of the sun, we saw what appeared, and afterwards proved, to be a clump of cottonwood trees. Our hopes and courage were renewed, for we well knew the cottonwood usually grows near flowing water." About one o'clock that afternoon, they finally reached "the bank of the great river down which we had floated more than a month before" and immediately "recognized objects which we had seen while on our way down."[32]

McMahon clearly recognized where he was on the Green, perhaps observing familiar landmarks and the direction of bends of the river. He even pinpointed his exact location: "According to our map, our

Morgan McMahon and Richard Field arrived in the Uinta Basin at the confluence of the Duchesne and Green Rivers after traveling in a northward direction for fifteen days.

recollections of different objects, and present appearances we were now a little above the mouth of the Uinta [Duchesne] river which comes in from the northwest, all of which proved true."[33] This places the two men at river mile 128, about 125 river miles north of where the Old Spanish Trail crosses the Green River.

It can be estimated that McMahon on foot and sometimes-ill Field on mule averaged ten miles a day or less. This total of 160 miles is consistent with the miles traveled in my re-creation of McMahon's land journey, which totaled 156 miles. At river mile 128, the men were only thirty-two miles north of Desolation Canyon. With McMahon having in his possession a map and compass to help orient him as to this location, his observations are credible: after fifteen days of traveling east, northeast, and northwest, McMahon and Field ended up in the Uinta Basin. McMahon's account, then, makes it clear that the Manly party did not end their river voyage in the Uinta Basin but must have traveled through Desolation and Gray Canyons and into the San Rafael Desert.

After drinking the life-saving waters of the Green, McMahon and Field eagerly began to devise plans to cross it and travel up the Duchesne River to Fort Uinta. They did not know if anyone was there, but it was identified on McMahon's map. Field made an attempt to cross the Green, his "trusty old mule . . . swimming faithfully," but when they arrived at midstream, the current was too strong: "the mule made a complete somerset backwards plunging Field, the pack, and himself entirely under the water. . . . I heard him call for help and on going a little further down, found him stuck fast in the mud." The problems from this near-disastrous event were soon compounded when Field once again became extremely sick from foods that he had eaten. "The pain was intense, and we feared that he would surely die," McMahon related, "and earnestly prayed all the rest of the night that he might be relieved, and get well. Towards morning most violent vomiting came on, which continued for thirty hours, or more. He was not able to walk for three days."[34]

By the morning of the fourth day after arriving at the Green, McMahon had built a raft to float across the Green, using "remnants of log cabins, a number of which had been built and occupied more than half a century before, but by whom I do not know."[35] Research regarding log structures constructed on the east banks of the Green River across from its confluence with the Duchesne turned up several important documents helping corroborate McMahon's story. In 1935, Albert B. Reagan wrote an article in the *New Mexico Historical Review* about the location of a fort called Fort Kit Carson, used in the winter of 1832–1833. Carson's quarters, he wrote, "were somewhere in the vicinity of Ouray [Utah] at the junction of the Green, White and Winty [Uinta] rivers, the latter now being called the Duchesne in its lower course. We looked for this winter fort and found it, now reduced to wall mounds, in the woods on the east side of Green River, about a mile opposite the mouth of the Duchesne." The fort was about ninety-five by seventy-eight feet, with two lookout towers outside its walls.[36] The 1836 diary of Warren Angus Ferris included a map showing the location of Fort Kit Carson. Though not at all drawn to scale, the map clearly shows the fort on the east side of the Green, just east of the confluence with the "Euinta R.," a contemporaneous source verifying what McMahon wrote.[37]

Finding safe haven at the abandoned Fort Kit Carson, Field recovered from food poisoning while McMahon used the decaying logs from the old fort to construct a crude raft. They then safely crossed the Green

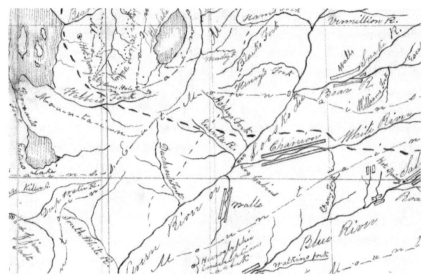

In the 1830s fur trapper Warren Angus Ferris prepared an elaborate map of the intermountain West, including details of log cabins on the east side of the Green River near the mouth of the Uinta River. Morgan McMahon and Richard Field would pass by this location in 1849. COURTESY OF L. TOM PERRY SPECIAL COLLECTIONS, HAROLD B. LEE LIBRARY, BRIGHAM YOUNG UNIVERSITY, PROVO, UTAH

and, once across the river, found their way up the Duchesne River to Fort Uinta and on to the snow-covered Uinta Mountains, which they successfully crossed. After many hardships in this stage of their journey, including near-death experiences, they parted company, both eventually finding their separate ways back to Fort Bridger and on to Utah Territory.

Before recounting his journey from Fort Carson to Salt Lake City, McMahon noted incredulously that it had been only three months since "the seven dug up the little flatboat from its sandy bed." Here he gives the date of commencing the journey down the Green as "the fifth day of August,"[38] which is incorrect, since as previously reviewed, both James Hutchings and Robert Morris confirm the date as August 19.[39] McMahon traveled with a "Government train" the last leg of the journey, arriving in Salt Lake City November 15, 1849. Field arrived seventeen days later, December 2.[40]

In Salt Lake City, both found safety and spent the winter months of 1849–1850 with the Mormons. They joined forces again in the spring and traveled to Sacramento together, where they arrived "in good condition on the fourth day of July, 1850, and pitched our tent under a large oak tree where the State Capitol now stands."[41]

Author's Note: With McMahon giving so few details for this portion of his journey, I was not able to trace his path exactly or know how many miles he and Field traveled. If they continued their rate of about ten miles per day, they would have traveled seventy miles in the seven days, the approximate distance from Westwater Creek to the Green River at Ouray, Utah.

10/20–10/21/2013, McMahon and Field Trek Days 10–16

Westwater Canyon to Ouray, Utah

A beautiful morning greets me today as I silently watch Westwater Creek flow by. At the canyon junctions of East Canyon, Middle Canyon, and Hay Canyon, all are surrounded by a chalky gray soil that mounds upward into hills and plateaus. On the top of one of the plateaus lies a crusted layer of brown sandstone that protects the plateau from erosion. At the base where the three canyons meet is an unbelievable pictograph etched in tan sandstone by Antoine Robidoux, a well-known trapper and explorer of this western region. Above the pictograph are the writings in French by Robidoux giving the date of 1837. I stop and look at Robidoux's inscription on the wall. A piece of it has broken off the wall and is leaning against the other parts of the inscription. What a fantastic piece of history.

Across middle canyon on the eastern wall of Westwater Canyon are Indian pictographs as well. Ghost-like figures that are painted on the wall in dark red colors seem to float hauntingly above me with an eerie sense of unknown meanings. They silently stare at me as if I were the one that needed to walk their path to knowledge. Near these figures is a painting of a buffalo, proving that buffalo were in the region. Such rare and beautiful work. I hope it always stays in its pristine form for future generations to view and appreciate.

This canyon area, with water flowing, must have been such a welcome sight for Wákara's party with McMahon and Field. At the base of Westwater Canyon, where the canyon gives way to the flat and barren lands, stands a settler's home made of wood and mud. Expertly crafted, the logs still interlock exactly with each other, maintaining the dream that was so long ago built. What dreams these settlers had and hardships they endured. I will always stand in respect of such fortitude and willpower. In direct contrast and only several hundred feet apart, a gas compression station surrounded by a chain-link fence has been installed with several large brown holding tanks. They look so out of place in a land that time has truly forgotten.

It is within this region or area that McMahon leaves Wákara and travels to the northeast over the Roan/Book Cliff Mountains. My inclination is to follow up the canyon to the northeast called East Canyon. It runs in the direction McMahon describes. It is a dry canyon and winds its way northeast for almost twenty miles. I wish he had left more written evidence as to the exact canyon that he entered, but he did not. Many natural gas wells are in the canyon, and visible gas lines lay on the ground like long spider legs extending from the ground-sucking pumps. The land is very dry, with no water visible. The canyon gives way to the strong gray and brown towering walls of the Roan/Book Cliff Mountains overlooking Grand Valley. As East Canyon steadily winds upward nineteen miles to the northeast, the vegetation begins to change as pine, cedar, and piñon trees along with scrub oak begin to cover the canyon and ridgelines. I think of McMahon and what a hard climb this would have been for him. He was walking while Field rode. Again, I don't know exactly what canyon he went up because of his lack of detail in his accounting, but any of these canyons in the surrounding area would have been difficult due to the climb in altitude and dry conditions.

Finally, reaching the top of East Tavaputs Plateau overlooking the Roan/Book Cliff Mountains, I can see for untold miles in all directions. Looking northward I can see the Uinta Mountains, their peaks dressed in snow. To the east of the Uinta Mountains, I recognize the red strata of Cliff Ridge where the Green River flows from Lodore Canyon. I wonder if McMahon would have recognized this ridge. That would have given him a bearing as to where he was. Looking southwest I can see the Henry Mountains, also in snow.

With my retracing McMahon's path at the same time of year of late September/early October, I know McMahon would be concerned with the snow. Still no visible water sources or springs. It is so dry, which McMahon vividly recounts. Once on top and traveling northwest as McMahon did, I follow the East Tavaputs Plateau for thirty-nine miles until I begin to drop down into the Wonsits Valley in the Uinta Basin South. The trees now are gone and very scant vegetation remains. Looking down at lower elevations, I see more and more gas lines and pump stations that fill the open landscape. They look like ants on a flat tortilla. While driving across the plateau, I travel on a newly constructed road called Cliff Ridge Road. It is a very wide road that is being expanded and paved. Construction workers are working on the road and paving it as I pass. The value of natural gas has conquered all.

I know McMahon would have been so discouraged as he continually moved to the northwest without finding water or food. I am surprised that at this elevation of 8,000 to 10,000 feet, it is so dry. Small clumps of grass that have turned brown in the fall are all that have grown in these arid lands. Continuing to drop off the plateau, I have changed my direction and travel in a northwestern direction, as McMahon stated. With the Uinta Basin now directly in front of me to the north and northwest, it is very large and opens in all directions. Once I arrived on the valley floor sixty-five miles since the mouth of Westwater Canyon, I began to see cottonwood trees in the far distance to the west, which marks a change of water present. McMahon also knew that, once he arrived on the Uinta Valley floor, he would soon find water with the Green River flowing through the basin, and he turned west. It is very satisfying from a researcher's point of view to experience the same conditions that McMahon felt and wrote about.

What a wonderful sight McMahon had in seeing the shimmering golden cottonwood trees. Water at last! I am greeted by the same cottonwood trees that greeted McMahon, traveling west on the Uinta Basin, and it is hard to realize that he traveled four days without water. How desperate they must have been. Arriving at the river, McMahon mentions that he recognizes objects by the river as they floated down a month prior. I wonder what those objects were? The landscape in this region is very nondescript. No massive rock ledges or noticeable outcroppings. The land is flat with a quiet demeanor of infertile soil. The confluence of the Duchesne and the Green could have been the noticeable object that he refers to, or perhaps an old campsite they stayed at on their river journey down.

Arriving at the Green River in the late afternoon by Ouray, Utah, I quickly notice the life that the river brings. Having traveled for so long in dry and desolate lands, it is refreshing to see ducks on the river and deer on the shore drinking. I look across and see the Duchesne flowing into the Green. I have such wonderful memories of floating by here in 2006. Wow, this book has taken a long time to complete. It truly is a labor of love. Looking over at the east bank, I wish I knew the exact location that McMahon found the logs from Fort Kit Carson to cross the Green. Though McMahon and Field cross the river and continue their quests to reach Fort Bridger, which both do separately, wintering in Salt Lake City, this is where I end researching McMahon's journey. Now, firmly establishing that he reached the confluence of the Green and Duchesne, the validation that Manly and his men floated past this area of the Uinta Basin and on to Gunnison Valley has been proven. Walking along the eastern riverbank through the quiet cottonwoods, I imagine where Fort Kit Carson might have been. The Ferris map places the long cabins just above the Duchesne on the east side of the river. . . . Watching the gently flowing waters silently drift past me, it would have been amusing to see McMahon and Field attempt to cross the Green. It is amazing both survived with the little wilderness skills each possessed.

Having now traveled the same barren lands of desert, plateau, and mountains that McMahon and Field crossed with such hardships and encounters, I silently sit on the riverbank of the Green and contemplate their unstoppable spirit to survive. I truly appreciate these two men and their unshakeable drive to reach the Pacific Coast and the gold fields of California. McMahon and Field, your once-silent story is now appreciated by many. Well done.

CONCLUSION

IN THE WORDS OF WILLIAM LEWIS MANLY HIMSELF, WRITTEN AS HE concluded his story of *Death Valley in '49*, "This story is not meant to be sensational, but a plain, unvarnished tale of truth—some parts hard and very sad. It is a narrative of my personal experience, and being in no sense a literary man or making any pretense as a writer, I hope the errors may be overlooked, for it has been to me a difficult story to tell, arousing as it did sad recollections of the past. I have told it in the plainest, briefest way, with nothing exaggerated or overdone."[1] Manly valued truth and honesty, and his life was a rich tapestry of meaningful friendships, with others often dependent upon his skills and compassion as he made his way through the untamed American wilderness, the lands he loved.

One encounter that vividly portrays Manly's life experiences and compassion occurs many years later, when he is present with his dear friend and associate, Sarah Bennett, as she lives out her last days with him by her bedside. "She reached out her arms and drew me down to her," he remembered, "and embraced me and said in a faint whisper—'God bless you:—you saved us all till now, and I hope you will always be happy and live long.'"[2] The following day, Sarah Bennett passed away knowing the man she called Lewis had always cared for her and seen to the safety of her family as they endured the many hardships on the long journey westward to California. Manly was a true leader, outdoorsman, and humanitarian, not ashamed to show compassion and love to both family and friends that walked with him through life.

Uncovering the past enlightens the present and gives hope to the future for the betterment of all humankind through knowledge and understanding. Manly's love, respect, and appreciation of the land grew as he traveled westward. His firmly embedded character traits, appreciating

open lands and the freedoms he enjoyed, parallel recreationists and outdoor enthusiasts of today. Manly's love for the land and those individuals
who respectfully use its resources is evident. He appreciated the opportunity to explore an environment free of barriers and restrictions, values
that persist in today's outdoor enthusiasts. While the environment has
changed, as have the laws and regulations determining land use, the purest
form of recreational experience in wilderness areas remains the same: to
breathe in Mother Nature. As Daniel Dustin wrote: "The wilderness is my
well of souls. . . . It offers the kind of challenge that is increasingly rare, a
paring down to the essentials, a stripping away of the civilized veneer that
shields us all so that we can once again experience the basic nature of our
existence."[3] Establishing this common experience in wilderness unlocks
the grounding values within our own lives.

Manly's deep respect for both humankind and Mother Nature
weave together to form a rich heritage. When he met with Wákara on
the bank of the Green, two men of different races, religious beliefs, and
background showed mutual respect and admiration, a model in today's
untrusting world. Their encounter unfolded in and was founded on the
vast southwest deserts of the Utah Territory, their mutual respect for the
environment, and their ability to survive in an unforgiving land. Each
man recognized in the other an undaunted spirit in lands where others
had failed. Manly recognized the reverence Wákara and his band showed,
living in a wild, desolate land. As the open lands of the American West
have gradually diminished due to population growth, lack of respect,
ignorance, and unsound resource management policies, the values Manly
held produce a sense of sadness for what can never be felt again. Experiencing that void gives motivation to change and reclaim open wilderness.

I give the final word to Lewis Manly himself, to sum up his wilderness experience overland and down the river, to reflect on what he
accomplished and demonstrate the respect and compassion that ema-
nated from him:

And on some rolling stone you may inscribe the name of WIL-
LIAM LEWIS MANLY, born near St. Albans, Vermont, April
[6th], 1820, . . . who went to Michigan . . . then onward to Wis-

consin . . . traveled across western prairies and lofty mountains and sunken deserts. . . .

I was always a great admirer of Nature and things which remained as they were created. . . .

We floated and tumbled down the deep cañon of Green River till we emerged into an open plain and were compelled to come on shore by the Indians. . . . We found a Chief and his tribe, Walker and his followers who were as humane and kind to White people as could be expected of any one. I have often wondered at the knowledge of this man respecting the country. . . . I have for these more than forty years credited the lives of myself and comrades to the thoughtful interest and humane consideration of old Chief Walker, . . . We shook hands with quivering lips as we hoped the other would meet good luck. . . .

I always felt better when I got around to the determination as I always did, to stand by my friends, their wives and children let come what might . . . wherein, after 40 years of earnest toil, I rest in the midst of family and friends, and can truly say I am content.[4]

NOTES

PREFACE

1. Shafer, *Guide to Historical Method,* 48.
2. See, for example, LeRoy and Jean Johnson, eds., *Escape from Death Valley* (Reno: University of Nevada Press, 1987); and Richard E. Lingenfelter, *Death Valley and the Amargosa: A Land of Illusion* (Berkeley: University of California Press, 1986), 40–71.
3. Because her work represents some of the most recent and best scholarship on the Ute people, I am following the spelling of Wákara found in Sondra Jones's *Being and Becoming Ute.* Alternate spellings in historical sources include Walkara, Wakara, and Walker.

INTRODUCTION: ON THE TRAIL WITH LEWIS MANLY

1. See, for example, Dolnick, *Down the Great Unknown;* and Worster, *A River Running West.*
2. Manly, *Death Valley in '49,* 75.
3. See, for example, LeRoy and Jean Johnson, eds., *Escape from Death Valley* (Reno: University of Nevada Press, 1987); and Richard E. Lingenfelter, *Death Valley and the Amargosa: A Land of Illusion* (Berkeley: University of California Press, 1986), 40–71.
4. Manly, *Death Valley in '49,* 437–439.
5. William Lewis Manly, "From Vermont to California," *Santa Clara Valley,* June 1887–July 1890; William Lewis Manly, *Death Valley in '49: Important Chapter of California Pioneer History. The Autobiography of a Pioneer, Detailing His Life from a Humble Home in the Green Mountains to the Gold Mines of California; and Particularly Reciting the Sufferings of the Band of Men, Women and Children Who Gave "Death Valley" Its Name* (San Jose, CA: Pacific Tree and Vine, 1894).
6. Dellenbaugh, *Romance of the Colorado River,* 132.
7. See, for example, Webb, *If We Had a Boat,* 45–47. On the other hand, historians LeRoy and Jean Johnson conclude in *Death Valley in '49,* 52, and in their later publications that Manly went as far as Green River. Also, on pages 60–61 of his 1982 *Colorado River Country,* historian David Lavender concludes, based on Manly's mention of the Old Spanish Trail, that the party went as far as "near the site of today's Green River, Utah," but Lavender devotes only a few paragraphs and a single endnote to the story. Likewise, Utah historian Wade Allinson has recently concluded that Manly traveled as far as the Old Spanish Trail. (Email correspondence with Wade Allinson, in possession of the author.) On the spelling of Wákara, see note 3 in the preface to this volume.
8. Shafer, *Guide to Historical Method,* 3.

9. Manly, *Death Valley in '49*, 496.
10. Leedy, *Practical Research*, 87 (emphasis in original).
11. Manly, *Death Valley in '49*, 387–388.

CHAPTER 1: AMERICAN EXPLORERS OF THE WEST

1. Lewis, Journal, Apr. 7, 1805.
2. Ambrose, *Undaunted Courage*, 482–483.
3. Powell, *Exploration of the Colorado River*, 80.
4. Powell, *Exploration of the Colorado River*, 99; see also Dolnick, *Down the Great Unknown*, ix.
5. Qtd. in Clokey, *William H. Ashley*, 141.
6. Clokey, *William H. Ashley*, 12, 152.
7. Manly, *Death Valley in '49*, 98.
8. Manly, *Death Valley in '49*, 194.
9. Lewis, Journal, Apr. 25, 1805.
10. Manly, *Death Valley in '49*, 247–248.
11. Powell, *Exploration of the Colorado River*, 70.

CHAPTER 2: EARLY LIFE ON THE FRONTIER

1. See *Yale Book of Quotations*, c.v. "Go West, Young Man," for a discussion of the ambiguous source of this quote.
2. Woodward, *Jayhawkers' Oath*, 49.
3. Manly, *Death Valley in '49*, 11–12, 64.
4. Manly, *Death Valley in '49*, 30–31.
5. Manly, *Death Valley in '49*, 21; Sleath, "Manley/Manly Family History and Genealogy," 92.
6. Manly, *Death Valley in '49*, 21.
7. Manly, *Death Valley in '49*, 21–22.
8. See Manly, *Death Valley in '49*, 31–32.
9. Manly, *Death Valley in '49*, 38, 62.
10. Manly, *Death Valley in '49*, 22.
11. Manly, *Death Valley in '49*, 23–24.
12. Manly, *Death Valley in '49*, 23.
13. Manly, *Death Valley in '49*, 24.
14. Manly, *Death Valley in '49*, 30.
15. Manly, *Death Valley in '49*, 30–32.
16. Manly, *Death Valley in '49*, 31.
17. Manly, *Death Valley in '49*, 43.
18. Manly, *Death Valley in '49*, 36.
19. Manly, *Death Valley in '49*, 40.
20. Manly, *Death Valley in '49*, 46.
21. Manly, *Death Valley in '49*, 47.
22. Manly, *Death Valley in '49*, 53, 55.
23. Manly, *Death Valley in '49*, 56.

24. Manly, *Death Valley in '49*, 57.
25. Manly, *Death Valley in '49*, 31.
26. Manly, *Death Valley in '49*, 45.
27. Manly, *Death Valley in '49*, 51.
28. Manly, *Death Valley in '49*, 53.
29. Manly, *Death Valley in '49*, 56.

CHAPTER 3: WESTWARD HO

1. Manly, *Death Valley in '49*, 59.
2. Brands, *Age of Gold*, 24.
3. Schlissel, *Women's Diaries of the Westward Journey*, 24.
4. Cross, *March of the Regiment*, 29.
5. Qtd. in Journal History of the Church, May 28, 1849.
6. Stansbury, *Expedition to the Great Salt Lake of Utah*, 24.
7. Manly, *Death Valley in '49*, 59.
8. Manly, *Death Valley in '49*, 39.
9. Manly, *Death Valley in '49*, 61.
10. Manly spells it "Lynn." There was no city in Iowa with the name of Lynn, but there is a county named Linn. It was established on January 15, 1839, and is located in the eastern side of the state. The county seat is Cedar Rapids.
11. Manly, *Death Valley in '49*, 63.
12. Manly, *Death Valley in '49*, 64.
13. Letter, *Daily Missouri Republican*, Oct. 25, 1849.
14. Hannon, *Boston-Newton Company Venture*, 138–139.
15. Manly, *Death Valley in '49*, 66.
16. Cross, *March of the Regiment of Mounted Riflemen*, 13, 27.
17. Royce, *Frontier Lady*, 14.
18. Manly, *Death Valley in '49*, 62.
19. Manly, *Death Valley in '49*, 64.
20. Welch, Log, 7–11. The original journal is held in the Adonijah Strong Welch Papers at Iowa State University and is reproduced in Theodore C. Ressler's 1964 publication, *Trails Divided*. Ressler incorrectly attributes the journal to David Switzer.
21. Lorton, Diary, Sept. 26, 1849.
22. Clayton, *Latter Day Saints Emigrants' Guide*, 7, 22.
23. Further details of Manly's travel miles per day are reviewed in the discussion of his crossing of the Wyoming Territory from Fort Laramie to the banks of the Green River.
24. Manly, *Death Valley in '49*, 66.
25. Slaughter and Landon, *Trail of Hope*, 85.
26. Manly, *Death Valley in '49*, 66.
27. Manly, *Death Valley in '49*, 68.
28. Clayton, *Latter Day Saint Emigrants' Guide*, 64, 74.
29. Sargent, *Seeking the Elephant*, 13.
30. Sargent, *Seeking the Elephant*, 20.
31. Hutchings, Journal, in Sargent, *Seeking the Elephant*, 110.

32. Hafen and Young, *Fort Laramie and the Pageant of the West*, 138, 141.
33. Sargent, *Seeking the Elephant*, 18.
34. Manly, *Death Valley in '49*, 86.
35. Hutchings, Journal, in Sargent, *Seeking the Elephant*, 144.
36. Manly, *Death Valley in '49*, 71.
37. Manly, *Death Valley in '49*, 75.
38. Manly, *Death Valley in '49*, 74; Sargent, *Seeking the Elephant*, 18–19.
39. Cross, *March of the Regiment of Mounted Riflemen*, 52.
40. Manly, *Death Valley in '49*, 71.
41. Manly, *Death Valley in '49*, 68–69.
42. Hutchings, Journal, in Sargent, *Seeking the Elephant*, 130.
43. Morris, Journal, July 25, 1849.
44. Hutchings, Journal, in Sargent, *Seeking the Elephant*, 134.
45. Manly, *Death Valley in '49*, 69.
46. Hutchings, Journal, in Sargent, *Seeking the Elephant*, 134.
47. Manly, *Death Valley in '49*, 69.
48. Hutchings, Journal, in Sargent, *Seeking the Elephant*, 135.
49. Morris, Journal, July 31, 1849.
50. Hutchings, Journal, in Sargent, *Seeking the Elephant*, 140.
51. Hutchings, Journal, in Sargent, *Seeking the Elephant*, 139.
52. Hutchings, Journal, in Sargent, *Seeking the Elephant*, 140–141; see also Clayton, *Latter Day Saints Emigrants' Guide*, 15.
53. Morris, Journal, Aug. 9, 1849.
54. Manly, *Death Valley in '49*, 72.
55. Ruth, *Landmarks of the West*, 286; see also Hannon, *Boston-Newton Company Venture*, 139.
56. See, for example, Manly, *Death Valley in '49*, 22, 106, 125, 195.
57. Manly, *Death Valley in '49*, 79.
58. Manly, *Death Valley in '49*, 72.
59. Hutchings, Journal, in Sargent, *Seeking the Elephant*, 144.
60. Morris, Journal, Aug. 16, 1849.
61. Manly, *Death Valley in '49*, 70, 71.
62. Manly, *Death Valley in '49*, 69.
63. Sargent, *Seeking the Elephant*, 20.
64. Manly, "From Vermont to California," 94.

CHAPTER 4: DECISION AT THE GREEN RIVER
1. Manly, *Death Valley in '49*, 70.
2. Manly, *Death Valley in '49*, 74.
3. Manly, *Death Valley in '49*, 70.
4. Sargent, *Seeking the Elephant*, 144.
5. Sargent, *Seeking the Elephant*, 146.
6. Morris, Journal, Aug. 19, 1849.
7. Manly, "From Vermont to California," 110.

8. Clayton, *Latter Day Saints Emigrants' Guide*, 70, 72.

9. Manly, *Death Valley in '49*, 73–74.

10. Manly, *Death Valley in '49*, 74, 76; see also Manly, "From Vermont to California," 110.

11. See Barney, *Mormon Vanguard Brigade of 1847*, 189–190.

12. William Clayton, Diary, June 30, 1847, in Smith, *Intimate Chronicle*, 353.

13. Cross, *March of the Regiment of Mounted Riflemen*, 59–60.

14. Manly, "From Vermont to California," 142.

15. Sargent, *Seeking the Elephant*, 146–147.

16. Manly, "From Vermont to California," 110.

17. Manly, "From Vermont to California," 110.

18. Manly, *Death Valley in '49*, 74.

19. Manly, *Death Valley in '49*, 75.

20. Sargent, *Seeking the Elephant*, 147.

21. Manly, *Death Valley in '49*, 76.

22. Manly, *Death Valley in '49*, 76.

23. Hugh B. Heiskell, Journal, in Steel, *A Forty-Niner from Tennessee*, 17.

24. Another possibility is that both Hutchings and Heiskell intended Quemby, which according to the Internet Surname Database is an "English locational name from 'Quenby' in Leicestershire." According to this database, "Locational surnames were originally given as a means of identification to those who left their village or place of origin to settle elsewhere." Though perhaps unlikely, it is possible that Hutchings was the origin of the name Quenby, which he may have given as a nickname to Manly because he fit the description of one leaving home and village to settle elsewhere. (Internet Surname Database, s.v. "Quemby.")

25. Manly, *Death Valley in '49*, 74.

26. Manly, *Death Valley in '49*, 97.

27. Manly, *Death Valley in '49*, 76–77.

28. Manly, *Death Valley in '49*, 288.

29. Manly, *Death Valley in '49*, 288.

30. Manly, *Death Valley in '49*, 78.

31. Manly, *Death Valley in '49*, 281.

32. Frémont, *Map of the Exploring Expedition to the Rocky Mountains in the Year 1842*.

33. Frémont, *Map of Oregon and Upper California from the Surveys of John Charles Frémont and Other Authorities*.

34. Manly, *Death Valley in '49*, 94.

35. Manly, *Death Valley in '49*, 288.

36. Zwinger, *Run, River, Run*, 4.

37. Irving, *Adventures of Captain Bonneville*, 260.

38. Frémont, *Memoirs of My Life*, 199.

39. Frémont, *Memoirs of My Life*, 200.

40. Zwinger, *Run, River, Run*, 5.

41. Farnham, *Travels*, 15.

42. Zwinger, *Run, River, Run*, 162, 156.

43. Frémont, *Memoirs of My Life,* 200.
44. Zwinger, *Run, River, Run,* 174–175.
45. Zwinger, *Run, River, Run,* 183, 185.
46. Cosco, *Echo Park,* 5.
47. Vélez de Escalante, Diary, Sept. 13, 1776, in Warner, *Dominguez-Escalante Journal.*
48. Belknap, *Dinosaur River Guide,* 25.
49. Belknap, *Dinosaur River Guide,* 19.
50. Zwinger, *Run, River, Run,* 183, 5.

CHAPTER 5: SETTING OUT ON THE GREEN RIVER
1. Manly, *Death Valley in '49,* 496.
2. Manly, *Death Valley in '49,* 75.
3. Manly, *Death Valley in '49,* 76. In Manly's earlier serialized account, this selection occurred on the second day of travel. (Manly, "From Vermont to California," 110.)
4. Manly, *Death Valley in '49,* 76.
5. Manly, *Death Valley in '49,* 76, 77.
6. Manly, "From Vermont to California," 110.
7. See, for example, Manly, *Death Valley in '49,* 77.
8. Lorton, Diary, July 28, 1849. The next day, another traveler, David Staples, observed that the Green "is a beautifull stream, 200 yards wide, swift current and clear water." (Staples, Journal, July 29, 1849, in Hannon, *Boston-Newton Company Venture,* 149.)
9. Manly, *Death Valley in '49,* 77, 78.
10. Manly, *Death Valley in '49,* 74, 83.
11. Manly, *Death Valley in '49,* 77–78.
12. Manly, *Death Valley in '49,* 82. Wildlife was indeed abundant in the secluded lands bordering the Green. Historian Roy Webb writes: "Like the rest of North America before the coming of the Europeans and their guns, railroads, and livestock, the country around the Green was teeming with wildlife; as Bill Purdy put it, there were so few people that the whole area 'belonged to the animals.'" (Webb, *Lost Canyons of the Green River,* 6.)
13. Manly, *Death Valley in '49,* 89.
14. Manly, *Death Valley in '49,* 82.
15. Manly, *Death Valley in '49,* 77.
16. Manly, "From Vermont to California," 110.
17. Manly, *Death Valley in '49,* 78.
18. As later discussed, this was not in fact Browns Hole, which is below what is now Flaming Gorge Dam.
19. Manly, *Death Valley in '49,* 78.
20. Dellenbaugh, *A Canyon Voyage,* 17, 20. Manly estimated the cliffs at "2000 feet or more." (Manly, *Death Valley in '49,* 78.)
21. Webb, *Lost Canyons of the Green River,* 47.
22. Manly, "From Vermont to California," 110.
23. Manly, "From Vermont to California," 110.
24. Qtd. in Ghiglieri, *First through Grand Canyon,* 87.
25. Manly, *Death Valley in '49,* 79.

Chapter 6: Into the Canyons

1. Manly, *Death Valley in '49*, 79.
2. Manly, "From Vermont to California," 110.
3. Manly, *Death Valley in '49*, 79–80.
4. William Ashley to Gen. Henry Atkinson, Dec. 1, 1825, in Dale, *Ashley-Smith Explorations*, 142.
5. Qtd. in Ghiglieri, *First through Grand Canyon*, 95–96.
6. Dellenbaugh, *Canyon Voyage*, 22.
7. Manly, *Death Valley in '49*, 80.
8. Manly, "From Vermont to California," 110; Manly, *Death Valley in '49*, 80.
9. Dellenbaugh, *Canyon Voyage*, 112; see also Ghiglieri, *First through Grand Canyon*, 100.
10. Webb, *Lost Canyons of the Green River*, 70.
11. Jones, Journal, 32.
12. William Ashley to Gen. Henry Atkinson, Dec. 1, 1825, in Dale, *Ashley-Smith Explorations*, 142; for Powell's summary of Ashley Falls, see Ghiglieri, *First through Grand Canyon*, 100.
13. Dellenbaugh, *Canyon Voyage*, 112.
14. Dellenbaugh, *Canyon Voyage*, 112.
15. Dellenbaugh, *Romance of the Colorado*, 62–63.
16. In similar fashion, Powell also camped above the rocks of Ashley Falls in both expeditions of 1869 and 1871; as Dellenbaugh noted, "In the morning soon after leaving this camp a dull roar ahead told of our approach to Ashley Falls, for which we were on the lookout." (Dellenbaugh, *Canyon Voyage*, 26–27; see also Ghiglieri, *First through Grand Canyon*, 100.)
17. Manly, "From Vermont to California," 110.
18. Manly, *Death Valley in '49*, 80.
19. Qtd. in Ghiglieri, *First through Grand Canyon*, 99.
20. William Ashley to Gen. Henry Atkinson, Dec. 1, 1825, in Dale, *Ashley-Smith Explorations*, 142.
21. Manly, *Death Valley in '49*, 80.
22. Manly, "From Vermont to California," 110.
23. Manly, *Death Valley in '49*, 80.
24. See Manly, *Death Valley in '49*, 80.
25. Manly, "From Vermont to California," 110.
26. Manly, *Death Valley in '49*, 81.
27. Dellenbaugh, *Canyon Voyage*, 28.
28. Manly, *Death Valley in '49*, 81. In his book *Age of Gold*, historian H. W. Brands estimates it took most of a week. (Brands, *Age of Gold*, 156.)
29. Manly, "From Vermont to California," 126.
30. Manly, *Death Valley in '49*, 81–82.
31. Manly, "From Vermont to California," 110. This suggests Brands may have overestimated the time for the two earlier-built canoes.
32. Manly, "From Vermont to California," 126.

33. Manly, *Death Valley in '49*, 31.
34. Manly, *Death Valley in '49*, 82.
35. Manly, *Death Valley in '49*, 83.
36. Manly, *Death Valley in '49*, 279–280.
37. Manly, "From Vermont to California," 126.
38. Qtd. in Ghiglieri, *First through Grand Canyon*, 113.
39. Manly, *Death Valley in '49*, 82.
40. Zwinger, *Run, River, Run*, 136.
41. Qtd. in Ghiglieri, *First through Grand Canyon*, 105.
42. Manly, *Death Valley in '49*, 83; see also Zwinger, *Run, River, Run*, 137.
43. As identified at note 47 below, these were most likely squawbush berries.
44. Powell, *Exploration of the Colorado River and Its Canyons*, 149.
45. Zwinger, *Run, River, Run*, 140–141.
46. Manly, *Death Valley in '49*, 83; he called them "bush cranberries" in "From Vermont to California," 126.
47. Merriam-Webster.com, c.v., "squawbush," https://www.merriam-webster.com/dictionary/squawbush; see also Zwinger, *Run, River, Run*, 145.
48. Qtd. in Ghiglieri, *First through Grand Canyon*, 104–105; see also Dellenbaugh, *Canyon Voyage*, 31.
49. Manly, *Death Valley in '49*, 43.
50. Manly, "From Vermont to California," 126
51. Qtd. in Zwinger, *Run, River, Run*, 151.
52. Zwinger, *Run, River, Run*, 155.
53. Qtd. in Ghiglieri, *First through Grand Canyon*, 108, 113.
54. William Ashley to Gen. Henry Atkinson, Dec. 1, 1825, in Dale, *Ashley-Smith Explorations*, 145.
55. Dellenbaugh, *Canyon Voyage*, 32–34.
56. Manly, "From Vermont to California," 126.
57. Manly, *Death Valley in '49*, 85.
58. Manly, *Death Valley in '49*, 84.
59. William Ashley to Gen. Henry Atkinson, Dec. 1, 1825, in Dale, *Ashley-Smith Explorations*, 145.
60. George Bradley, qtd. in Ghiglieri, *First through Grand Canyon*, 120.
61. Dellenbaugh, *Canyon Voyage*, 40–41.
62. Qtd. in Ghiglieri, *First through Grand Canyon*, 113, 114.
63. Manly, *Death Valley in '49*, 84.
64. Qtd. in Ghiglieri, *First through Grand Canyon*, 121. Powell even provided a story for what he believed had happened: "Though some of his companions were drowned, Ashley and one other survived the wreck, climbed the canyon wall, and found their way across the Wasatch Mountains to Salt Lake City, living chiefly on berries, as they wandered through an unknown and difficult country. When they arrived at Salt Lake, they were almost destitute of clothing, and nearly starved. Of their subsequent history, I have no knowledge." (Powell, *Exploration of the Colorado River and Its Canyons*, 158.)

65. Dellenbaugh, *Romance of the Colorado River*, 54. Fort Davy Crockett was a trading post in what is now the northwest corner of Colorado, and it operated from the late 1830s to the early 1840s.

66. Dellenbaugh, *The Romance of the Colorado River* 63.

67. Dellenbaugh, *Romance of the Colorado River*, 92.

68. Manly, *Death Valley in '49*, 84.

69. Qtd. in Ghiglieri, *First through Grand Canyon*, 120.

70. Manly, *Death Valley in '49*, 85.

71. Powell, *Exploration of the Colorado River and Its Canyons*, 153; compare Dellenbaugh, *Canyon Voyage*, 43, 44.

72. Manly, *Death Valley in '49*, 85.

73. Powell, *Exploration of the Colorado River and its Canyons*, 159, 160.

74. Dellenbaugh, *Canyon Voyage*, 44; see also George Bradley, qtd. in Ghiglieri, *First through Grand Canyon*, 120. According to Dellenbaugh, it was John F. Steward who suggested the name in 1871.

75. Manly, *Death Valley in '49*, 85.

76. Manly, "From Vermont to California," 126.

77. Manly, *Death Valley in '49*, 86. Powell experienced a similar capsizing and near-drowning at this point in the river. "I heard a shout, and looking around, saw one of the boats coming over the falls," he recalled. "The *No Name* had not seen the signal in time, and the swift current had carried him to the brink. I saw he was going over the inevitable. . . . The men were thrown into the river and carried beyond my sight. Very soon I turned the point, and could see a man's head above the waters seemingly washed about by a whirlpool below a rock. . . . I saw Howland trying to go to his aid from the island. He finally got near enough to Frank to reach him by the end of the pole, and letting go of the rock, he grasped it, and was pulled out. Seneca Howland, the Captain's brother, was washed farther down the island on to some rocks, and managed to get on shore in safety, excepting some bad bruises. This seemed a long time, but 'twas quickly done." (Qtd. in Ghiglieri, *First through Grand Canyon*, 113–114.)

78. Manly, "From Vermont to California," 126.

79. Manly, "From Vermont to California," 126.

80. See Dellenbaugh, *Canyon Voyage*, 48.

81. Powell, *Exploration of the Colorado River and Its Canyons*, 165.

CHAPTER 7: DEEPER AND DEEPER

1. Manly, *Death Valley in '49*, 88.

2. See Powell, *Exploration of the Colorado River and Its Canyons*, 168.

3. Qtd. in Ghiglieri, *First through Grand Canyon*, 130.

4. Dellenbaugh, *Canyon Voyage*, 49.

5. William Ashley to Gen. Henry Atkinson, Dec. 1, 1825, in Dale, *Ashley-Smith Explorations*, 145–146.

6. Manly, *Death Valley in '49*, 88.

7. Powell, *Exploration of the Colorado River and Its Canyons*, 168.

8. Manly, *Death Valley in '49*, 88.

9. Zwinger, *Run, River, Run*, 175.

10. Manly, *Death Valley in '49*, 89. In "From Vermont to California," 126, Manly wrote, "There seemed to be no more mountains down the river as far as we could see, which caused us to believe we had now passed the troublesome part of our journey, and would be able to reach the sea coast in a few more days." Clearly his geography concerning the location of the Pacific was in error, and again he failed to describe Desolation and Gray Canyons, which I try to account for in the following paragraphs.

11. Webb, "Green River."

12. Aton, *The River Knows Everything*, iv.

13. Clint Goode, statement, copy in author's possession.

14. Clint Goode, statement, copy in author's possession.

15. Qtd. in Ghiglieri, *First through Grand Canyon*, 137–138.

16. Qtd. in Ghiglieri, *First through Grand Canyon*, 136.

17. Powell, *Exploration of the Colorado River and Its Canyons*, 174, 176.

18. Powell, *Exploration of the Colorado River and Its Canyons*, 176.

19. Dellenbaugh, *Canyon Voyage*, 55.

20. Dellenbaugh, *Canyon Voyage*, 56.

21. For an analysis of days Manly spent on the river, see p. 201 herein.

22. Qtd. in Ghiglieri, *First through Grand Canyon*, 141.

23. Dellenbaugh, *Canyon Voyage*, 60.

24. Dellenbaugh, *Romance of the Colorado River*, 117.

25. Starting here, the journal entries are out of chronological order because we floated from Split Mountain Campground to the Duchesne River before we launched from Lombard Crossing at Green River, Wyoming. It was necessary to float these seventy miles before we began the full expedition so as to keep our time schedule for permits and upcoming public events. The permit to enter Dinosaur National Monument was for September 2, and our plans to attend the festivities of Watermelon Days in Green River, Utah, on September 16 left us insufficient time to run the whole river in chronological order. Although the next four days reported in the journal were floated out of sequence, they are logged in numerical order with the other expedition days to preserve the time spent on the Green River for comparison with Manly's account.

26. Powell, *Exploration of the Colorado River and its Canyon*, 182.

27. Qtd. in Ghiglieri, *First through Grand Canyon*, 145.

28. See Ghiglieri, *First through Grand Canyon*, 146, 152.

29. Dellenbaugh, *Canyon Voyage*, 60.

30. William Ashley to Gen. Henry Atkinson, Dec. 1, 1825, in Dale, *Ashley-Smith Explorations*, 149–150.

31. Manly, *Death Valley in '49*, 89.

32. Powell, *Exploration of the Colorado River and Its Canyons*, 191.

33. Dellenbaugh, *Romance of the Colorado River*, 118.

34. Qtd. in Ghiglieri, *First through Grand Canyon*, 161.

CHAPTER 8: BEYOND THE UINTA BASIN

1. Dellenbaugh, *Canyon Voyage*, 77, 80.
2. Dellenbaugh, *Canyon Voyage*, 119.
3. Qtd. in Ghiglieri, *First through Grand Canyon*, 165; see also 166–167. Powell renamed it Gray Canyon during his 1871 expedition. (Zwinger, *Run, River, Run*, 228.)
4. Manly, *Death Valley in '49*, 89.
5. Warner, *Dominguez-Escalante Journal*, 52–53.
6. Manly, "From Vermont to California," 126.
7. Manly, *Death Valley in '49*, 496; Manly, "From Vermont to California," 192.
8. Zwinger, *Run, River, Run*, 230.
9. Manly, *Death Valley in '49*, 89–90. In his earlier "From Vermont to California," Manly recounted more succinctly, "While we were moving silently along we thought we heard the sound of a distant gun, and soon another more plainly, and were quite sure we were not mistake, and we did not think it possible that there could be any settlement in such a worthless country." (Manly, "From Vermont to California," 142.)
10. Manly, "From Vermont to California," 142.
11. Manly, *Death Valley in '49*, 90.

CHAPTER 9: ENCOUNTER WITH WÁKARA

1. Jones, *Being and Becoming Ute*, 66.
2. Sonne, *World of Wakara*, 6.
3. Jones, *Being and Becoming Ute*, 48.
4. Qtd. in *Latter-day Saints' Millennial Star*, June 15, 1851, 180.
5. Bailey, *Walkara, Hawk of the Mountains*, 14.
6. Hafen and Hafen, *Old Spanish Trail*, 327.
7. Carvalho, *Incidents of Travel and Adventure in the Far West*, 188, 195.
8. Smart and Smart, *Over the Rim*, 43.
9. Bailey, *Walkara, Hawk of the Mountains*, 18, 73.
10. Qtd. in *Latter-day Saints' Millennial Star*, 15 June 1851, 180.
11. Hafen and Hafen, *Old Spanish Trail*, 248.
12. Jones, *Being and Becoming Ute*, 54–55.
13. Jones, *Being and Becoming Ute*, 35.
14. See Justesen, "Brigham Young and Chief Walkara," 19.
15. Qtd. in Jones, *Being and Becoming Ute*, 196.
16. Jones, *Being and Becoming Ute*, 83.
17. Sonne, *World of Wakara*, 199.
18. Jones, *Being and Becoming Ute*, 73.
19. Sonne, *World of Wakara*, 180.
20. "Synopsis of President Young's Address," *Deseret News*, Nov. 24, 1853.
21. Qtd. in Sonne, *World of Wakara*, 180.
22. Qtd. in *Latter-day Saints' Millennial Star*, June 15, 1851, 181.
23. M. S. Martenas [Martinez], Statement, Salt Lake City, 6 July 1853, Brigham Young Office Papers (MS 1234, Box 58, Folder 14), Church History Library; transcription by

Will Bagley. Martinez was a common name in New Mexico. In his sketch of the life of Denis Julien, Otis "Doc" Martin noted Manuel Martinez's 1827 report of a party sent "to retrieve some caches in the direction of the lands of the Utes." (Hafen, *Mountain Men and Fur Trade of the Far West*, 7:185.) Bancroft mentioned a Miguel Martinez at San Bernardino in 1846. I have been unable to make a more precise identification.
24. Bailey, *Indian Slave Trade in the Southwest*, 149. The importance of the Old Spanish Trail to Wákara and his group's survival is also documented by Virginia Simmons, who explains, "The most famous Ute to loot travelers on the Old Spanish Trail was Walkara, also known as Walker or Wakara, meaning 'yellow.' . . . Walkara halted traders and, later, emigrants on the portion of the trail between Utah and California to exact tolls in gifts." (Simmons, *Ute Indians of Utah, Colorado, and New Mexico*, 49.)
25. Bailey, *Indian Slave Trade in the Southwest*, 146.
26. Jones, *Being and Becoming Ute*, 53.
27. Sonne, *World of Wakara*, 136. Further legislation on March 7 authorized "binding out," or a form of indenture, rather than slavery. This indenture of "any prisoner, child, or woman who came into the possession of white settlers" could last no more than twenty years, and the master was required to provide servants with schooling, training in a trade, clothing, food, and "the care he would give to his own offspring." The next year, in a sermon in the Salt Lake Tabernacle, Brigham Young spoke specifically of Wákara's slave trade: "Walker, with a small band, has succeeded in making all the Indian bands in these mountains fear him. He has been in the habit of stealing from the Californians, and of making every train of emigrants that passed along the Spanish trail to California pay tithing to him. He finally began to steal children [from] those bands to sell to the Spaniards; and through fear of him, he has managed to bring in subjection almost all the Utah tribes. I will relate one action of Walker's life, which will serve to illustrate his character. He, with his band, about last February, fell in with a small band of Payedes [Paiutes], and killed off the whole of the men, took the squaws prisoners, and sold the children to the Mexicans, and some few were disposed of in this Territory." (Sonne, *World of Wakara*, 144; Brigham Young, qtd. in Carvalho, *Incidents of Travel and Adventure in the Far West*, 56.)
28. See, for example, Jones, *Being and Becoming Ute*, 93–105; and Foster, "Indian Life," 23.
29. Jones, *Being and Becoming Ute*, 46, 52; see also page 54.
30. Foster, "Indian Life," 22.
31. Jones, *Being and Becoming Ute*, 32, 65.
32. Sonne, *World of Wakara*, 66; see also Foster, "Indian Life," 23.
33. Jones, *Being and Becoming Ute*, 82–83.
34. Crawford, *Early History of Manti*, 1; Carter, *Our Pioneer Heritage*, 105–106; Boren, "The Untold Story of Chief Walker and the Mormons," 2.
35. Foster, "Indian Life," 23; Antrei, *The Other Forty-Niners*, 8; Boren, "The Untold Story of Chief Walker and the Mormons," 7.
36. Lorton, Diary, Aug. 22 and 23, 1849.
37. Crampton and Madsen, *In Search of the Spanish Trail*, 11; Sonne, *World of Wakara*, 72.
38. Manly, *Death Valley in '49*, 142.

39. Bryan Justesen points out that Wákara naturally situated their encampments at the intersection of the trail and water to meet trade and survival needs. (Justesen, "Brigham Young and Chief Walkara," 23.)

40. Nevins, *Frémont*, 385–386; see also Sonne, *World of Wakara*, 46.

41. Qtd. in Hafen and Hafen, *Old Spanish Trail*, 369.

42. Brewerton, *Overland with Kit Carson*, 118.

43. Heap, *Central Route to the Pacific*, 84.

44. Beckwith, *Report of Explorations for a Route for the Pacific Railroad*, 62.

45. Qtd. in Kessler, *Old Spanish Trail North Branch*, 302.

46. Manly, *Death Valley in '49*, 91.

47. Manly, *Death Valley in '49*, 91.

48. Manly, "From Vermont to California," 142.

49. Manly, "From Vermont to California," 142.

50. Manly, *Death Valley in '49*, 83.

51. Manly, *Death Valley in '49*, 94.

52. Manly, "From Vermont to California," 142.

53. Manly, *Death Valley in '49*, 97.

54. See Ghiglieri, *First through Grand Canyon*, 165, 171.

55. Lorton, Diary, Sept. 30, 1849. Despite this error in reporting, Lorton's diary provides an early corroboration of Manly's travels, which Manly himself detailed only later.

56. Manly, *Death Valley in '49*, 279. John Sumner of the Powell expedition also described the proximity to the upcoming Colorado River, which he called the Grand, as they float through the San Rafael Desert. "Grand River can't be very distant for it must flow to the right of the mountains we can see to the east of us. Think we must reach it this week of the river don't canon badly between here and the confluence" (Qtd. in Ghiglieri, *First through Grand Canyon*, 165.)

57. Manly, *Death Valley in '49*, 94.

58. Simmons, *Ute Indians of Utah, Colorado, and New Mexico*; McCormick, *Utah Adventure*.

59. Email correspondence with Sondra Jones, in possession of the author.

60. See Jones, *Being and Becoming Ute*, 27, 53.

61. Manly, *Death Valley in '49*, 94.

62. Manly, "From Vermont to California," 142.

63. Manly, *Death Valley in '49*, 94.

64. Manly, *Death Valley in '49*, 94–95.

65. Manly, *Death Valley in '49*, 96.

66. Manly, "From Vermont to California," 142.

67. Manly, "From Vermont to California," 142.

68. Manly, "From Vermont to California," 142.

69. Manly, *Death Valley in '49*, 96.

70. Manly, *Death Valley in '49*, 95.

71. Manly, "From Vermont to California," 142; Manly, *Death Valley in '49*, 97.

72. This is the last time Manly saw McMahon until he was reunited with him in San Jose, California, several years later. By request of Manly, McMahon wrote chapter 12 of

Death Valley in '49 about his experiences and survival after separating from Manly. This chapter provides one of the strongest validating records of Manly's river travels to the San Rafael Desert, and it is considered separately in chapter 12 of the present book.

CHAPTER 10: DESERT AND PLATEAU

1. Manly, *Death Valley in '49*, 98.
2. Manly, *Death Valley in '49*, 98.
3. Email correspondence with Wade Allinson, in possession of the author.
4. Manly, *Death Valley in '49*, 98–99.
5. Jones, *Being and Becoming Ute*, 104, 105.
6. Sonne, *World of Wakara*, 218–220.
7. Manly, *Death Valley in '49*, 98.
8. Manly, *Death Valley in '49*, 98.
9. Crampton and Madsen, *In Search of the Spanish Trail*, 11.
10. Lavender, *Colorado River Country*, 61–62, 204; email correspondence with Wade Allinson, in possession of the author.
11. Manly, "From Vermont to California," 142.
12. Manly, *Death Valley in '49*, 92, 97–98.
13. Qtd. in Hafen and Hafen, *Old Spanish Trail*, 350.
14. Heap, *Central Route to the Pacific*, 84–85.
15. Qtd. in Kessler, *Old Spanish Trail North Branch*, 259, 260. Later, in the twentieth century, people were still commenting on the barren land. In the *Guidebook of the Western United States Part E, The Denver & Rio Grande Western Route*, Marius Campbell combines two vivid descriptions of the lands west of Green River, Utah. He writes, "After the train surmounts the slight rise out of the valley of Green River the traveler will see spread wide before him one of the most desolate landscapes that he has thus far passed in his western trip. For miles the surface of the plain consists of bare clay or shale without so much as a clump of sagebrush or greasewood to break its monotony. . . . Beckwith Plateau is one of the landmarks west of Green River. . . . It stands in the midst of one of the most desolate flats that the traveler will see east of Salt Lake City. Scarcely a shrub or plant of any kind breaks the monotony of this expanse of barren clay" (pp. 206, 210). The Denver & Rio Grande Railroad considered a route partially following the Old Spanish Trail to the Wasatch Plateau, only to decline and construct a route north from Green River to Price, Utah.
16. Manly, *Death Valley in '49*, 98, 99.
17. Qtd. in Hafen and Hafen, *Old Spanish Trail*, 350.
18. Huntington, *Diary of Oliver B. Huntington*, 97–98.
19. DeLafosse, *Trailing the Pioneers*, 18–19.
20. Qtd. in Kessler, *Old Spanish Trail North Branch*, 301.
21. Manly, *Death Valley in '49*, 99.
22. Manly, "From Vermont to California," 142. Allinson further details "Big Holes" and the fortunate encounter by Manly and his men to find water in such a desolate valley: "Manly reports that they had traveled for one day, camped for the night and found water in some pools or holes in the flat rocks which held the rain. This perfectly

describes Big Holes in the Chimney Rock area that is along the Santa Fe to Los Angeles Trail. Having spent the last 25 years explor[ing] this area, Big Holes is the only place in that region that fits this description." (Email correspondence with Wade Allinson, in possession of the author.)

23. Manly, "From Vermont to California," 142.

24. Manly, *Death Valley in '49*, 99.

25. Qtd. in Ghiglieri, *First through Grand Canyon*, 166–167. Another expedition member, George Bradley, called it "in[con]ceivably desolate."

26. Warner, *Dominguez-Escalante Journal*, xix.

27. Hafen and Hafen, *Journals of Forty-Niners*, 17.

28. Warner, *Dominguez-Escalante Journal*, 52.

29. Warner, *Dominguez-Escalante Journal*, 54–55.

30. Warner, *Dominguez-Escalante Journal*, 56–57.

31. Warner, *Dominguez-Escalante Journal*, 57–58.

32. For example, Oliver Huntington noted in May 1848: "Left the wagon trail and took the old spanish Trail being led by some Indians from Huntington Creek [east slope of the Wasatch Plateau] who said we could save 6 days travel in going to Green river [across Buckhorn Flat, Furniture Draw, and the San Rafael Desert, like Manly]. Traveled hard that day & found no water until near night" (Huntington, Journal, May 15, 1848).

33. Manly, *Death Valley in '49*, 95.

34. Heap, *Central Route to the Pacific*, 85.

35. Manly, "From Vermont to California," 42.

36. Crampton and Madsen, *In Search of the Spanish Trail*, 59.

37. Beckwith, *Report of Explorations for a Route for the Pacific Railroad*, 65.

38. Manly, "From Vermont to California," 142.

39. Qtd. in Smart and Smart, *Over the Rim*, 41.

40. Simmons, *Ute Indians of Utah, Colorado, and New Mexico*, 97; Sonne, *World of Wakara*, 219.

41. Manly, *Death Valley in '49*, 99.

42. Manly, "From Vermont to California," 142.

43. McEwan, Diary, 113–114.

44. McEwan, Diary, 117, 119.

45. Manly, *Death Valley in '49*, 95.

46. Manly, *Death Valley in '49*, 100; Manly, "From Vermont to California," 158.

47. See, for example, Dehler et. al, *Uinta Mountain Geology*, 5, 290.

48. Manly, "From Vermont to California," 158.

49. Warner, *Dominguez-Escalante Journal*, 58.

50. Warner, *Dominguez-Escalante Journal*, 59.

51. Warner, *Dominguez-Escalante Journal*, 60.

52. Warner, *Dominguez-Escalante Journal*, 60–62.

53. See Warner, *Dominguez-Escalante Journal*, 62–63.

54. Manly, *Death Valley in '49*, 100.

55. Warner, *Dominguez-Escalante Journal*, 60, 62–63.

56. Manly, "From Vermont to California," 142, 158.
57. Manly, *Death Valley in '49*, 100.
58. "Our horse-tracks came out into a large trail which was on a down grade leading in a northward direction." (Manly, *Death Valley in '49*, 101.)
59. September 20, 1776: "We went southwest . . . then swung west . . . and at a quarter league's travel south-southwest we turned west again . . . crossed the river, and to the southwest we went." September 21: "We set out . . . toward the southwest . . . a quarter league we swung west. . . . [A]fter going one league south-southwest . . . we took the southern slope of a forested narrow valley . . . after going west for half a league . . . this ridge we went southwest for a quarter league . . . after having traveled a league west." September 22: "We set out to the southwest . . . traveled six long leagues. . . . [T]hey must have amounted to three leagues toward the west-southwest." September 23: "Heading southwest . . . we turned west." (Warner, *Dominguez-Escalante Journal*, 60–63.)
60. Manly, *Death Valley in '49*, 100.
61. Manly, *Death Valley in '49*, 100.
62. Though the first initial "M" is hard to make out, Cory Jensen, the national register coordinator with the Utah State Historic Preservation Office, confirmed, "My team did a little digital enhancement and there is definitely an M but it's so eroded it's hard to fully identify."
63. Manly, *Death Valley in '49*, 98, 100; see also Manly, "From Vermont to California," 142.
64. Manly, *Death Valley in '49*, 100.
65. Justesen, "Brigham Young and Chief Walkara," 40.
66. Manly, *Death Valley in '49*, 100.
67. Madsen, "The Fremont."
68. Gunnerson, *Fremont Culture*, 134.
69. Kilbourne, "Wasatch Plateau."
70. Simmons, *Ute Indians of Utah, Colorado, and New Mexico*, 26. Another possibility besides wild potato is the yampa root, which also grows at high elevation and looks like a carrot.
71. Hijmans and Spooner, "Geographic Distribution of Wild Potato Species," 2101–2102.
72. Manly, *Death Valley in '49*, 100.
73. Manly, "From Vermont to California," 158; Manly, *Death Valley in '49*, 100.
74. Manly, *Death Valley in '49*, 100.
75. Manly, "From Vermont to California," 142; Lorton, Diary, Sept. 30, 1849.
76. Manly, *Death Valley in '49*, 100.
77. Lorton, Diary, Sept. 30, 1849.
78. Manly, *Death Valley in '49*, 100–101.
79. Manly, "From Vermont to California," 158.
80. Manly, *Death Valley in '49*, 101.
81. Manly, *Death Valley in '49*, 98.
82. Manly, "From Vermont to California," 158.
83. Manly, *Death Valley in '49*, 101.

CHAPTER 11: ARRIVAL AND REUNION IN UTAH VALLEY

1. See Manly, "From Vermont to California," 158.
2. Manly, "From Vermont to California," 158.
3. Manly, *Death Valley in '49*, 101.
4. Lorton, Diary, Sept. 30, 1849.
5. Manly, *Death Valley in '49*, 101.
6. Similarly, researcher Michael Ghiglieri wrote of John Wesley Powell's 1869 expedition members: "The men were frequently forced to wade deep into the river. Their rotting boots consistently slid on the silt lubricated boulders hidden under the muddy surface of the roiling flow." (Ghiglieri, *First through Grand Canyon*, 58.)
7. Manly, "From Vermont to California," 158.
8. Manly, *Death Valley in '49*, 496.
9. Manly, *Death Valley in '49*, 101.
10. Manly, "From Vermont to California," 158; see also Manly, *Death Valley in '49*, 101.
11. Manly, *Death Valley in '49*, 107–108.
12. Welch, Log, 192A.
13. Manly, *Death Valley in '49*, 101.
14. Manly, *Death Valley in '49*, 101.
15. Manly, "From Vermont to California," 158; see also Hoover, "Notes for an Overland Guide."
16. Manly, *Death Valley in '49*, 102. Other histories have followed Manly's reference and mistakenly placed Manly at Hobble Creek; see Webb, *If We Had a Boat*, 46.
17. Madsen, *A Forty-Niner in Utah*, 78.
18. Manly, "From Vermont to California," 158. Sarah and Lewis shared a special bond and he was at her side when she died; see the Conclusion in this volume.
19. Manly, *Death Valley in '49*, 102.
20. Manly, "From Vermont to California," 158.
21. Manly, *Death Valley in '49*, 102.
22. Manly, *Death Valley in '49*, 61.
23. Manly, *Death Valley in '49*, 102.
24. Manly, *Death Valley in '49*, 102; Manly, "From Vermont to California," 158.
25. Manly, *Death Valley in '49*, 105.
26. Manly, *Death Valley in '49*, 101; see also Sutak, *Into the Jaws of Hell*, 290; Hafen and Hafen, *Journals of Forty Niners*, 28.
27. Manly, "From Vermont to California," 158.
28. Manly, *Death Valley in '49*, 106.
29. Manly, "From Vermont to California," 158.
30. Welch, Log, Oct. 3, 1849.
31. Sutak, correspondence with the author; Manly, *Death Valley in '49*, 107; see also Hafen and Hafen, *Journals of Forty-Niners*, 62–63.
32. Welch, Log, Oct. 3, 1849.
33. Manly, *Death Valley in '49*, 108; Sutak, *Into the Jaws of Hell*, 317.
34. Sutak, *Into the Jaws of Hell*, 317.
35. Manly, *Death Valley in '49*, 113.

CHAPTER 12: M. S. MCMAHON'S STORY

1. Manly, *Death Valley in '49*, 319.
2. 1860 U.S. Census, Union, Davis Co., IA, microfilm 803,317, Family History Library, Salt Lake City, UT.
3. Van Buren County, Iowa, Records, Mar. 28, 1848, familysearch.org.
4. Alumni College of Physicians and Surgeons, Keokuk Medical College, Records, 1850–1898, University of Iowa, Iowa City.
5. 1860 U.S. Census, Union, Davis Co., IA.
6. California State Library, California History Section, Great Registers, 1866–1898, Collection Number 4-2A, microfilm 978,585, Family History Library, Salt Lake City, UT.
7. 1870 U.S. Census, San Jose, Santa Clara Co., CA.
8. "M. S. McMahon, M. D.," *Santa Cruz Surf*, Mar. 31, 1898.
9. Manly, *Death Valley in '49*, 279.
10. Manly, *Death Valley in '49*, 279, 93.
11. Qtd. in Kessler, *Old Spanish Trail North Branch*, 280.
12. Manly, *Death Valley in '49*, 96–97.
13. Manly, "From Vermont to California," 142. In *If We Had a Boat*, historian Roy Webb writes that McMahon and Field "followed the river into Desolation Canyon, but just as Wákara predicted, they were soon forced to abandon it. They tried to follow their comrades, but ran into the Ute chief, who took them along on his buffalo hunt." As the letter in *Death Valley in '49* makes clear, though, McMahon and Field never left Wákara's camp at the Old Spanish Trail. (Webb, *If We Had a Boat*, 46.)
14. Manly, *Death Valley in '49*, 280.
15. Manly, *Death Valley in '49*, 281.
16. Ferris, *Life in the Rocky Mountains*, 10.
17. Van Hoak, "The Other Buffalo," 172–173; see also Brewerton, *Overland with Kit Carson*, 118. An Indian pictograph of a buffalo is located at the mouth of Hay Canyon, adjacent to Westwater Creek flowing from the Book Cliffs, sixty miles east of Green River and fifteen miles from the Utah/Colorado state line. This pictograph would have been in the direct traveling path from the Old Spanish Trail to the headwaters of the Colorado River.
18. Manly, *Death Valley in '49*, 281.
19. See Sutak, working paper.
20. Manly, *Death Valley in '49*, 281.
21. Heap, *Central Route to the Pacific*, 83; Carvalho, *Incidents of Travel and Adventure*, 104; see also Sutak, working paper.
22. Manly, *Death Valley in '49*, 282.
23. Manly, *Death Valley in '49*, 282.
24. Manly, *Death Valley in '49*, 284.
25. Manly, *Death Valley in '49*, 303.
26. Manly, *Death Valley in '49*, 283–284.
27. Manly, *Death Valley in '49*, 284.
28. Manly, *Death Valley in '49*, 284.
29. Nelson, *Forgotten Pathfinders*, 51.

30. Manly, *Death Valley in '49,* 285, 286.
31. Manly, *Death Valley in '49,* 285.
32. Manly, *Death Valley in '49,* 287–288.
33. Manly, *Death Valley in '49,* 288.
34. Manly, *Death Valley in '49,* 289, 290.
35. Manly, *Death Valley in '49,* 294.
36. Reagan, "Forts Robidoux and Kit Carson in Northeastern Utah," 130, 131; see also Reagan, "Some Notes on the History of the Uintah Basin," 55–64.
37. Ferris, *Life in the Rocky Mountains;* Sutak, working paper; see also Hafen, *Mountain Men and Fur Trade,* 152.
38. Manly, *Death Valley in '49,* 311.
39. Sargent, *Seeking the Elephant,* 146; Morris, Journal, Aug. 19, 1849.
40. Manly, *Death Valley in '49,* 318.
41. Manly, *Death Valley in '49,* 318.

CONCLUSION
1. Manly, *Death Valley in '49,* 496.
2. Manly, *Death Valley in '49,* 474.
3. Dustin, *Wilderness Within,* 10, 14.
4. Manly, *Death Valley in '49,* 43, 97, 99, 123, 486–498.

WORKS CITED

Ambrose, Stephen E. *Undaunted Courage: Meriwether Lewis, Thomas Jefferson, and the Opening of the American West.* New York: Simon & Schuster, 1996.

Antrei, A. C. *The Other Forty-Niners: A Topical History of Sanpete County Utah, 1849 to 1983.* Salt Lake City, UT: Western Epics, 1983.

Aton, James M. *The River Knows Everything: Desolation Canyon and the Green.* Logan: Utah State University Press, 2009.

Bailey, Lynn R. *Indian Slave Trade in the Southwest.* Los Angeles, CA: Westernlore Press, 1966.

Bailey, Paul. *Walkara, Hawk of the Mountains.* Los Angeles, CA: Westernlore Press, 1954.

Bancroft, Hubert Howe. *History of Utah, 1540–1886.* San Francisco, CA: The History Company, 1889.

Barney, Ronald O., ed. *Mormon Vanguard Brigade of 1847: Norton Jacob's Record.* Logan: Utah State University Press, 2005.

Beckwith, E. G. *Report of Explorations for a Route for the Pacific Railroad, by Capt. J.W. Gunnison, Topographical Engineers, near the 38th and 39th Parallels of North Latitude, the Mouth of the Kansas River, Mo., to the Sevier Lake, in the Great Basin.* Washington, DC: Government Printing Office, 1855.

Belknap, Buzz. *Dinosaur River Guide.* Denver, CO: Eastwood Printing, 1974.

Boren, K. R. "The Untold Story of Chief Walker and the Mormons." Copy at Manti Public Library, Manti, UT.

Brands, H. W. *The Age of Gold: The California Gold Rush and the New American Dream.* New York: Anchor Books, 2003.

Brewerton, George D. *Overland with Kit Carson.* Lincoln: University of Nebraska Press, 1993.

Brown, Randy. *Historic Inscriptions on Western Emigrant Trails.* Independence, MO: Oregon-California Trails Association, 2004.

Campbell, Marius. *Guidebook of the Western United States Part E. The Denver & Rio Grande Western Route.* Washington, DC: Government Printing Office, 1922.

Carter, Kate B. *Our Pioneer Heritage.* Salt Lake City: Utah Printing Company, 1974.

Carvalho, Solomon Nunes. *Incidents of Travel and Adventure in the Far West with Colonel Frémont's Last Expedition.* Lincoln: University of Nebraska Press, 2004.

Christy, Howard. "The Walker War: Defense and Conciliation as Strategy." *Utah Historical Quarterly* 47, no. 4 (1979), 395–420.

Clayton, William. *The Latter-Day Saints' Emigrants' Guide*. St. Louis, MO: Republican Steam Power Press–Chambers & Knapp, 1848.

Clokey, Richard M. *William H. Ashley: Enterprise and Politics in the Trans-Mississippi West*. Norman: University of Oklahoma Press, 1980.

Cosco, Jon M. *Echo Park: Struggle for Preservation*. Boulder, CO: Johnson Printing, 1995.

Crampton, C. Gregory, and Steven K. Madsen. *In Search of the Spanish Trail*. Salt Lake City, UT: Gibbs-Smith, 1994.

Crawford, Elizabeth. *Early History of Manti*. Salt Lake City: Daughters of the Utah Pioneers, 1928.

Cross, Osborne. *March of the Regiment of Mounted Riflemen to Oregon in 1849*. Fairfield, WA: Ye Galleon Press, 1967.

Dale, Harrison Clifford, ed. *The Ashley-Smith Explorations and the Discovery of a Central Route to the Pacific, 1822–1829*. Cleveland, OH: Arthur H. Clark, 1918.

Dehler, Carol M., Joel L. Pederson, Douglas A. Sprinkel, B. J. Kowallis. *Uinta Mountain Geology*. Logan: Utah Geological Association Publication, 2005.

DeLafosse, Peter. H. *Trailing the Pioneers*. Logan: Utah State University Press, 1994.

Dellenbaugh, Frederick Samuel. *A Canyon Voyage*. New York: G. P. Putnam's Sons, The Knickerbocker Press, 1908.

Dellenbaugh, Frederick Samuel. *The Romance of the Colorado River*. 3rd ed. New York: G. P. Putnam's Sons, The Knickerbocker Press, 1909.

Dolnick, Edward. *Down the Great Unknown: John Wesley Powell's 1869 Journey of Discovery and Tragedy through the Grand Canyon*. New York, NY: Harper Collins, 2001.

Dustin, Daniel L. *The Wilderness Within*. Champaign, IL: Sagamore Publishing, 2006.

Farnham, Thomas. *Travels in the Great Western Prairies. The Anahuac and Rocky Mountains and in the Oregon Territory. Part II*. London: Richard Bentley, 1843.

Ferris, Warren Angus. *Life in the Rocky Mountains: A Diary of Wanderings on the Sources of the River Missouri, Columbia, and Colorado 1830–1835*. Denver, CO: Fred A. Rosenstock Old West Publishing, 1940.

Foster, Robert L. "Indian Life." *Wild West* 24, no. 1 (June 2011), 20–25.

Frémont, John Charles. *Map of Oregon and Upper California from the Surveys of John Charles Frémont and Other Authorities. Drawn by Charles Preuss under the Order of the Senate of the United States*. Washington, DC, 1848.

Frémont, John Charles. *Map of the Exploring Expedition to the Rocky Mountains in the Year 1842 and to Oregon and Upper California in the Years 1843–44 by Brevet Capt. J. C. Frémont of the Corps of Topographical Engineers under the Orders of Col. J. J. Abert, Chief of the Topographical Bureau*. Washington, DC, 1845.

Frémont, John Charles. *Memoirs of My Life*. Reprint. New York: Cooper Square Press, 2001.

Ghiglieri, Michael Patrick. *First through Grand Canyon: The Secret Journals and Letters of the 1869 Crew Who Explored the Green and Colorado Rivers*. Flagstaff, AZ: Puma Press, 2003.

Gunnerson. James H. *The Fremont Culture*. Salt Lake City: University of Utah Press, 1969.

Hafen, LeRoy R. *Mountain Men and the Fur Trade of the Far West*. Ten vols. Glendale, CA: Arthur H. Clark Company, 1965–1972.

Hafen, LeRoy R., and Ann W. Hafen. *Journals of Forty Niners: Salt Lake to Los Angeles with Diaries and Contemporary Records of Sheldon Young, James S. Brown, Jacob Y. Stover, Charles C. Rich, Addison Pratt, Howard Egan, Henry W. Bigler and Others.* Glendale, CA: Arthur H. Clark, 1954.

Hafen, LeRoy R., and Ann Woodbury Hafen. *Old Spanish Trail: Santa Fé to Los Angeles; with Extracts from Contemporary Records and Including Diaries of Antonio Armijo and Orville Pratt.* Lincoln: University of Nebraska Press, 1954.

Hafen, LeRoy R., and Francis Marion Young. *Fort Laramie and the Pageant of the West, 1834–1890.* Glendale, CA: Arthur H. Clark. 1938.

Hannon, Jessie G., ed. *The Boston-Newton Company Venture: From Massachusetts to California.* Lincoln: University of Nebraska Press, 1969.

Heap, Gwinn Harris. *Central Route to the Pacific.* New York: Arno Press, 1981.

Hijmans, Robert J., and David M. Spooner. "Geographic Distribution of Wild Potato Species." *American Journal of Botany* 88.11 (2001): 2101–2112.

Hoover, Vincent A. "Notes for an Overland Guide." Typescript. Dale Lowell Morgan Papers. Bancroft Library, University of California, Berkeley.

Huntington, Oliver. *Diary of Oliver B. Huntington 1847–1900. Part II.* Copy at Brigham Young University Library, 1942.

Internet Surname Database. http://www.surnamedb.com.

Irving, Washington. *The Adventures of Captain Bonneville, U.S.A. in the Rocky Mountains and the West.* Rev. ed. New York: G. P. Putnam, 1868.

Johnson, LeRoy, and Jean Johnson, eds. *Escape from Death Valley.* Reno: University of Nevada Press, 1987.

Jones, Sondra G. *Being and Becoming Ute: The Story of an American Indian People.* Salt Lake City: University of Utah Press, 2019.

Jones, Stephen Vandiver. Journal. Published in *Utah Historical Quarterly* 16–17 (1948–1949): 19–174.

Journal History of The Church of Jesus Christ of Latter-day Saints, Church History Library, Salt Lake City, UT.

Justesen, Bryan Howard. "Brigham Young and Chief Walkara : a Study of Colliding Concepts of Authority." Master's thesis, University of Utah, 2003.

Kessler, Ron. *Old Spanish Trail North Branch.* Santa Fe, NM: Sunstone Press, 1943.

Latter-day Saints' Millennial Star. Liverpool. 1840–1970. Copy at Church History Library, Salt Lake City, UT.

Lavender, David. *Colorado River Country.* New York: E. P. Dutton, 1982.

Leedy, Paul. D. *Practical Research: Planning and Design.* New York: Macmillan, 1989.

Lewis, Meriwether. Journal. *Journals of the Lewis & Clark Expedition.* https://lewisand clarkjournals.unl.edu.

Lorton, William B. Diary, 1849–1850. Bancroft Library, University of California, Berkeley.

Lyman, Edward Leo. *The Overland Journey from Utah to California.* Reno: University of Nevada Press, 2004.

Madsen, Brigham D. *A Forty-Niner in Utah.* Salt Lake City: Tanner Trust Fund/ University of Utah Library, 1981.

Madsen, David B. "The Fremont." *Utah History Encyclopedia.* https://heritage.utah.gov /history/uhg-first-peoples-fremont. Accessed June 27, 2017.

Manly, William Lewis. *Death Valley in '49.* San Jose, CA: The Pacific Tree and Vine Co., 1894.

Manly, William Lewis. "From Vermont to California." *Santa Clara Valley* 4, no. 4–7, no. 5 (June 1887–July 1890).

McCormick, John S. *The Utah Adventure.* Salt Lake City: Gibbs Smith, 2005.

McCourt, Tom, and Wade Allinson. *The Elk Mountain Mission: A History of Moab, Mormons, The Old Spanish Trail and the Shereetch Utes.* Price, UT: Southpaw, 2017.

McEwan, John. Diary. L. Tom Perry Special Collections, Harold B. Lee Library, Brigham Young University, Provo, UT.

Morris, Robert M. Journal. Beinecke Library, Yale University, New Haven, CT.

Nelson, Jack W. *Forgotten Pathfinders Along the North Branch of the Old Spanish Trail 1650–1850.* Grand Junction, CO: 2003.

Nevins, Allan. *Frémont: Pathmarker of the West.* Lincoln and London: University of Nebraska Press, 1992.

Powell, John W. *The Exploration of the Colorado River and Its Canyons.* New York: Dover, 1961. Reprint of John W. Powell, *Canyons of the Colorado* (Flood & Vincent, 1895).

Reagan, Albert B. "Forts Robidoux and Kit Carson in Northeastern Utah." *New Mexico Historical Review* 10 (Apr. 1835), 121–132.

Reagan, Albert B. "Some Notes on the History of the Uintah Basin." *Proceedings of the Utah Academy of Sciences, Arts and Letters* 11 (1934), 55–64.

Ressler, Theodore C. *Trails Divided.* Williamsburg, IA: By the author, 1964.

Royce, Sarah. *A Frontier Lady: Recollections of the Gold Rush and Early California.* Lincoln, NE: Bison Books, 1977.

Ruth, Kent. *Landmarks of the West.* Lincoln: University of Nebraska Press, 1993.

Sargent, Shirley, ed. *Seeking the Elephant, 1849: James Mason Hutchings' Journal of His Overland Trek to California Including His Voyage to America, 1848 and Letters from the Mother Lode.* Glendale, CA: Arthur H. Clark Company, 1980.

Schlissel, Lillian. *Women's Diaries of the Westward Journey.* New York: Schocken Books, 2004.

Shafer, Robert J. *A Guide to Historical Method.* Belmont, CA: Dorsey Press, 1974.

Simmons. Virginia M. *The Ute Indians of Utah, Colorado, and New Mexico.* Boulder: University Press of Colorado, 2000.

Slaughter, William W., and Michael Landon. *Trail of Hope.* Salt Lake City, UT: Shadow Mountain, 1997.

Sleath, Doris Holloway. "Manley/Manly Family History and Genealogy." 1993. Copy at Death Valley National Park.

Smart, William B., and Donna T. Smart. *Over The Rim: The Parley P. Pratt Exploring Expedition to Southern Utah, 1849–50*. Logan: Utah State University Press, 1999.

Smith, George D. *An Intimate Chronicle: The Journals of William Clayton*. Salt Lake City: Signature Books, 1995.

Sonne, Conway B. *World of Wakara*. San Antonio, TX: Naylor, 1962.

Stansbury, Howard. *Expedition to the Great Salt Lake of Utah*. Philadelphia, PA: Lippincott, Grambo & Co., 1852.

Steel, Edward M., ed. *A Forty-Niner from Tennessee*. Knoxville: University of Tennessee Press, 1998.

Stephens, Hal G., and Eugene M. Shoemaker. *In the Footsteps of John Wesley Powell*. Boulder, CO: Johnson Books, 1987.

Sutak, Tom. *Into the Jaws of Hell*. California: Pine Park Publishing, 2012.

Sutak, Tom. Working paper. 2012. Copy in possession of the author.

Van Hoak, Stephen P. "The Other Buffalo: Native Americans, Fur Trappers, and Western Bison, 1600–1860." *Utah Historical Quarterly* 72, no. 1, 168–180.

Warner. Ted J., ed. *The Dominguez-Escalante Journal: Their Expedition through Colorado, Utah, Arizona, and New Mexico in 1776*. Transl. Fray Angelico Chavez. Salt Lake City: University of Utah Press, 1995.

Webb, Roy. "Green River." *Utah History Encyclopedia*. https://historytogo.utah.gov/utah_chapters/the_land/greenriver.html. Accessed August 24, 2018.

Webb, Roy. *If We Had a Boat: Green River Explorers, Adventurers, and Runners*. Salt Lake City: University of Utah Press, 1986.

Webb, Roy. *Lost Canyons of the Green River: The Story before Flaming Gorge Dam*. Salt Lake City: University of Utah Press, 2012.

Welch, Adonijah Strong. Log. 1849. In Theodore C. Ressler, ed., *Trails Divided* (Williamsburg, IA: By the author, 1964), 255–274 (misattributed to David Switzer).

Woodruff, Wilford. Journals, 1833–1898. Church History Library, Salt Lake City, UT. Available in *Wilford Woodruff's Journals, 1833–1898*, edited by Scott G. Kenney (Midvale, UT: Signature Books, 1983–1985).

Woodward, Arthur. *The Jayhawkers' Oath and Other Sketches*. Los Angeles, CA: Warren F. Lewis, 1949.

Worster, Donald. *A River Running West: The Life of John Wesley Powell*. New York: Oxford University Press, 2001.

The Yale Book of Quotations. Edited by Fred R. Shapiro. New Haven, CT: Yale University Press, 2006.

Young, Brigham. Office Papers. MS 1234. Church History Library, Salt Lake City, UT.

Zwinger. Ann. *Run, River, Run: A Naturalist's Journey Down One of the Great Rivers of the West*. New York: Harper & Row, 1975.

Index

A

Allinson, Wade, 158
Arapeen, 174
Ashley Falls, 71
Ashley, William H., 9, 10, 70, 87, 90, 95, 105, 122
Aton, James, 110

B

Bailey, Lynn, 141
Bailey, Paul, 136
Bashore, Mel, 26, 28
Bassett, Sam, 86
Beckwith, E. G., 171
Bennett, Asabel, 18, 23, 34, 206, 209
Bennett, Mrs. Asabel (Sarah), 206, 208, 235
Big Holes, 161
Birdseye, Utah, 199
bison, 216
Black's Fork, 60
boat, Manly's, 39, 41
boat, Mormon, 39
Book Cliffs, 157, 220
Bradley, George, 122, 126
Brewerton, George Douglass, 145
Browne, Baptiste, 84
Browns Hole, 46, 62, 82
Browns Park, 45, 81. *See* Browns Hole.
Browns Wash Spring, 217, 220
Buckhorn Flat, 170
Bureau of Land Management rangers, 83
Butch Cassidy and the Sundance Kid, 83

C

Campbell, Robert, 174
canoes, 19, 54, 61, 75, 79, 88, 94, 99, 120, 128
Carvalho, Solomon Nunes, 136, 215, 217
Castle Dale, Utah, 172
Castle Valley, 171
cattle theft, 26
Cedar Mountain, 163, 169
Chimney Rock, 169
chokecherries, 82
cholera, 25
Choteau, B., 145
Church of Jesus Christ of Latter-day Saints, 28
Cisco Springs, 223
Clark, William, 9
Colorado River, 44, 46, 49, 216

About the Author

Michael D. Kane received his BS, MS, and PhD from the University of Utah, studying recreation and hospitality management. Under his direction, Zion Ponderosa Ranch Resort has been named one of the Top 6 adventure resorts in America by *U.S. News and World Report*. He is also an instructor and a former director of basketball operations for the University of Utah and an advisory council member to the University of Utah Department of Parks, Recreation, and Tourism.

His research into the historical documents from the 1800s to present, and then his experiences following the trail of William Lewis Manly in a dugout canoe and on foot, helps him re-create routes taken, hardships shared, and the benevolent brotherhood demonstrated by these American forty-niners and the American Indians they encountered. Kane lives in West Jordan, Utah.